Applied Epistemology

An Introduction

Applied Epistemology

An Introduction

GORDON BARNES

HACKETT PUBLISHING COMPANY
INDIANAPOLIS

Copyright © 2025 by Hackett Publishing Company, Inc.

All rights reserved
Printed in the United States of America

28 27 26 25   1 2 3 4 5 6 7

For further information, please address
    Hackett Publishing Company, Inc.
    P.O. Box 44937
    Indianapolis, Indiana 46244-0937

    www.hackettpublishing.com

Cover design by Laura Clark
Interior design by Laura Clark
Composition by Aptara, Inc.

Library of Congress Control Number: 2025930396

ISBN-13: 978-1-64792-231-3 (pbk.)
ISBN-13: 978-1-64792-232-0 (PDF ebook)
ISBN-13: 978-1-64792-233-7 (epub)

The paper used in this publication meets the minimum requirements of American National Standard for Information Sciences—Permanence of Paper for Printed Library Materials, ANSI Z39.48–1984.

∞

CONTENTS

Acknowledgments   *ix*
Introduction   *x*

Chapter One: Trusting Others   1
Chapter Two: Deferring to Experts   29
Chapter Three: Responding to Disagreement   58
Chapter Four: Acknowledging Bias   84
Chapter Five: The Threat of Polarization   111
Chapter Six: Propaganda, Nudging, and Big Data   137
Chapter Seven: Artificial Intelligence and Human Understanding   162
Chapter Eight: Thinking about Conspiracy Theories   181

Conclusion   *209*
Index   *213*

For my sister, Martha Jones, and my sister-in-law, Heidi Fine.

They accept our humanity, and love us as we are.

ACKNOWLEDGMENTS

This book is deeply indebted to the late Joe Shieber. In the spring of 2023, I taught a seminar on the Epistemology of Testimony at SUNY Brockport, and I used Joe's book *Testimony: A Philosophical Introduction* as the principal text for that course. It's a wonderful book. Joe's writing is excellent—it's engaging and accessible without sacrificing any rigor. We worked our way through Joe's book, chapter by chapter, and at the end of the semester, Joe visited, as a guest of the Center for Philosophic Exchange. The students in the seminar formulated questions for Joe, and he spent the entire class answering. He was great with them. He was thoughtful, patient, and always respectful. Over dinner, I told Joe that I had an idea for an introduction to applied epistemology—one that would be engaging and accessible for undergraduates. He offered encouragement and support beyond what I ever would have expected from someone I had just met. Over the next several months, we corresponded about Joe's own work on testimony and many other issues in applied epistemology. Joe was extremely generous with his time and encouragement. I was deeply saddened when he passed on April 7, 2024. Joe was an outstanding philosopher, an exceptional teacher, and just a great human being. In the short time that I knew him, he left a deep impression on me. He will be missed.

Thanks are due to Matt Davidson and an anonymous reviewer, who read the entire manuscript and gave copious comments. They saved me from many errors. Throughout this process, I received invaluable advice and support from Jeff Dean. Jeff read the entire manuscript multiple times and gave insightful suggestions at every point. He has made the entire process of writing this book a great experience.

Finally, I am deeply grateful to my wife, Marnie Barnes, for all of her love and support throughout this process. Life with her makes everything better, including this book.

INTRODUCTION

Many people believe that philosophy is abstract, esoteric, and practically irrelevant. It might be fun to think about in your spare time, but it isn't useful for anything else. This common perception applies equally to *epistemology*—the theory of knowledge. If you ask, "How do you know you're not dreaming right now?" at a cocktail party, that could be fun, but if you ask it in the middle of a job interview, it will seem a little odd, to say the least. That question just isn't *practical*. And that is how people perceive philosophy, in general. It's fun, but it isn't practical. Hopefully, this book will demonstrate that this is very far from the truth. Many of the problems that we face in our everyday lives are actually philosophical problems; they just aren't *recognized* as philosophical problems.

Consider just one example. In the modern world, most of our knowledge comes from other people and through books, magazines, broadcasts, and podcasts. Of course, we know that there is a lot of deception in the world. This forces us to ask the question: *Who should I trust?* Well, when we trust other people, what is our goal? We trust people for lots of different reasons—to cooperate, to build friendships, to gain their trust in return. But sometimes, we trust people simply because there are things we want to *know*. When that is our goal, we should trust people when, and only when, we will get knowledge from them. If that is our goal, then in order to know who to trust, we need to answer another question: *When does trusting another person's testimony produce knowledge?* That is a philosophical question. It's practical, and it's also philosophical. This book is about those kinds of questions.

Each chapter of this book will begin with a true story. As we will see, each story poses an epistemological problem—a problem about knowledge. In Chapter 1, we begin with the story of Bernie Madoff, who deceived everyone on Wall Street and defrauded thousands of people from their life savings. Madoff's story illustrates exactly what we want to avoid when we trust others. How can we do that? Under what conditions do we *know* that a person is telling us the truth? That is the question addressed in Chapter 1. In Chapter 2, we begin with the economic crisis of the late 1970s, in which both unemployment and inflation were on the rise. President Jimmy Carter needed to find someone who could fix the economy. He needed an expert. Since Carter was not himself an expert in economics, how could he know who the experts were? That is the question addressed in Chapter 2.

Chapter 3 begins with the extraordinary friendship between Francis Collins and Christopher Hitchens. Collins, a renowned scientist, was also an evangelical Christian, while Hitchens was an avowed atheist. Each of them was highly intelligent and well-informed, yet they completely disagreed about religion. How should they each respond to their disagreement? Should it lead them to revise their own beliefs? That is the question addressed in Chapter 3. In Chapter 4, we begin with a story about cognitive bias in a murder investigation. This story illustrates a general truth about all human beings—we all suffer from many cognitive biases. In fact, the extent of our biases is so great that it casts doubt on our ability to know the truth in many cases. What should we infer from this? That is the subject of Chapter 4.

In Chapter 5, we begin with the story of political polarization, which is on the rise today. Many people form their political beliefs by trusting the people in their community or in-group. In an age of polarization, this seems to imply that many people must be forming false beliefs in this way. How do you know that it isn't *you* who are forming false beliefs in this way? That is the subject of Chapter 5. Chapter 6 starts with the story of an American propaganda campaign in several countries in eastern Europe and central Asia. The existence of propaganda threatens our ability to acquire knowledge from news outlets. Chapter 6 also investigates what is called "nudging" and "Big Data." Like propaganda, these are ways in which our beliefs can be manipulated. Do they all deprive us of knowledge, and if so, then why?

Chapter 7 begins with some recent successes of artificial intelligence. AlphaGo—the computer program that plays the strategy game Go—stunned the world by beating the world champion Go player, and AlphaFold predicted the structures of many proteins, which even the best biologists had been unable to do. Can AI give us scientific knowledge? Can it do this on its own, independently of human researchers? That is the question addressed in Chapter 7. Finally, in Chapter 8, we begin with a conspiracy theory. In the wake of Hurricane Katrina, many people believed that the levees around New Orleans had been bombed deliberately to destroy black neighborhoods. Is it always irrational to believe a conspiracy theory like this? Why or why not? That is the subject of Chapter 8.

Throughout this book, you will see that our everyday lives pose epistemological problems. You can use the concepts and theories developed in epistemology to solve these problems for yourself. They will also give you the tools you need to solve new problems in life as they arise. As you will soon see, epistemology is a very useful, practical discipline.

In the remainder of this Introduction, I will define some key terms, as I will use them throughout this book. I will also explain one key assumption that I will make. I will not assume any particular theory of knowledge. As we will see, different theories sometimes give different answers to the questions we discuss, so we will not assume any particular theory at the outset. However, in order to avoid confusion, I will clarify how I use some key terms, as well as one basic assumption that I will make.

First, knowledge requires that you have a *true belief*. You can know that the earth is round because it is true that the earth is round. By contrast, no one knows that the earth is flat, simply because it is false that the earth is flat. You cannot know what is false. That is part of our ordinary concept of knowledge—it is part of how we use the term "knows," and I will follow that ordinary usage in this book.

Second, while true belief is necessary for knowledge, it is not sufficient for knowledge. In other words, it is possible to have a true belief without *knowing* that your belief is true. Suppose that you think of a number between one and ten, and you ask me to guess the number. I guess that you are thinking of the number seven. It just so happens that you *are* thinking of the number seven. Then I have a true belief—I believe that you are thinking of the number seven, and it is *true* that you are thinking of the number seven, so my belief is true. But do I *know* that you are thinking of the number seven? No, I don't know. I just made a lucky guess. So, just having a true belief is not yet knowledge. Knowledge requires something more.

What more is required to have knowledge? As the example above illustrates, if you were just lucky that your belief is true, then you don't really know that it is true. Thus, we can infer that knowledge is true belief that is *not just true by accident*. What does that mean? Here is one way to understand this.[1] Some ways of forming beliefs are *reliable*—they usually lead to true beliefs. For example, if you have typical adult human vision, then using your vision to form beliefs about what is right in front of you is a very reliable way of forming beliefs. That process will lead to true beliefs most of the time because your vision is very reliable, at least at very close range. Thus, typical adult vision, at close range, is a reliable way of forming beliefs.

Remember that knowledge is true belief that is not just true by accident. Suppose I have typical adult vision, and I use my vision to form a belief about what is right in front of me. In those circumstances, if I form a true belief about what is in front of me, *it will not be an accident that I form a true belief*. That is because I form my belief by using a process that is very reliable. It is a process that leads to true beliefs most of the time. Thus, it will not be an accident if that process leads me to form a true belief since that is what it tends to do. When you use your eyes to determine what is right in front of you, you will usually form a true belief, and so it will not be an accident if you form a true belief in that way. Now suppose that I use my vision to form a belief about what is right in front of me, and I thereby form a true belief. Now I have a true belief *that is not just true by accident*; thus, I have *knowledge*. Finally, here is what we can infer from this: *if you form*

---

1. In what follows, I will use the terminology of a particular theory of knowledge, which is called *reliabilism*. However, this is only to illustrate the fact that knowledge can be *fallible*. As I will explain, it is that latter claim—that knowledge can be fallible—that I will assume in this book. I will not be assuming the reliabilist theory of knowledge.

a belief in a reliable way—a way that usually leads to true beliefs—and you thereby form a true belief, then you have knowledge.

I have said this in order to explain an important assumption I will make in this book. I will assume that *knowledge is fallible*. To understand this, consider again a case of using my vision to form a belief about what is right in front of me. Suppose that I look directly in front of me, I see a laptop computer in front of me, and I form the belief that there is a laptop computer in front of me. In this situation, I have used a reliable process—my vision—to form a true belief. Thus, I *know* that there is a laptop computer in front of me. However, the process that I used to form this belief—trusting my vision—is not an *infallible* process. Even that process can lead to error. On this particular occasion, it did *not* lead to error, but it is always *possible* that it led to error. Consider just a couple of ways in which this could happen. If I had been drugged with a hallucinogenic drug, then I might hallucinate a laptop computer, even if there is not one there. Alternatively, someone in the physics department might decide, as a prank, to project a hologram of a laptop computer onto my desk, and I cannot tell the difference just by looking at it. These are unusual examples, but they illustrate the point: even adult human vision at close range is *fallible*—it can lead to false beliefs.

However, despite its fallibility, my vision often gives me knowledge. In ordinary circumstances, when my vision is working properly and it produces a true belief, I *know* that my belief is true. Since I formed my belief through a process that usually leads to true beliefs, it is not an accident that my belief is true. Thus, I have a true belief that is not just true by accident, and that is knowledge. In summary then, if a way of forming beliefs is *reliable*—it usually leads to true beliefs—then it can give us knowledge, even if it is *fallible*. A way of forming beliefs need not be infallible in order to give us knowledge. It only needs to be reliable. This view is called *fallibilism* about knowledge, and in this book, I will assume that it is true. It is certainly true with respect to *testimony*. Testimony is fallible, but it often gives us knowledge. The question is *how* and *when* testimony gives us knowledge. It is to that question that we now turn.

CHAPTER ONE

Trusting Others

Gordon Bennett worked very hard for over twenty years, running his own natural foods business. Eventually, he decided to sell the business and retire. He was able to sell the business for $1 million, and he invested $100,000 of that money through two accountants, Frank Avellino and Michael Bienes. His investment generated steady returns, and he was pleased with the results. Then, the Securities and Exchange Commission (SEC) investigated Avellino and Bienes and determined that they had violated federal regulations. Bennett followed the story closely, discovering that Avellino and Bienes had been investing all of their money through a single financial advisor, Bernard Madoff. When the SEC investigated Madoff, they found no evidence of fraud. Bennett did his own research on Madoff, and he learned that Madoff was seen as a mover and shaker on Wall Street. He was a leader in the growing field of electronic trading. The fact that the SEC had investigated Madoff and found no evidence of fraud simply confirmed Madoff's status as a trustworthy financial advisor. With these assurances, Bennett decided to invest the rest of his life savings directly in Madoff. He sent Madoff a wire for $900,000.

Once again, Bennett's investment generated steady returns, and before long, his account with Madoff was worth about $3 million. Feeling secure, Bennett decided to make extensive renovations to his home in Marin County, north of San Francisco. Everything seemed to be going well for Bennett. All of his hard work and financial planning had paid off. Then, on December 11, 2008, Bernard Madoff was arrested for fraud. When he learned of Madoff's arrest, Bennett told his wife, Kate Carolan: "Kate, we just lost the house." Indeed, Gordon Bennett and Kate Carolan lost everything—all of their life savings, as well as their home. Nearly 5,000 of Madoff's investment clients were tricked into investing in the largest Ponzi scheme in history. All told, it was a $64 billion fraud. Madoff's client list included Kevin Bacon, Steven Spielberg, Larry King, and Zsa Zsa Gabor. The Holocaust survivor Elie Wiesel lost most of his $15.2 million in assets. Even institutions, like Tufts University, had invested money in Madoff and lost it all.[1]

The Madoff fraud was exposed in 2008, amid the worst financial crisis since the Great Depression. Much like the Madoff fraud, the financial crisis was precipitated by deception and the failure of regulators to expose it. First, mortgages were given to people who could not afford to pay them, and the financial institutions that issued these mortgages misrepresented their clients' ability to pay back the loans. Second, these subprime mortgages were then bundled into mortgage-backed securities that were given a high rating by the major credit rating agencies.[2] The agencies said, in effect, "These are good investments." Major financial institutions then invested in these securities without doing their own due diligence to determine if they were good investments. The result was catastrophic. American households lost an estimated $16 trillion in net worth. One-quarter of households lost at least 75 percent of their net worth, and more than half lost at least 25 percent. In many ways, the financial crisis was like the Madoff fraud but on a much, much larger scale. In both cases, there was trust, followed by deception, followed by the failure of regulators, and the end result was great harm to many people.[3]

Both the Madoff fraud and the 2008 financial crisis illustrate a problem we face in trusting others. In a modern society with a complex division of labor, we have no choice but to trust other people. We

---

1. The story of Gordon Bennett and Kate Carolan is told in the documentary film *Madoff: The Monster of Wall Street*, directed by Joe Berlinger (United States: Netflix, 2023).
2. A mortgage-backed security is a tradable financial asset created by combining many mortgage debts into a single package that can be bought and sold. Investors can then purchase other people's mortgage debts in this single package.
3. For a summary of the financial crisis, see H. Davies, *The Financial Crisis: Who is to Blame?* (Cambridge: Polity Press, 2010).

trust other people to do their jobs and to tell us the truth. We depend on them, and that dependence makes us vulnerable, as dependence always does. The people who trusted Bernie Madoff were vulnerable, and Madoff exploited their vulnerability. The American people trusted banks and other financial institutions to manage their money responsibly. That made them vulnerable, and some of those institutions exploited their vulnerability.

So here is the problem. In a modern society, trust is indispensable. We cannot live our lives without it. However, trust also makes us vulnerable to exploitation by deception. And even when we are not deceived, people sometimes fail us through their incompetence. The SEC did not intend to deceive people about Madoff; they were simply incompetent. Likewise, the credit rating agencies did not intend to deceive people about the value of mortgage-backed securities; they simply failed to do their job. Our trust makes us vulnerable in two ways—vulnerable to deception and vulnerable to incompetence. So we have no choice but to trust other people, but we want to avoid being deceived or failed by incompetence. What can we do?

One way to approach this question is through *epistemology—the theory of knowledge*.[4] Sometimes, our goal in trusting the testimony of other people is to acquire knowledge. Other people have knowledge that is useful to us, and trusting their testimony is often the only way for us to acquire that knowledge. Gordon Bennett wanted to know how to invest his money, so he sought people who knew the answer to that question and trusted them in order to get that knowledge. Of course, Bennett could have picked stocks randomly and invested in those. And he could have gotten lucky and chosen stocks that performed well. Or he could have picked a financial advisor at random and trusted them. Why didn't he do that? He didn't do that because he didn't want to depend on sheer luck. He wanted to *know* the best way to invest his money.

---

4. For the etymology of the term "epistemology," see Matthias Steup and Ram Neta, "Epistemology," *The Stanford Encyclopedia of Philosophy*, ed. Edward N. Zalta, Fall 2020 Edition, https://plato.stanford.edu/archives/fall2020/entries/epistemology.

This illustrates an important fact about knowledge. As I noted in the Introduction, knowledge is more than merely true belief. To see this, consider the following example. Suppose that I buy a lottery ticket, and through wishful thinking, I get myself to believe that my ticket is the winning ticket. I have no reason to believe this—no evidence that this is the winning ticket. I just believe it because I want it to be true. Now suppose that it just so happens that my ticket is, in fact, the winning ticket. Then, my belief that I have the winning ticket is true. But did I *know* that I had the winning ticket? No. My belief was just a lucky guess, and a lucky guess isn't knowledge. This example shows that knowledge is more than just true belief. A lucky guess is a true belief, but it isn't knowledge. Knowledge is true belief that is not just true by accident, and that is exactly why we want knowledge. A lucky guess is fine in the short run, but in the long run, luck eventually runs out. So we don't want to depend on luck to get the truth. We want to *know* that our beliefs are true. In order to get knowledge, we need to form our beliefs in ways that make it likely that they are true. Then, we will get the truth in a way that is more stable and dependable than mere luck. Perhaps that is why Gordon Bennett didn't just guess how to invest his money—he wanted to know.

Of course, there are ways of trusting testimony that would also be completely vulnerable to luck. If Bennett had chosen someone randomly and asked them how to invest his money, then the result would have been a matter of sheer luck. Maybe that's why Bennett didn't do that. He wanted to find someone he could trust—someone whose testimony was reliable. In general, that is the way to get knowledge through testimony—to trust testimony when, and only when, it is reliable. For that purpose, it would be nice to have a general rule or policy that tells us when to trust testimony and when to doubt it. And that brings us to the central question in this chapter: *What policy regarding testimony will enable us to get knowledge through testimony and avoid being deceived?* We can never completely rule out the possibility of deception or incompetence, but we might be able to make it very unlikely that we trust people who are lying or incompetent. How could we make it very unlikely that we fall prey to deception or incompetence? One option would be to stop trusting testimony altogether. However, that will cut us off from a vast store of information that other people possess, and in the modern world, that is not a viable option for most of us. What we want is a policy that will filter out most cases of deception and incompetence so that testimony becomes a secure source of knowledge. Then, we will get knowledge from testimony. What policy will enable us to achieve that?

This brings us to the first view on this subject, which I will call *The Demanding View*.

The Demanding View: You should trust testimony only when you have evidence that the speaker of the testimony is a reliable source of information.

We often say, "Don't believe everything you hear." The Demanding View embodies that advice in a specific way. In order to get knowledge from testimony, you should trust testimony only when you have evidence that the speaker of the testimony is a reliable source, which is to say that the speaker is both honest and competent. To consider this view, let's apply it to Gordon Bennet's decision to trust Bernie Madoff. Did Bennett have evidence that Madoff was a reliable source of information—both honest and competent? Yes, he did. The SEC had investigated Madoff and found no evidence of fraud, so Bennett had evidence that Madoff was honest. As it turned out, that was misleading evidence, but it was evidence nonetheless. If you had asked Bennett, "Why do you believe that Bernie Madoff is honest?" Bennett had an answer—that the SEC had investigated Madoff and found no evidence of any wrongdoing. So Bennett had evidence that Madoff was honest. Did Bennett have evidence that Madoff was competent? Yes, he did. Many financial news outlets on Wall Street reported that Madoff was a great financial mind. They all said that he was a leader in electronic trading. So Bennett had evidence that Madoff was competent as well. Thus, Bennett had evidence that Madoff was both honest and competent and thus a reliable source of information.

However, notice that Bennett's evidence for the reliability of Bernie Madoff was *also* based on the testimony of other people. Bennett's evidence for Madoff's honesty was that the SEC had investigated Madoff and declared that he had committed no fraud. Bennett's evidence for Madoff's competence was based on the reporting of financial news outlets. So Bennett's evidence for Madoff's reliability was, itself, based on the testimony of other people. Of course, that was the source of the problem. Both the SEC and the financial news outlets had been incompetent in their investigation of Madoff, so their statements about Madoff were false. Now notice something else: when Bennett trusted the testimony of the SEC and the financial news outlets, the Demanding View says that Bennett needed to have evidence that the SEC and the financial news outlets were reliable sources. Otherwise, Bennet did not really *know* that the SEC and the financial news outlets were right about Madoff. Did Bennett have evidence that the SEC and the financial news outlets were reliable sources? One might reply that sources like the SEC and the financial news outlets are obviously reliable. However, the Madoff case tells us that this is not always so. More importantly, we are looking for a general policy for responding to all testimony, and that includes even sources like the SEC and major news outlets. According to the Demanding View, Bennett needed to have evidence that the SEC and the financial news outlets were reliable sources of information. Otherwise, Bennet did not really know that they were speaking the truth.

One might say that he did have evidence of their reliability. After all, the SEC has a reputation of being generally reliable in financial matters, and the same is true of the major financial news outlets.[5] Bennett knew that they had this reputation, and that was his evidence that they were reliable sources of information. However, notice that this evidence—the reputation of these institutions—is also based on the testimony of other people. That is what a reputation *is*, essentially—it is the testimony of many people. So this evidence is also based on the testimony of other people. Once again, the Demanding

---

5. In addition, the functional role of the SEC, in a democracy, is to protect people from financial fraud or incompetence. Thus, the SEC is also subject to government oversight. That is yet another reason for someone like Bennett to trust the SEC.

View requires that Bennett have evidence that this source is reliable. In order to know that the reputation of the SEC and the financial news outlets is correct, the Demanding View says that Bennett must have evidence that the opinions of many people about these institutions are reliable. It is now more difficult to see just what kind of evidence Bennett could possibly have for the reliability of many, many people's opinions. If there is such evidence, it seems likely that it will be based on yet more opinions of other people, which will just raise the same question all over again. The problem we are facing here is an instance of an ancient philosophical problem known as *The Regress Problem*. The Regress Problem is a serious problem for the Demanding View. To understand this, we need to take a detour through this ancient problem.

Suppose that I make a claim. I claim that P is true.[6] Now suppose you ask, "How do you know that P is true?" One way for me to answer would be to say, "I know that P is true, because Q," where Q is another statement. What I am saying is that I know that P is true because I know that Q is true, and that is a reason to believe that P is true. Now, at this point, you might say, "OK. But how do you know that Q is true?" Suppose I say, "Oh, I don't know that Q is true. I just assumed it." In that case, I don't really know that P is true after all. If my belief that P is based on my belief that Q, and Q is just an unjustified assumption, then my belief that P is based on an unjustified assumption. But a belief that is based on an unjustified assumption is not knowledge, so in this case I do not really know that P is true. In order for me to know P by inferring it from Q, I must know that Q is true. But then the same problem arises for Q. How do I know that Q is true? If I say that I know Q because R, then the same problem arises all over again. I can know Q by inferring it from R only if I also know that R is true, and this raises the same question about R—"How do I know that R is true?" Now we are off on a regress, but that is just the

---

6. I will use capital letters, like "P" and "Q," as variables that stand for any statement.

beginning of the problem. The problem gets serious when we realize that there are only three ways this regress can continue.[7]

1. The regress keeps going infinitely without end. I just keep giving reasons and never stop.
2. The regress eventually goes in a circle, coming back to P itself as a reason.
3. The regress ends with a belief Z, and I cannot support Z with any other belief.

This is the Regress Problem: *none of these answers seems to yield genuine knowledge.*

Let's start with the first answer—that the regress just keeps going infinitely. This view is called *infinitism*. The infinitist says that my belief is justified if I can give reasons for each one of my beliefs without ever ending. For each belief in the regress, I can give a reason for that belief. The problem with this answer seems obvious. No one can really do that. We only have a finite amount of time, after all, even if we use our entire lives giving reasons for our beliefs. Therefore, no finite human being ever completes the task of giving an infinite series of reasons for their beliefs. However, the infinitist replies that this objection is based on a misunderstanding of her view. In order for my belief to be justified, I don't actually have to give the reason for each of my beliefs. All that is required is that *there are* reasons for each belief in my series of beliefs, and so *I could* give a reason for each of those beliefs *if I had the time*. Unfortunately, even this seems to require too much. It seems doubtful that anyone even *could* give a reason for every belief in an infinite series. To see this, consider a simple belief. Suppose I believe that it is raining outside. What is my reason for this belief? My reason is that I hear a pitter-patter sound on the roof above me, and I remember that in the past, that sound was caused by rain falling on the roof. Now let's proceed to the next stage of the regress. Why do I believe that I hear a pitter-patter sound on the roof? My reason is that I *seem* to hear a pitter-patter

---

7. This problem is known as *Agrippa's Trilemma*. It is attributed to the ancient Greek skeptic Agrippa, who lived sometime near the end of the first century CE.

sound on the roof. That sounds good. But now, let's proceed to the third stage of the regress. Why do I believe that I *seem* to hear a pitter-patter sound on the roof? I now need a reason for believing that I am having an experience—*seeming* to hear a sound. At this point, it is very hard to think of any further reason for believing that I am having really having this experience. If there is a reason for this belief, it seems to be *the experience itself* that gives me a reason for believing that I am having the experience. But if that is correct, then when I get to the experience itself, I cannot give any further reason for believing that I am having that experience. Thus, it seems that, at one of these stages, I simply cannot go on giving any further reasons, infinitely. For that reason, let's set that option aside.

What about option (2)? What if my series of reasons eventually goes in a circle, coming all the way back to the original belief P? Then my reasoning looks like this. I believe P because Q, and I believe Q because R, and I believe R because S, and I believe S because . . . P. The problem with this reasoning is pretty obvious: it is *circular*, and circular reasoning is not good reasoning. To see that, consider the following example. Suppose I believe that every statement in the Bible is true. You ask me why I believe that. In reply, I quote a statement from the Bible that says that every statement in the Bible is true. Suppose you then ask me why I believe that this particular statement in the Bible is true. In reply, I say, "Every statement in the Bible is true, so this statement in the Bible must be true." This is circular reasoning. To support my belief that every statement in the Bible is true, I appeal to a particular statement in the Bible. Then, to support that particular statement in the Bible, I appeal to my belief that every statement in the Bible is true. I have reasoned in a circle, and that is not good reasoning.

Defenders of option (2) reply that this objection misrepresents their view. According to their view, *coherentism*, our reasons for our beliefs are not *linear*—they do not go in a straight line. Rather, we should think of our beliefs as forming a sort of *web*, and in that web, our beliefs give each other mutual support. According to this view, if our beliefs are logically consistent with each other, and they hold together well in other ways, then we have good reason to think that they are true. The problem with this view is that even fairy tales can be logically consistent and hold together well. Thus, the fact that a set of beliefs is logically consistent and holds together well in other ways does not rule out the possibility that it is mere fiction. For that reason, let's set that option aside as well.

That brings us to option (3)—that the regress ends with a belief that cannot be supported by any other belief. Some philosophers think that option (3) can actually give us knowledge. And since we *do* know some things, after all, option (3) must be correct. This view is called *foundationalism*. According to the foundationalist, some beliefs are *basic beliefs*—a basic belief is a belief that is rational to hold even if it cannot be proven by any inference or argument from another belief. Foundationalists say there must be some basic beliefs since that is the only way to solve the Regress Problem. As we give reasons for our beliefs, we eventually come to beliefs that do not need any further evidence or proof. These are things that we know to be true without having to prove them. An example of a basic belief would be my belief that I *seem* to hear a pitter-patter sound on the roof above me. This is a belief about my own sense experience and nothing more. Foundationalists say this is something that I know to be true, and I do not have to give any further reason for the belief in order to know that it is true. The same can be said for my other beliefs about my own experiences. Beliefs about what I am experiencing are basic beliefs. What other kinds of beliefs can be basic in this sense? As we will now see, the Demanding View about testimony implies that beliefs based on testimony cannot be basic beliefs. As we will also see, that is a significant problem for the Demanding View.

According to the Demanding View, in order to get knowledge from testimony, a person must have evidence that the source of the testimony is reliable. That means that every belief based on another person's testimony must be supported by evidence that the source is reliable. Suppose that some of this evidence is itself based on the testimony of another person. Then that latter belief must also be supported by evidence that the source of that testimony is reliable. Thus, the Demanding View entails that no beliefs based on testimony can be basic beliefs. It is important to see exactly what this means.

According to the Demanding View, every belief based on testimony must be based on reasons that can be traced back to evidence that is *not* based on any testimony of any other person. Thus, the Demanding View concerning testimony entails that *no beliefs that are based on testimony are basic beliefs*.[8] However, it is very doubtful that this condition can be met in all of the cases in which we get knowledge from testimony.

Most of what we know about the world comes from the testimony of other people. Just consider what you know about places far away, where you have never been. Everything you know about those places is based on the testimony of other people. Consider everything you know about the history of the world long before you were born. Everything you know about that is also based on the written testimony of other people. Even in science today, most people have to trust scientists when they say that they conducted certain experiments and when they describe the results of those experiments. All of this knowledge—of faraway places, the past, and the experiments of scientists, is based on the testimony of other people. You might think that our trust in these people, when it is appropriate, is based on evidence that they are reliable sources. However, when we consider our evidence carefully, it often turns out to be based on more testimony. I trust *National Geographic* magazine because it has a track record of being very reliable. But how do I know that? Have I, myself, traveled to all of the distant places described in the magazine? No. I am told by many other people that *National Geographic* is generally reliable. That is my evidence, and it is based on more testimony. In fact, this is usually the case—our evidence for the reliability of a source is based on more testimony, and our evidence for the reliability of that source is still more testimony. It appears that many of our sources of knowledge are based on testimony, *all the way down*.

---

8. To say that a belief is a basic belief is to say two things: (1) it is not based on any other beliefs, and (2) it constitutes *knowledge* without being inferred from anything else. The Demanding View is saying that no belief that is based on testimony can be basic in this way. In other words, either a belief based on testimony must be supported by another belief, or it does not constitute knowledge.

If that is correct, then the Demanding View cannot be right. As we have seen, the Demanding View prohibits trusting any testimony without having evidence that the source is reliable. If some trust in testimony is ultimately based on more testimony, then the Demanding View would prohibit trusting testimony in those cases. However, those cases include much of what we know about the world. Thus, the Demanding View entails a large degree of *skepticism*. Skeptics deny that we have knowledge. Complete skepticism denies that we have any knowledge at all. The Demanding View does not entail complete skepticism since we could still acquire knowledge through our own senses and reason. However, the Demanding View seems to entail that I do not know anything that I have learned from a book, a documentary, or the daily news unless I can somehow confirm that the source is reliable *and* confirm it without ever relying on any further testimony unless I can confirm the reliability of *that* source. It is doubtful I can do that for very many of the sources that I trust. Consequently, we can accept the Demanding View only if we are willing to deny that we know a lot of what we take ourselves to know—about geography, history, and the natural world. Before we accept such a radical conclusion, we should see if there are any other possibilities.

Before we consider the next view, we should stop to consider how this applies to the case of Gordon Bennett. It is tempting to say that in order to know that Madoff was telling the truth, Gordon Bennett needed to have evidence that Madoff was reliable; if that evidence was based on the testimony of the SEC and the financial news outlets, then Bennett needed to have evidence that they were also reliable, and so on. However, as we have now seen, that view implies that you and I do not know most of the things we have learned from history books, science books, and even the daily news. So we can apply that standard of knowledge to Gordon Bennett only if we are willing to say that we do not know many of the things that we all think we know. If that seems implausible, then Bennett's failure to meet that standard cannot be what went wrong in his case. Moreover, that standard is not a viable solution to the problem of getting knowledge from testimony in the modern world. Is there a more reasonable standard that will enable us to achieve knowledge through testimony? Some people would say there is, and it is what I will call *The Credulous View*.

The Credulous View: You should always trust testimony unless you have some reason to doubt that the speaker is reliable or to doubt that their statement is true.

According to the Credulous View, testimony is innocent until proven guilty. Our default position should be to trust testimony unless we have some specific reason to doubt it. At first glance, the Credulous View might seem *too* credulous. It sounds like we are supposed to believe everything we hear. However, that is not what it says. The Credulous View does not say we should always trust testimony, *no matter what else we know*. It only says that we should always trust testimony *unless* we have some reason to doubt that the speaker is reliable or to doubt that their statement is true. That qualification is important. To see that, consider how some people responded to Gordon Bennett. In a letter to the *Los Angeles Times* on May 2, 2009, Greg Daniels wrote, "The investors who gave money to Bernie Madoff did so in spite of the fact that he promised returns that were literally 'too good to be true.' . . . Mr. Bennett, you were a victim of your own greed." According to Daniels, Gordon Bennett had reason to doubt that Madoff was reliable—the returns that Madoff promised were unrealistic. If that is correct, then even the Credulous View implies that Bennett should not have trusted Madoff because he had reason to doubt that Madoff was reliable.

In his own defense, Bennett has said that Madoff "promised steady returns, averaging 9 percent a year. . . . It wasn't promising the moon. It was just steady." Madoff's returns turned out to be higher than that—between 12 percent and 24 percent. However, as Madoff himself noted in an interview in 1992, this rate of return was not that unusual. Between November 1982 and November 1992, Standard and Poor's 500 stock index generated an average annual return of 16.3 percent.[9] What *was* unusual was the *steadiness* of Madoff's returns. Markets are

---

9. Sital Patel, "My Interview with Madoff," *Wall Street Journal*, December 16, 1992.

volatile—they have ups and downs. But Madoff's returns were completely steady. It was as if his investments were somehow immune to the volatility of the market. Should the steadiness of Madoff's returns have led Bennett to doubt his reliability? That seems doubtful. Suppose, for the sake of argument, that the unusual steadiness of Madoff's returns was some reason to doubt Madoff. If that was the only evidence that Bennett possessed, then perhaps he should have doubted Madoff. However, that was not Bennett's only evidence on the matter. Remember that Bennett had evidence from both the SEC and the financial news outlets that Madoff was reliable. Arguably, that evidence was enough to counterbalance any reasons to doubt Madoff. Be that as it may, the important point is that the Credulous View does *not* give us a blank check to trust any testimony whatsoever. The Credulous View says that we should trust testimony unless we have some specific reason to doubt that the source is reliable or that their statement is true. In many cases, that implies that we should *not* trust a particular piece of testimony. Whenever we know that someone has a history of lying or that they have a motive to lie on this occasion, we will have reason to doubt that they are a reliable source. Likewise, whenever we know that someone has poor judgment in some area, we will have a reason to doubt that they are reliable in that area. Thus, the Credulous View often tells us to doubt testimony rather than to trust it. The view is not as naïve as it first sounds.

Nevertheless, one might still think that this is too credulous. If I know absolutely nothing about a person, then the Credulous View seems to imply that I should believe everything they say just because they said it. However, we know that people often deceive us and that they often say false things out of incompetence. If we trust people whenever we have no reason to doubt them, then we are bound to form some false beliefs. At this point, defenders of the Credulous View note that even our best sources of information are fallible. Consider vision. People often say, "Seeing is believing." If there is one source of information that we trust, it is our own vision. However, even our own vision is fallible. A stick submerged in water looks bent, even though it isn't. What appears to be an oasis in the desert is actually a mirage. In many cases, our eyes deceive us. Even vision is fallible. Yet, we should trust our vision unless we have a specific reason to doubt it. If I seem to see a tree, then I should believe that it is a tree, even if it is possible that I am mistaken. Defenders of the Credulous View argue that we should treat testimony in the very same way. Just like vision, testimony is fallible, but it is generally reliable. Most of the time, vision is accurate, and most of the time, people tell the truth. So, in both cases, vision and testimony, our default position should be to trust unless we have a specific reason to doubt.

Unfortunately, there are significant differences between vision and testimony. The function of vision is to give us accurate information about the world around us. It does not achieve that perfectly, but that is what it evolved to do. By contrast, the function of testimony is not always to convey accurate information. Sometimes, when a person gives testimony, their principal aim is to get us to believe what they say, *whether or not it is true*. People often have an interest in *being believed*. In many cases, that is why they give testimony—to get other people to believe what they say. Sometimes, this interest coincides with what is true, but not always. Even when people lie, they usually have an interest in being believed. Even when they are incompetent, they usually want to be believed. Thus, unlike our own vision, the testimony of other people is not essentially aimed at giving us accurate information. Moreover, when people lie or when they are incompetent, they are capable of being just as convincing as when they are honest and competent.

In summary, then, there's an important difference between vision and testimony. Normally, my environment is not trying to deceive my eyes, nor does it have the ability to disguise itself for that purpose. There are exceptions to this, of course. Animals use camouflage to disguise themselves. But for the most part, the environment is not trying to deceive me, nor does it have the intelligence to outwit my own eyes. By contrast, people who give testimony are often trying to deceive me, and they have the intelligence to do so. Thus, the analogy between vision and testimony is imperfect, to say the least.

However, the case of vision does show that the mere fact that a source of information is fallible does not prove that it should not be trusted. Vision is fallible, but we should not stop trusting our own eyes. In the same way, a defender of the Credulous View says that the mere fact that testimony is fallible does not show that we should not trust testimony as long as we recognize when we have some specific reason to doubt it. Nevertheless, this might demand too little to give us secure knowledge from testimony.

To see the problem, imagine the following situation. Suppose that a sales representative comes to my door and offers to sell me a piece of land in Florida. He describes this land in superlative terms: it is the most beautiful piece of land that he has ever seen; it is perfect in every way, and so on. However, when I ask him questions about the land and how he got it, his answers are very vague, and he gets irritated. Moreover, there appear to be inconsistencies in some of his answers. Nevertheless, suppose that I agree to buy the land, and I eventually discover that I have been swindled. The land is entirely in a swamp. You might well say to me, "You should not have believed him." And you would be right. Since we know that people sometimes deceive us, a reasonable person will always be on the lookout for signs of dishonesty. If I had been paying attention and looking for signs of dishonesty, I would have detected many such signs in this person's testimony. The Credulous View does not require that I actively monitor people in this way. The Credulous View seems to license my acceptance of the salesperson's testimony, and that seems mistaken. Thus, critics say that the Credulous View demands too little.

A defender of the Credulous View might say that, in the case of the land salesman, I have a good reason to doubt the salesman. The vagueness of his answer, his irritation at being asked questions, and the inconsistencies in his answers give me good reason to doubt what he is saying. If that is correct, then the Credulous View does *not* imply that I should trust the salesman. But what if I fail to pay attention to any of this? Suppose that this man reminds me of my elderly uncle, whom I adore. For that reason, suppose that I fail to look for any signs of dishonesty in this salesman, and so I fail to see them. Then, I will be unaware of any reason to doubt the salesman. In that case, the Credulous View seems to permit trusting him. Critics of the Credulous View contend that if we want to get secure knowledge from testimony, then we must monitor people for signs of honesty or dishonesty and for signs of competence or incompetence.[10] There is room for debate here, and I will leave it to the reader to think about this further.

This brings us to the third view, which I will call *The Monitoring View*.

The Monitoring View: You should always monitor those who give testimony for signs of dishonesty or incompetence. If you find no signs of dishonesty or incompetence, then you should trust testimony unless you have some other reason to doubt that the source is reliable or that this statement is true.

The Monitoring View is more demanding than the Credulous View but less demanding than the Demanding View. The Monitoring View requires that we always be on the lookout for signs of dishonesty or incompetence. If we find such signs, then we should not trust the testimony, but if we find no such signs, then we should trust the testimony unless we have some other reason to doubt it. The Monitoring View aims to make us a bit less gullible than the Credulous View without requiring that we have independent evidence for the reliability of every source we trust. Thus, the Monitoring View aims to be demanding enough to give us secure knowledge without being so demanding that it leads to skepticism about most of what we learn from other people.

Unfortunately, the Monitoring View faces a very serious problem. Recent work in psychology suggests that we are not very good at monitoring other people for dishonesty or incompetence.[11] We trust attractive people more than unattractive people, even though attractiveness is independent of both honesty and competence. We believe

---

10. This argument is developed and defended by Elizabeth Fricker in "Against Gullibility," in *Knowing from Words: Western and Indian Philosophical Analysis of Understanding and Testimony*, ed. Bimal Krishna Matilal and Arindam Chakrabarti (New York: Springer, 1994), 125–161.

11. For an excellent discussion of the empirical evidence on this question and its relevance for the epistemology of testimony, see Joseph Shieber, *Testimony: A Philosophical Introduction*, chap. 2 (New York: Routledge, 2015). The following summary is based on that work.

that "keeping a straight face" is a sign of honesty, but liars actually keep a straight face more consistently than people telling the truth. We believe that sustained eye contact indicates sincerity, but liars actually maintain eye contact more consistently than truth-tellers. We see confidence as a sign of competence, but studies have found that confidence is independent of competence. In fact, people who know less are often more confident in their judgments than people who know more. Generally speaking, studies have found that people are not very good at determining when someone is lying. We rarely get it right more than 60 percent of the time, which is only 10 percent better than chance. Thus, the evidence suggests that we are just not very good at monitoring people for dishonesty or incompetence. If that is correct, then monitoring does not put us in a significantly better position to determine whether someone is telling the truth. If we were good at monitoring people, then monitoring might help, but it looks like our actual monitoring is simply inept.

Perhaps this just shows that we need to get better at monitoring. However, there is an even deeper problem here. Intelligent deceivers will tailor their behavior to their particular situation and their particular audience in each act of deception. Moreover, deceivers' personalities will vary from person to person as well. Consequently, deceivers are likely to behave differently in different situations—it is doubtful that there is any single behavior or set of behaviors, that is a reliable indicator of deception. If that is correct, then it makes effective monitoring even more difficult. The case of Bernie Madoff illustrates this very problem. Madoff fooled everyone on Wall Street, including everyone at the SEC. At one point, a journalist, Michael Ocrant, went to see Madoff in person. Ocrant was an experienced journalist who had actually exposed Ponzi schemes before. After visiting Madoff, he gave the following report.

> This guy was as cool as can be. I mean, I didn't see the slightest indication that anything was wrong. In fact, rather than worrying about the story I was writing, he acted like he was inviting me over for Sunday tea. He doesn't act like he's got something to hide. He spent more than two hours with me. He showed

me around the whole operation. He even offered to answer any other questions. Guilty people usually don't act this way.[12]

This illustrates the difficulty of monitoring effectively. Bernie Madoff did not show any of the signs that we tend to associate with lying. He was not nervous or withdrawn. He was calm and friendly. He did not resist questions. Rather, he invited them. Thus, not even an experienced reporter could tell that Madoff was lying. Diana Henriques, the author of *The Wizard of Lies: Bernie Madoff and the Death of Trust*, summed it up this way:

> The lesson of the Madoff story is really: this is what a Ponzi scheme looks like—charming, successful, widely admired, facile at telling lies and winning your trust.[13]

Monitoring is simply no match for such deception.

If monitoring will not give us secure knowledge from testimony, then is there anything that will? The fourth and final view that we will consider proposes a different kind of solution to the problem. According to this view, the problem of getting knowledge through testimony cannot be solved by individuals acting alone. Rather, the only possible solution to this problem is a *social* solution. This view is what I will call *The Reliable Network View*.

> ***The Reliable Network View:*** *Testimony transmits knowledge when it is embedded in a socially distributed cognitive network that is generally reliable.*[14]

If this view seems very different from the other views we have considered, that is because it *is* very different. We will consider objections to this view in due course, but only after it has been explained fully. To understand the Reliable Network View, it will help to consider the

---

12. Harry Markopolos, *No One Would Listen: A True Financial Thriller* (Hoboken, NJ: Wiley, 2010), 82.
13. *Madoff: The Monster of Wall Street* (2023).
14. The Reliable Network View has been developed and defended most fully by Shieber. See *Testimony*, chap. 6.

way that natural science is often practiced today. In a seminal article on the role of trust in knowledge, the philosopher John Hardwig explains how modern science often works.

> Modern science is collegial, not only in the sense that scientists build on the work of those who have preceded them, but also in the sense that research is increasingly done by teams and, indeed, by larger and larger teams. This is true for two reasons. (1) The process of gathering and analyzing data sometimes just takes too long to be accomplished by one person. . . . (2) Even more important, research is increasingly done by teams because no one knows enough to be able to do the experiment by herself. Increasingly, no one could know enough—sheer limitations of intellect prohibit it. The cooperation of researchers from different specializations and the resulting division of cognitive labor are, consequently, often unavoidable if an experiment is to be done at all. No one particle physicist knows enough to measure the lifespan of charm particles.[15]

Modern science is not practiced by lone individuals acting in isolation. Rather, it is practiced by groups of people who are organized into teams in order to perform the task of scientific discovery. The organization of these teams involves a division of labor—each member performs one specific task, and then they pass the results on to the next member of the team, or to the entire team, to perform the next task. In this way,

> it is the testimony of one scientist or mathematician to another that connects the bits of evidence gathered by different researchers into a unified whole that can justify a conclusion. By accepting each other's testimony, individual researchers are united into a team that may have what no individual member of the team has: sufficient evidence to justify their mutual conclusion.[16]

---

15. John Hardwig, "The Role of Trust in Knowledge," *Journal of Philosophy* 88 (1981): 694.
16. Hardwig, "The Role of Trust in Knowledge," 697.

Scientists who work together in teams like this constitute a *socially distributed cognitive network*. A socially distributed cognitive network is a group of people who are organized for the purpose of performing a certain cognitive task, like conducting an experiment and reporting the results. The organization of the group involves a division of cognitive labor between the members of the group, in which different members perform different cognitive tasks. No single member of the group is directly aware of all of the tasks that are performed by all of the other members of the group. The cooperation of the members of the group in performing their collective task is achieved through testimony. Testimony is the channel through which information passes between members of the group. If each member of the group performs their own task well and reports it accurately, then the whole network will succeed in performing the cognitive task for which it exists. If a network succeeds in this respect most of the time, then I will say that it is a *reliable* network. According to the Reliable Network View, testimony transmits knowledge from one person to another when, and only when, that testimony is embedded in a reliable cognitive network.

The Reliable Network View takes a radically different approach to the problem of testimony. All the other approaches to the problem of testimony are *individualistic*. They ask how an individual should respond to testimony. By contrast, the Reliable Network View suggests that the problem of testimony—the problem of getting secure knowledge from testimony—cannot be solved by any individual acting alone. Rather, the only solution to the problem of testimony is a *social* solution. In order for a person to get knowledge by trusting testimony, they must belong to a reliable network—a group of people organized in such a way that they transmit information reliably through testimony. There is nothing that an individual can do unilaterally to achieve this. It requires the cooperation of many people. Thus, the Reliable Network View takes the problem of testimony out of the hands of individuals and puts it into the hands of communities, acting together.

To see what this means in practice, let's apply it to the case of Gordon Bennett. According to the Reliable Network View, Gordon

Bennett can get knowledge from testimony only if he is embedded in a reliable network of people. Suppose that Bennett's network, with respect to his investments, consists of the following people: the accountants with whom he first invested—Avelino and Bienes—and Bernie Madoff. Since Avelino, Bienes, and Madoff were all guilty of multiple counts of fraud, this is clearly an unreliable network. According to the Reliable Network View, that is why Gordon Bennett did not get secure knowledge from the testimony of these people. Bennett was embedded in a very *unreliable* cognitive network. Of course, that was not Bennett's fault. According to the Reliable Network View, individuals are often blameless for being situated in an unreliable network. In some cases, like this one, a person's failure to get knowledge from testimony is not their fault.

Suppose that we widen the scope of Bennett's network to include all of the people at the SEC, and all of the people at the major financial news outlets. Was that wider network a reliable network? At first glance, the answer to this question is less obvious. Remember that a reliable network does not have to be *infallible*. In order to be reliable, a cognitive network only needs to be accurate most of the time. If we include both the SEC and the major financial news outlets in Bennett's network, then one might say that this was, in fact, a reliable cognitive network. In that case, Bennett was just unlucky to be the victim of one of the relatively few failures of this network. However, that answer seems plausible only if we ignore the fact that in 2008, the entire financial system was in crisis. At that time, the entire financial system had failed to transmit information reliably. This suggests that, even if we widen the scope of Bennett's network to include the entire financial system, Bennett was embedded in a very unreliable cognitive network. That is why he could not get secure knowledge by trusting testimony. The entire system was broken.

As noted above, the Reliable Network View takes a radically different approach to the problem of testimony. The other views *give advice to individuals*—they tell each person when to trust the testimony of other people. By contrast, the Reliable Network View does not give advice to individuals, at least not directly. Instead, it tells us what an individual's environment must be like in order for them to get knowledge from testimony. Of course, the environment that a person finds themselves in is not always in their control. Thus, the Reliable Network View implies that getting knowledge from testimony is not in the control of any individual acting alone.

One might object to the Reliable Network View for this reason: it doesn't tell us—each of us, as individuals—what we should *do* or what we should *believe* with respect to testimony. For each of us, as individuals, it just isn't very helpful to say, "Well, you need to belong to a reliable network," since that is not something that is in our control as individuals. A defender of the Reliable Network View has at least two replies to this. First, she might say that the problems with each of the other views show that there simply isn't anything that an individual can do unilaterally to get secure knowledge from testimony. When we look at the advice given by the Demanding View, the Credulous View, and the Monitoring View, we see that each of them is either too demanding, too permissive, or simply ineffective. If that is correct, then the prospects for individualistic approaches seem very dim. In that case, we should turn to a collective approach, like the Reliable Network View. I will leave it to the reader to decide whether this reply is correct.

Second, a defender of the Reliable Network View will insist that she *does* offer advice concerning testimony—it's just that it is advice to *whole communities of people* rather than to individuals acting alone. The Reliable Network View instructs us to act together, in communities, to build reliable cognitive networks and maintain them as such. This is not something that any one individual can do unilaterally, but it *is* something that whole communities of people can do acting together. Thus, the Reliable Network View does give advice—it's just a different kind of advice.[17]

The Reliable Network View tells us to construct reliable cognitive networks. How can we do that? That is a large, complex question, and I will not try to give a complete answer here. However, in the

---

17. There is yet another significant objection to the Reliable Network View based on the fact that it is an *externalist* view of knowledge. This objection will be discussed at length in the next chapter.

remainder of this chapter, I will argue that, in many cases, a reliable cognitive network needs to include some *doubters*—people who do not simply trust the testimony of others. Not everyone in a reliable network should be a doubter. In fact, the majority should *not* be doubters. If most people were doubters, then the flow of information in the network would break down. A team of scientists would never complete their research if everyone in the group doubted the testimony of the other members of the group. However, in some cases, doubters perform a very important function in a reliable cognitive network. To see that, consider a recent episode in the history of science.[18] In the 1870s, scientists entertained two hypotheses concerning the cause of peptic ulcer disease (PUD). One hypothesis attributed PUD to the presence of bacteria in the stomach, while the other attributed it to excess acid in the stomach. For the next several decades, scientists explored each of these two hypotheses. Then, in 1954, a prominent gastroenterologist, Walter Palmer, published a study claiming to show that no bacteria were capable of colonizing the human stomach. As a result of Palmer's study, the scientific community abandoned the bacterial hypothesis. As one author put it, "[Palmer's study] ensured that the development of bacteriology in gastroenterology would be closed to the world as if frozen in ice. . . . [It] established the dogma that bacteria could not live in the human stomach. . . ."[19] As it turned out, Palmer was mistaken, but it would take the scientific community another fifty years to figure that out. In 1958, John Lykoudis, a Greek doctor, began treating his PUD patients with antibiotics with some success. However, no one would publish his results, nor would the Greek government accept his treatment. He was eventually fined

---

18. The following story is recounted by Kevin Zollman in "The Epistemic Benefit of Transient Diversity," *Erkenntnis* 72 (2010): 17–35.
19. See Y. T. Fukuda, T. Shimoyama, and B. J. Marshall, "Kasai, Kobayashi and Koch's Postulates in the History of Helicobacter Pylori," in *Helicobacter Pioneers: Firsthand Accounts from the Scientists Who Discovered Heliobacters*, ed. Barry Marshall (Hoboken, NJ: Wiley-Blackwell, 2002), 15–24.

for it.[20] Decades later, Robin Warren and Barry Marshall returned to the bacterial hypothesis, and in 2005, they won the Nobel Prize for their discovery that PUD is primarily caused by bacteria. In retrospect, it would have been better if not everyone in the scientific community had trusted Palmer's study. If some members of the scientific community had doubted Palmer's study, they would have continued to explore the bacterial hypothesis, and they would have discovered the truth sooner. This example illustrates how the presence of doubters can make a cognitive network more reliable.[21]

That is precisely what was missing from Gordon Bennett's cognitive network when he invested in Bernie Madoff—some doubters. No one at the SEC doubted Madoff. No one at the financial news outlets doubted Madoff. Eventually, one man doubted Madoff and is now credited with exposing Madoff's Ponzi scheme. That man was Harry Markopolos. Markopolos was a portfolio manager at Rampart Investment Management when he first heard about a hedge fund manager who delivered returns of 1 percent to 2 percent a month. His employers at Rampart learned that the manager in question was Bernie Madoff, and they asked Markopolos to design a product similar to Madoff's. When Markopolos got a copy of Madoff's revenue stream, he could tell something was wrong. No one could produce returns like that. Right away, Markopolos suspected that Madoff was either running a Ponzi scheme or committing some other kind of fraud. Markopolos wrote to the SEC, laying out the evidence for his conclusion. Unfortunately, no one would listen.[22] It would take

---

20. See B. Rigas and E. D. Papavassiliou, "John Lykoudis: The General Practitioner in Greece Who in 1958 Discovered the Etiology of, and a Treatment for, Peptic Ulcer Disease," in *Helicobacter Pioneers: Firsthand Accounts from the Scientists Who Discovered Heliobacters*, ed. Barry Marshall (Hoboken, NJ: Wiley-Blackwell, 2002), 75–87.

21. Not just any doubters will serve the purposes of a reliable cognitive network. A reliable network needs doubters who raise the right sorts of doubts and who raise them in the right sort of way.

22. Hence the title of Markopolos's book, *No One Would Listen: A True Financial Thriller*.

several more years and billions of dollars stolen before Bernie Madoff was exposed to the world.

A reliable cognitive network needs people like Markopolos—people who do not simply trust what others' say but question and doubt it. Without such doubters, cognitive networks are vulnerable to exploitation by people like Bernie Madoff. Furthermore, those doubters need to be *heard*. If people had listened to the Greek doctor, John Lykoudis, and considered his claims, the truth about peptic ulcer disease would have been discovered much sooner. Likewise, if people had listened to Harry Markopolos, then Bernie Madoff would have been caught much sooner. Reliable cognitive networks need some doubters, and those doubters need to be heard. However, as I noted above, not everyone should be a doubter. In fact, in most cases, a reliable cognitive network needs the majority of people to trust the testimony of the people around them. In a reliable cognitive network, trust is necessary for the flow of information, so it is best if most people trust the testimony of other people. At the same time, in order to prevent frequent exploitation of that trust, there need to be some doubters to expose those who seek to exploit our trust. This is one particular way a reliable cognitive network will employ a division of cognitive labor. In the following chapter, we will consider another way whole societies divide their cognitive labor.

Study Questions

1. If Gordon Bennett did some research on Bernard Madoff and found many sources that said that Madoff was trustworthy, then would his trust in Madoff satisfy the Demanding View? What problem does this raise? Explain your answer.
2. Suppose that Gordon Bennett met Madoff in person, and Bennett saw signs that Madoff was dishonest. According to the Credulous View, should Bennett continue to trust Madoff? Explain your answer.
3. Suppose that Gordon Bennett met Madoff in person, and he looked closely for any signs of dishonesty in Madoff. Suppose that Bennett saw no signs of dishonesty in Madoff. Then, should Bennett trust Madoff? Explain your answer.
4. If the Reliable Network View is correct, then can Gordon Bennett, through his own thoughts and actions, guarantee that he knows the truth about Madoff? Explain your answer.
5. If a network of people is generally reliable, then should everyone in that network accept what they hear uncritically without questioning it? Explain your answer.

For Further Reading

The best introduction to the epistemology of testimony is Joseph Shieber's book *Testimony: A Philosophical Introduction* (New York: Routledge, 2015). To dive even deeper, see the essays in Jennifer Lackey and Ernest Sosa's collection, *The Epistemology of Testimony* (New York: Oxford, 2006). Lackey's contribution to that collection proposes an interesting compromise between individualist and collectivist approaches. The most prominent champion of the Monitoring View is Elizabeth Fricker, and her position is well-defended in her essay in that collection. Finally, for an excellent defense of the Demanding View, see Tim Kenyon's article "The Informational Richness of Testimonial Contexts," *The Philosophical Quarterly* 63 (2013): 58–80. For a different approach to the epistemology of financial markets, see Lisa Warenski, "Disentangling the Epistemic Failings of the 2008 Financial Crisis," in *The Routledge Handbook of Applied Epistemology*, ed. David Coady and James Chase (New York: Routledge, 2018), 196–201. Warenski emphasizes the importance of responsible belief-forming practices in financial institutions.

CHAPTER TWO

Deferring to Experts

In the mid-1970s, the United States faced a new kind of economic problem—one that many economists had thought impossible. They called it *stagflation*. The economy was stagnant, but inflation was rising rapidly. In May 1975, unemployment reached 9 percent, and inflation reached 10 percent. The problem continued through the election of President Jimmy Carter in 1976 and persisted through his presidency. By 1979, Carter was looking for someone new to run the Federal Reserve and fix the economy. He settled on an economist named Paul Volcker. Volcker was a graduate of Princeton and Harvard and had been serving as president of the Federal Reserve Bank of New York since 1975. He was an outspoken advocate of taking whatever measures were necessary to reduce inflation. Sitting in the Oval Office, Volcker told Carter that he would favor a much tighter monetary policy than his predecessor. In reply, Carter told Volcker, "I need to get somebody in here who will take care of the economy." At that point, the president of the United States handed the reigns of the American economy over to Paul Volcker.[1]

At Volcker's confirmation hearing in July 1979, Wisconsin senator William Proxmire asked Volcker to assure him that he would not raise interest rates to a level that would be very difficult for small businesses, farmers, and working people. In his reply, Volcker made his intentions clear: "I don't think we have any substitute for seeking an answer to our problems in the context of monetary

---

1. This story is recounted by Binyamin Appelbaum in *The Economists' Hour: False Prophets, Free Markets, and the Fracture of Society* (New York: Little, Brown and Company, 2019), 70–83. The following summary is based on his account.

discipline."[2] Volcker was confirmed and in September 1979, he was sworn in as the chairman of the Federal Reserve. He proceeded to do exactly what he said he would. The Fed tightened the money supply, and interest rates rose sharply. The prime rate rose to over 20 percent, and other rates rose much higher than that. For some people, the effects were devastating. Consumers stopped buying certain goods, and as a result, millions of workers lost their jobs. Unemployment in the auto industry rose to 23 percent. In the steel industry, it climbed to 29 percent. Some of these people lost their homes and any chance of a comfortable retirement. However, Volcker believed that this was the only way to fix the economy, and it was worth the cost, including the heavy toll on some American workers. He told the journalist William Greider, "You just have to tell yourself that somehow it's in the larger interest of the country—and even of these people—to get this straightened out." Unfortunately, that generation of American workers never fully recovered from Volcker's choice. The median income of full-time, male workers in 1978, adjusted for inflation, was $54,392. That number would not be equaled or exceeded for the next four decades.

Jimmy Carter didn't know how to fix the economy. He needed to find someone who knew what to do. He needed an expert. The story of Jimmy Carter and Paul Volcker illustrates a pervasive feature of modern life. In order to get many of the things we want, we have to find people with expertise that we lack, and we have to defer to their judgment. I don't know how to fix my car, so I find a mechanic, and I ask him to fix it. I don't know how to cure my own illness, so I find a doctor, and I ask him how to cure it. I don't know how to fix the wiring in my house, so I find an electrician, and I ask him to do it. No one could be an expert in all of these areas. So we depend on other people to develop expertise in these areas, and then we defer to their judgment. Of course, to do that, we must be able to tell when another person is an expert. How do we do that? How do we know

---

2. Appelbaum, *The Economists' Hour*, 77.

that another person is an expert? That is the first question that we will explore in this chapter.³ An expert is someone who has more knowledge, skill, and understanding in a certain domain than most people have.⁴ In virtue of this knowledge, skill, and understanding, an expert is in a position to help novices solve problems they would otherwise be unable to solve.⁵ However, in order for novices to benefit from the services of an expert, they first have to *recognize* who the experts are. Throughout history, many people have claimed to be experts yet lacked the knowledge, skill, and understanding that makes someone a genuine expert. Thus, the mere fact that someone *claims* to be an expert does not guarantee that they really are an expert. How do we know when another person is a genuine expert? This is *The Recognition Problem*. If you are not yourself an expert in a certain domain, then how can you

---

3. This question is closely related to the question we explored in the previous chapter since trusting experts is a particular instance of trusting the testimony of another person. However, as we will see, this question poses additional problems unique to trusting experts.

4. It is possible for someone to be an expert without having a full understanding of their domain. As Thomas Grundmann notes, the Indian mathematician Srinivasa Ramanujan could solve many complex mathematical problems, but he could not prove any of his solutions. Thus, he had superior knowledge and skill in mathematics but not full understanding. However, in other cases, the lack of understanding implies a corresponding lack of expertise. If someone reads and believes everything written by a genuine expert, but they do not understand how it all fits together, or why it is true, then they are not an expert in the area. For our purposes, it will suffice to say that an expert has some combination of knowledge, skill, and understanding that is superior to most people. For discussion of the problem of defining expertise, see Alvin Goldman, "Expertise," *Topoi* 37 (2018): 3–10; Christian Quast, "Expertise: A Practical Explication," *Topoi* 37 (2018): 11–27; and Thomas Grundmann, "Experts: What Are They and How Can Laypeople Identify Them?" in *Oxford Handbook of Social Epistemology*, ed. Jennifer Lackey and Aidan McGlynn (New York: Oxford University Press, 2024).

5. I will use the term *novice* for anyone who is not an expert in the relevant domain.

tell if another person is really an expert in that domain?[6] Here is one possible answer to this question.

> *The Accessible Evidence View:* There are facts that constitute good evidence of expertise, and these facts are accessible to the average person; this enables the average person to know when another person is a genuine expert.[7]

According to the Accessible Evidence View, there are facts that constitute good evidence of expertise, and these facts are accessible to the average person. Thus, even a novice can acquire evidence that is sufficient for them to know that another person is a genuine expert. What kinds of facts constitute evidence of expertise? At least five types of facts seem to constitute evidence of expertise: *credentials*, *track record*, *argumentative capacity*, *agreement with consensus*, and *intellectual honesty*.[8] First, experts have credentials—degrees from accredited colleges and universities, publications in peer-reviewed journals, and recognition by other experts. Second, experts have a good track record of getting things right—they make statements that can be independently verified and predictions that come true. Third, experts have excellent argumentative capacity—they can rebut the objections of their critics convincingly. Fourth, experts usually agree with the consensus in their area of expertise. Fifth, experts are intellectually honest—they reveal conflicts of interest and retract false claims. If a person possesses enough of these qualities, then that is good evidence that they are a

---

6. The Recognition Problem is presented and discussed by Alvin Goldman in "Experts: Which Ones Should You Trust?," *Philosophy and Phenomenological Research* 63 (2001): 85–110.

7. A version of this view is defended by Elisabeth Anderson in "Democracy, Public Policy, and Lay Assessment of Scientific Testimony," *Episteme* 8 (2011): 144–164.

8. See Neil Levy, *Bad Beliefs: Why They Happen to Good People* (New York: Oxford University Press, 2022), 111. The following typology of the kinds of evidence for expertise is drawn from Levy.

genuine expert.[9] In many cases, it seems that even a novice can tell that a person possesses these qualities. That gives the novice evidence that this person is an expert, and if it is true, then the novice *knows* that this person is an expert. According to the Accessible Evidence View, this evidence solves the Recognition Problem.

In order to solve the Recognition Problem, these facts must meet certain conditions. First, a novice must be able to recognize the fact in question. It must be accessible to her. Second, it must be reasonable for a novice to take this fact as evidence of expertise *without already knowing that other people are experts*. To solve the Recognition Problem, a novice must have evidence of expertise that does not require already knowing that other people are experts. To understand this second condition, consider an analogy. Suppose I believe that a certain person—let's call him Axel—is a prophet, who has been appointed by God to reveal God's will to all of humanity. Suppose you ask me how I know that Axel is a prophet. I reply that Rhiannon told me Axel is a prophet. Naturally, you then ask me why I believe Rhiannon. I reply that I believe her because she is also a prophet, who was appointed by God. At this point, it should be clear that I have simply replaced one problem with another one, of the very same kind. What you want to know is how I can know that *anyone* is a prophet, who was sent by God. In answer to that question, it will not do to say that a prophet told me so. That raises the very same question all over again. If we are looking for an answer to the question "How does anyone who is not an expert ever know that another person is an expert?" then the evidence of expertise cannot consist in the testimony of another expert.

This requirement might seem overly skeptical. Unless we doubt that there are any experts at all, we should be free to use the testimony of some experts to provide evidence for the expertise of other experts.

---

9. This is a very abstract description of the capacities of experts. As such, it sets aside some significant differences between different areas of expertise. For example, some types of expertise consist of practical knowledge—*knowing how to do something*, rather than theoretical knowledge—*knowing that certain statements are true*. Expertise in an area of practical knowledge will not necessarily give the expert any argumentative capacity. Rather, such expertise will be manifested in the capacity to perform the relevant tasks better than the layperson.

However, if we allow this, then the resulting theory will be unable to help us with the hardest cases of identifying experts. Even if we know that there are genuine experts in the world, in some areas of expertise, there can be reasonable doubt about exactly *which* areas of study contain genuine experts. Even if I know that there are genuine experts in medicine and the other natural sciences, I might doubt that there are genuine experts in other areas, including economics. As we will see, the kind of evidence of expertise that is available varies from one discipline to another. In any area in which I am unsure that there is any expertise to be had, the testimony of experts in that area will not help me since I have just as much reason to doubt their expertise as that of anyone else in the field. If you, yourself, do not have this doubt with respect to economics, then consider another area of alleged expertise, such as alternative medicine. If you want to know if there are any genuine experts in alternative medicine, then it will not help to rely on the testimony of some practitioners of alternative medicine since you have reason to doubt their expertise as much as that of anyone else in that field. Thus, to solve the problem of recognizing experts in hard cases like these, we need evidence of expertise that does not rely on the testimony of other experts.[10]

In summary, then, good evidence of expertise must be accessible to the novice, and it must be accessible to the novice without already knowing which people are genuine experts. Third, and finally, the fact in question must make it more probable than not that a person is a genuine expert. If that is not the case, then the fact is not really evidence that the person is an expert. As we will now see, there is some reason to doubt in the case of Jimmy Carter and Paul Volcker.

Jimmy Carter needs to know if Paul Volcker is an expert who can help him fix the economy. How can he know this? The most

---

10. Could we use the testimony of an expert in an established discipline to support the claims of an expert in another, questionable discipline? That testimony will be reliable only if expertise in the former, established discipline gives an expert in that area the ability to recognize expertise in the other questionable discipline. In some cases, where the disciplines are related, that might be true. However, in other cases, there is too great a difference between the two disciplines for an established expert to make that judgment.

salient answer is that Volcker has the relevant credentials. He has degrees in economics from Princeton and Harvard. He has published articles in peer-reviewed journals. He is recognized as an expert by other experts. These facts seem to constitute evidence that Volcker is an expert. Do these facts satisfy the three conditions of evidence stated above? The first condition is clearly met. Carter knows that Volcker has these credentials. He can verify that for himself. What about the second condition? Can Carter take Volcker's credentials as evidence of expertise without already knowing that some other people are experts in economics? No. The reason is that Volcker's credentials—his academic degrees, publications, and reputation—consist in the testimony of other people who say that he is an expert. Credentials are nothing more than the testimony of others, saying that the recipient is an expert. When Jimmy Carter knows that Paul Volcker has these credentials, what he knows is that the faculties in the economics departments at Princeton and Harvard and the editors of the journals in economics say that Volcker is an expert. Thus, if Carter takes Volcker's credentials as evidence of expertise, Carter is relying on the testimony of these other people who say that Volcker is an expert. Why should Carter take their testimony as evidence that Volcker is an expert? Carter should take their testimony as evidence Volcker is an expert only if Carter knows that they are in a good position to know that Volcker is an expert. But how could they be in a good position to know that Volcker is an expert? The most plausible answer is that the faculty and editors who gave these credentials are, themselves, experts, and that is how they can know that Volcker is an expert. It follows that, in order for Carter to take Volcker's credentials as evidence of expertise, Carter must already know that the people who conferred those credentials are, themselves, experts. This shows that Volcker's credentials fail to meet the second condition for evidence stated above. Carter cannot take Volcker's credentials as evidence of expertise without already knowing that many other people are experts.

This argument does not show that credentials are never good evidence of expertise. It only shows that credentials alone are insufficient to solve the Recognition Problem. We can take credentials as evidence of expertise only if we have some *other* way of knowing that those who confer the credentials are experts. (To appeal to the credentials of those who confer the degrees would simply raise the very same question all over again.) Thus, credentials alone cannot solve the Recognition Problem. However, if we have some other way of knowing that those who give credentials are experts, then credentials will constitute good evidence of expertise. It is just not sufficient to solve the Recognition Problem. If the Accessible Evidence View is to succeed, then some other kinds of evidence will have to suffice. What could that be?

Arguably, the strongest evidence of expertise is a track record of getting things right. For the novice, the most accessible, compelling track record is a track record of accurate predictions. Experts often make predictions, and if those predictions come true, then that is evidence of their expertise. My doctor predicts that taking a certain medication will cure my illness. I take the medication, and it cures my illness. If that happened only once or twice, then it might be a coincidence. However, it happens repeatedly, and that gives me evidence that my doctor is an expert in medical science. When someone has a track record of making predictions that come true, then we have good evidence that they are a genuine expert. In some areas of expertise, this seems to solve the Recognition Problem. The success of modern medicine, which often involves making predictions that come true, is very strong evidence of genuine expertise. The same can be said for any science that makes precise predictions that come true. Experts in these "exact sciences" can certify their expertise by making predictions that come true. Consequently, the track record of experts in the exact sciences solves the Recognition Problem for those experts.

Unfortunately, not every area of expertise enables experts to make precise predictions. Moreover, even when precise predictions are possible, not every area of expertise has an equally good track record. Consider Paul Volcker's area of expertise—economics. Economics is not an exact science. That is because we cannot run controlled experiments in economics. Too many factors are relevant to human behavior in a complex society to control them all. When economists make predictions, they must rely on additional assumptions, called *auxiliary hypotheses*, which are distinct from the economic model itself. If an economic prediction does not come true, it is always possible that this is due to the falsehood of one of these additional assumptions. This means that economists cannot confirm their models in the same way that physicists, chemists, and doctors can confirm their theories. This does not imply that economics is not a genuine area of expertise, but it does make the Recognition Problem harder with respect to economics.

The difficulty of making predictions in economics is borne out by the track record of those who do. In 1891, Irving Fisher received the first PhD in economics granted by Yale, and he went on to have an illustrious career at Yale. His work is still highly regarded. In fact, he was once described as the greatest economist the United States has ever produced.[11] In September 1929, Fisher declared that "stocks have reached what looks like a permanently high plateau." The stock market crashed just nine days later, and the Great Depression began. In 1930, John Maynard Keynes predicted that within a hundred years, the average workweek would be just fifteen hours. Less than a decade from 2030, it does not look like that prediction will come true. In 1970, the economist Arthur Okun, who headed President Lyndon B. Johnson's Council of Economic Advisors, declared that the business cycle of growth and recession had come to an end. Unfortunately, the business cycle has continued.[12] In 1998, Paul Krugman wrote, "The growth of the Internet will slow drastically. . . . By 2005 or so, it will become clear that the Internet's impact on the economy has been no greater than the fax machine's."[13] The context of Krugman's prediction is especially instructive. Krugman made that prediction in an article for *Red Herring* magazine. The article was

---

11. Joseph Schumpeter, *Ten Great Economists: From Marx to Keynes* (New York: Oxford University Press, 1951), 223.

12. Arthur Okun, *The Political Economy of Prosperity* (Washington, DC: The Brookings Institution, 1970).

13. Paul Krugman, "Why Most Economists' Predictions Are Wrong," *Red Herring*, June 10, 1998, https://web.archive.org/web/19980610100009/https://www.redherring.com/mag/issue55/economics.html.

entitled "Why Most Economists' Predictions Are Wrong." In that article, Krugman argued that most economists make false predictions because they overestimate the impact of future technologies on the economy. In that context, Krugman made his own prediction—that the Internet would have very little impact on the economy in the future. Needless to say, that prediction did not come true. However, Krugman went on to win the Nobel Prize in economics.

If these were isolated incidents, they would not cast doubt on the track record of economists' predictions. Unfortunately, the false predictions of economists are much too frequent to be dismissed as isolated incidents. In 2018, the International Monetary Fund economist Prakash Loungani published a study of 153 recessions in sixty-three countries between 1992 and 2014. He found that economists failed to predict the vast majority of these recessions.[14] Of course, the most visible of these failures was the failure to predict the Great Recession of 2008. In the months leading up to that recession, leading economists, such as Ben Bernanke, repeatedly denied that there was any problem in the housing market or that the economy was in any serious trouble. Loungani's study shows that this failure to predict a recession was not an isolated incident. In recent decades, it has been much closer to the rule.

Even if the track record of economists is actually better than it seems, that will not solve the Recognition Problem for economics. According to the Accessible Evidence View, the facts that constitute evidence of expertise are accessible to the average person. With respect to economics, the relevant question is this: *Can the average person say that the track record of economists is good enough to certify their expertise?* That seems doubtful. To the average person, the track record of economists seems spotty at best. Thus, in the case of economics, there does not seem to be the sort of track record that would give the

---

14. Zidong An, Jão Tovar Jalles, and Prakash Loungani, "How Well Do Economists Forecast Recessions?" (IMF Working Papers, March 5, 2018), https://www.imf.org/en/Publications/WP/Issues/2018/03/05/How-Well-Do-Economists-Forecast-Recessions-45672#:~:text=The%20main%20finding%20is%20that,the%20year%20is%20almost%20over.

average person accessible evidence of genuine expertise. Therefore, neither credentials nor a good track record seems to provide the kind of evidence that the Accessible Evidence View requires.

There are three kinds of evidence left to consider: argumentative capacity, agreement with consensus, and intellectual honesty. If the Accessible Evidence View is correct, then these kinds of evidence must suffice to solve the Recognition Problem for economics. First, consider argumentative capacity—the ability to argue for one's claims and to rebut the claims of one's critics. Unfortunately, argumentative capacity is easily mimicked, and it is now often mimicked by people who lack genuine expertise. Pseudo-experts often appear to argue well for their claims and to rebut the claims of their critics. To the average person, it is difficult to tell if someone is demonstrating real argumentative capacity or just imitating it. In a world where argumentative capacity is mimicked very effectively and very often, the average person cannot take it as evidence of expertise.[15]

What about agreement with consensus? Just as argumentative capacity can be mimicked by pseudo-experts, so agreement with consensus can occur in a community of pseudo-experts. In an age of polarization, novices must choose between competing consensuses. Unless they already know which community is a community of genuine experts, they cannot use agreement with consensus to solve the Recognition Problem. That leaves just one kind of evidence—intellectual honesty. Can novices use intellectual honesty to determine who the genuine experts are? Unfortunately, a novice cannot determine who is being intellectually honest without already knowing the truth about the issues themselves. Once again, pseudo-experts can appear to be honest. Moreover, they can cast doubt on the honesty of genuine experts. When that happens, the average person will

---

15. Neil Levy develops and defends this point in *Bad Beliefs*, 110–115. He concludes that, in the present context, "The cues for expertise don't correlate well with its actual possession, [and this] reduces ordinary people's capacity to distinguish reliable from unreliable sources." I concur.

be unable to tell who is really being honest without already knowing who the genuine experts are.[16]

We have now considered all five types of evidence cited in the Accessible Evidence View. For each type of evidence, there appear to be serious obstacles to using that evidence to solve the Recognition Problem, at least with respect to inexact sciences like economics. Moreover, the very same problems arise with the other social sciences—psychology, sociology, anthropology, and political science. The appeal to credentials in these cases is circular, just as it is in economics. Moreover, these are *inexact* sciences in which it is not possible to conduct completely controlled experiments. Human behavior is subject to too many influences to control in that way. Thus, it is difficult for experts in these disciplines to make precise predictions. That, in turn, prevents them from establishing a track record accessible to novices. Finally, the other signs of expertise—agreement with consensus, argumentative capacity, and intellectual honesty—are just as easily imitated in these disciplines as in economics. Consequently, it is difficult to see how a novice could have sufficient evidence of expertise to solve the Recognition Problem for expertise in any of the social sciences.

Perhaps those obstacles can be overcome, but if they cannot, then where does that leave us? There is another possible solution to the Recognition Problem: *The Reliable Network View*.

> *The Reliable Network View: A novice knows that another person is an expert when the novice receives that information from a socially distributed cognitive network that is generally reliable.*

To understand the Reliable Network View, consider what it implies in the case of Jimmy Carter and Paul Volcker. There is a network of colleges, universities, academic journals, and academic publishers. Call this the *academic network*. The goal of the academic network is to transmit information from person to person within the network. If this network transmits genuine information (as opposed

---

16. Levy, *Bad Beliefs*, 120.

to misinformation) most of the time, then it is a *generally reliable* cognitive network. Notice: the network does not have to be *infallible* in order for it to be generally reliable. It only has to transmit genuine information *most of the time*. Let us suppose, for the sake of the example, that the academic network is generally reliable in that sense. One piece of information that the academic network transmits is the information that Paul Volcker is an expert in economics. Jimmy Carter receives that information from the academic network. Under these conditions, the Reliable Network View says that Jimmy Carter *knows* that Paul Volcker is an expert in economics. Carter knows it because he got the information from a reliable source. According to the Reliable Network View, if a person gets the information that someone is an expert from a reliable cognitive network, and the information is correct, then they *know* that the person in question is an expert. They need not have any further evidence, themselves, that the person is an expert to know that they are an expert. The reliability of the source is all that matters.

We have already seen a version of this view in Chapter 1 as a solution to the problem of testimony. Here, the view is being used to solve the Recognition Problem concerning expertise. As I noted in Chapter 1, this is a fundamentally different kind of solution to an epistemological problem. In Chapter 1, we did not delve into the theoretical foundations of the view. We will do so now. In Chapter 1, we noted that knowledge requires more than just true belief. Suppose you ask me a question, and I happen to guess the correct answer. Then, I have a true belief, but I do not know that my answer is correct. I was just lucky to guess the right answer. Thus, it is just an accident that I formed a true belief. In order for a true belief to constitute knowledge, it must not be just an accident that the person formed a true belief. Thus, we could say that knowledge is *non-accidentally true belief*. One of the central questions in epistemology is What is required for a true belief to be non-accidentally true, in such a way as to transform it into knowledge? Theories of knowledge aim to tell us, in general terms, what transforms a true belief into knowledge.

Philosophers now distinguish between two types of answers to this question—*internalist* and *externalist*. Broadly speaking, all theories of knowledge fall into one of these categories. According to an internalist theory of knowledge, what transforms a true belief into knowledge is something that is internal to the mind of the believer, such as the fact that the believer has good evidence for her belief, which makes it probable that her belief is true. According to an internalist, in order to know that something is true, the believer must have good evidence, internal to her own mind, that her belief is true. If she has good evidence and her belief is true, then she knows that it is true. However, if she does *not* have good evidence internal to her own mind, then she does *not* know that her belief is true. By contrast, according to an externalist theory of knowledge, what transforms a true belief into knowledge is that the belief was caused in a way that makes it probable the belief is true. If a person's true belief was caused by a process that does, in fact, produce mostly true beliefs, then that person *knows* her belief is true, *even if the process that caused her belief includes events that occur outside of her own mind.*[17] According to an externalist theory of knowledge, having good evidence internal to your own mind is *one way* to acquire knowledge, but it is not *the only way* to acquire knowledge. There are some processes that produce mostly true beliefs without producing evidence that is internal to the mind of the believer. Those processes also produce knowledge.

To understand the difference between internalism and externalism, notice that this is the fundamental difference between the two solutions to the Recognition Problem we have considered. The Accessible Evidence View is an example of an internalist view of knowledge. On that view, for a novice to know that someone is an expert, the novice must have good evidence that the person is an expert. If the novice knows that this person has relevant credentials and they have a good track record of making predictions that come true, then

---

17. Strictly speaking, this is just one kind of externalist theory, called *process reliabilism*, which was first developed by Alvin Goldman in "What Is Justified Belief?," in *Justification and Knowledge: New Studies in Epistemology*, ed. George Pappas (Boston, MA: Dordrecht Reidel, 1979), 1–25. This is not the only externalist theory of knowledge. However, for present purposes, it will illustrate the defining features of an externalist theory of knowledge.

the novice has good evidence that this person is a genuine expert. This is evidence that the novice herself must possess in order to know that the other person is an expert. Thus, the Accessible Evidence View is an internalist view of knowledge. It says that in order to know that something is true, a person must have good evidence, internal to their own mind, that makes it probable that their belief is true.

By contrast, the Reliable Network View is an example of an externalist view of knowledge. According to that view, if a novice believes that someone is an expert because the novice got that information from a reliable source, then the novice knows that this person is an expert. Notice: the novice does not need to prove that the source is reliable in order to get knowledge. The mere fact that the source *is* reliable is all that is required for the novice to get knowledge from that source. Thus, according to the Reliable Network View, if a reliable network tells Jimmy Carter that Paul Volcker is an expert, and it is true that Paul Volcker is an expert, then Jimmy Carter *knows* that Paul Volcker is an expert. Under those conditions, Carter does not need to possess any further evidence to know that Volcker is an expert. The reliability of the process caused Carter's belief, which transforms his belief into knowledge.

We have seen reason to doubt the Accessible Evidence View. Is there any reason to doubt the Reliable Network View? Critics say that there is. To understand their doubts, consider the following example.[18] Suppose that a man goes in for brain surgery, and unbeknownst to him, while he is unconscious, the surgeons plant a device in his brain. The device does two things: it detects the temperature outside, and then it causes this man to form a true belief about the temperature. If the temperature outside is exactly 67 degrees Fahrenheit, then this man will spontaneously believe that it is exactly 67 degrees Fahrenheit outside. However, this man has no idea that the surgeons have planted this device in his brain. Thus, when he finds himself believing that it is exactly 67 degrees Fahrenheit outside, he has no evidence for this belief. If you asked him, "Why do you believe it's exactly

---

18. This example is originally due to Keith Lehrer in *Theory of Knowledge* (Boulder, CO: Westview Press, 1990), 162.

67 degrees outside?" he could not give any evidence to support his belief. Call this man "Truetemp." When Truetemp believes that it is exactly 67 degrees outside, does he *know* that it is exactly 67 degrees outside? To many people, it seems that he does not. From Truetemp's point of view, his belief is no better than a hunch or a random guess. Truetemp has no reason—that he is aware of—to think that his belief is true. Thus, even though Truetemp has a true belief, it seems that he does not *know* that it is true. That poses a problem for the externalist theory of knowledge. Truetemp's belief was produced by a reliable cognitive process since the device in his brain always causes him to have a true belief. Thus, the externalist theory of knowledge implies that Truetemp *knows* the temperature outside is 67 degrees. However, that seems false. Thus, the externalist theory of knowledge must be false.

One possible reply to this argument is to maintain that Truetemp *does* know the temperature. According to this reply, Truetemp knows the temperature; he just doesn't *know that he knows*. On this view, it is possible to know something without knowing that you know it. For those who accept this view, the case of Truetemp does not undermine the externalist theory of knowledge. I will leave it to the reader to think about this. If one thinks that Truetemp does *not* know the temperature, then that poses a problem for externalism. However, Externalists have proposed several ways of solving this problem. Here is one such suggestion.[19] Not just any reliable process produces knowledge. Only *primal processes* generate knowledge. A primal process is a process that results solely from a combination of innate capacities and learning. To illustrate this, consider testimony. Human beings have an innate capacity to learn a language, understand what other people are saying, and then get information by trusting the testimony of other people. Over time, typical human beings develop these innate capacities through learning, and thereby start forming beliefs by trusting the testimony of other people. Thus, the process of forming beliefs by

---

19. This suggestion is due to Jack Lyons. See his *Perception and Basic Beliefs: Zombies, Modules, and the Problem of the External World* (New York: Oxford University Press, 2009).

trusting testimony counts as a primal process. It is solely the product of innate capacities and learning. By contrast, the process that produces Truetemp's beliefs about the temperature is *not* a primal process. The device planted in Truetemp's brain is not the result of innate capacities or Truetemp's own learning. Thus, the modified externalist theory correctly implies that Truetemp does *not* know it is 67 degrees outside. In this way, the modified externalist theory solves the problem of Truetemp.

There will be objections to the modified externalist theory as well. However, it is beyond the scope of this chapter to pursue them all here. It is time to take stock of our prospects for solving the Recognition Problem. We have considered two possible solutions to the problem—the Accessible Evidence View and the Reliable Network View. On close inspection, we found some reasons to doubt the Accessible Evidence View, at least with respect to some areas of expertise, like economics. There does not seem to be the kind of evidence that is required by that view, at least with respect to some areas of expertise. The other alternative is the Reliable Network View. Unless there is some additional solution, it seems that we now face a dilemma. Either the Reliable Network View is correct, or there is no solution to the Recognition Problem for some areas of expertise, like economics. In other words, if we reject the Reliable Network View, then it seems that we must accept the following skeptical view.

The Skeptical View: If an expert does not have a publicly accessible, clearly positive track record of making predictions that come true, then it is impossible for a novice to know that this person is an expert.

Faced with the difficulty of the Recognition Problem, it can be tempting to accept the skeptical view. However, this view requires a degree of skepticism that few people will be willing to accept. There are many areas of expertise that do not enable experts in those areas to make precise predictions. The skeptical view requires us to deny that any novice ever knows that someone is an expert in any of these areas. Historians are experts on the past. They acquire that expertise by studying the remains of the past, both written and unwritten. That expertise does not enable a historian to make precise predictions that are easily accessible to the novice in history. Consequently, the skeptical view implies that we novices in history never know that anyone is an expert in history. To many people, that is very hard to believe.

Henceforth, I will assume that there is some non-skeptical solution to the Recognition Problem. I will assume that it is possible for a novice to know that someone is an expert, even in areas like history and economics. When a novice recognizes that another person is an expert in a certain area, what is the appropriate stance for the novice to take to the expert? By definition, an expert is a person who is in a better position to have true beliefs in their area of expertise than a novice. Consequently, it seems that a novice should *defer* to the opinion of the expert in that area. There is a simple argument that supports this conclusion. I assume that the novice wants to have true beliefs rather than false beliefs. Many people would rather know the truth than be left in ignorance. If the novice wants to have true beliefs, and the expert is more likely to have true beliefs in their area of expertise than the novice, then the best way for the novice to get the true beliefs that she wants is to defer to the expert. Therefore, the novice should defer to the expert. It is in the novice's own interest to do so. Thus, we should accept what Jamie Carlin Watson calls *The Principle of Normative Deference*: "Other things being equal, novices ought to defer to the judgment of experts in their domain of knowledge or practice."[20]

If a novice recognizes that someone is an expert in a certain area, then insofar as they want to have true beliefs in that area, they should defer to the expert. If Jimmy Carter knows that Paul Volcker is an expert in economics, then Jimmy Carter should defer to Paul Volcker in economics, which is exactly what Carter did. If Carter knew that Volcker was an expert in economics, then the Principle of Normative Deference seems to vindicate Carter's choice to defer to Volcker in that area. However, on closer inspection, matters are not so simple. The Principle of Normative Deference begins with the phrase "other

---

20. Jamie Carlin Watson, *A History and Philosophy of Expertise* (New York: Bloomsbury Academic Press, 2021), 26.

things being equal," and that is for good reason. Under certain conditions, a novice should *not* defer to an expert. In the remainder of this chapter, we will consider three such conditions—*disagreement among experts*, *cognitive bias*, and *conflicting values*. We will begin with disagreement.

When Jimmy Carter appointed Paul Volcker to run the Federal Reserve, he was appointing someone whose opinions were controversial, even among economists. One of Volcker's predecessors in that position, Arthur Burns, refused to raise interest rates during his tenure at the Fed from 1970 to 1978. Burns believed that if the Fed raised interest rates, then unemployment would rise to above 6 percent. Burns's position was that the Fed should keep unemployment below 6 percent. In order to do that, the Fed had to allow inflation to remain well above the 2 percent that people like Volcker preferred.[21] When Jimmy Carter chose Paul Volcker to run the Fed, he was choosing to defer to Paul Volcker rather than to Arthur Burns. But Arthur Burns was also a trained economist. Why should Carter defer to Volcker rather than Burns? The Principle of Normative Deference does not answer that question. It tells us that we should defer to experts because they are more likely to know the truth than we are, but it does not tell us who to trust when the experts disagree.

One possible solution is to defer to the majority opinion among experts. If the majority of the experts in an area agree about something, then perhaps we should defer to them. This is especially plausible if two conditions are met: (1) there are many experts in this area, and (2) a large majority of the experts in this area agree about this matter. For example, there are over 30,000 economists in the United States alone. Suppose that 95 percent of those economists agree about some matter in economics. Then, it seems reasonable to defer to the opinion of the 95 percent, despite the disagreement of the other 5 percent. There is an argument in support of this conclusion, which

---

21. See Robert L. Hetzel, "Arthur Burns and Inflation," *Economic Quarterly* (The Federal Reserve Bank of Richmond) 84 (1998): 21–44.

is based on *Condorcet's Jury Theorem*.[22] Condorcet's Jury Theorem says that if each person in a group is more than 50 percent likely to be right about something, then the greater the number of people who hold the same belief on the matter, the greater the probability that their belief is true. Thus, if 95 percent of the people in a very large group hold the same opinion about something, then the probability that they are correct is very high. The basic idea of Condorcet's Jury Theorem is that if every member of a group is at least slightly better than chance to have a true belief about something, then the greater the percentage of people who agree, the more likely it becomes that they are correct. Condorcet's Jury Theorem can be proven mathematically, so it is clearly true. Now, if we apply Condorcet's Jury Theorem to the case in which 95 percent of 30,000 economists share the same opinion, it follows that it is very probable that the shared opinion of the majority of the economists is correct. Therefore, in that case, it seems that we should defer to the majority of the economists. The same point would apply to any case where a large majority of the experts agree about something. In a case like this, it seems that we can solve the problem of expert disagreement.[23]

Unfortunately, matters are not so simple. Condorcet's Jury Theorem assumes that the opinions of the people in the group are *probabilistically independent of one another*. If their opinions are not probabilistically independent of one another, then Condorcet's Theorem does not apply. To say that one opinion is probabilistically independent of another opinion is to say that the probability that the former opinion is true does not depend on the probability that the latter opinion is true. We can illustrate this with the following example. Suppose that there are twenty ancient manuscripts that attribute a certain statement to Cicero, and there is just one ancient manuscript that denies that Cicero made this statement. We can apply Condorcet's Jury Theorem and infer that it is more probable

---

22. Condorcet's Jury Theorem was first proposed by Nicolas de Condorcet in 1785 in his *Essay on the Application of Analysis to the Probability of Majority Decisions*.
23. This position is defended by David Coady in *What to Believe Now: Applying Epistemology to Contemporary Issues* (Hoboken, NJ: Wiley-Blackwell, 2011).

that the twenty concurring manuscripts are correct than that the sole dissenting manuscript is correct. However, suppose we discover that the twenty concurring manuscripts were all copied, verbatim, from a single, earlier manuscript. Then, it would be a mistake to apply Condorcet's Jury Theorem in this case. The reason is that the probability that each of these twenty manuscripts is correct depends entirely on the probability that the original manuscript was correct. Twenty copies of a single manuscript give us no more evidence for the truth than the original manuscript gave us. Thus, the value of the twenty manuscripts has been reduce to one. If we take this into account, then we will realize that we have just one manuscript on each side of the issue—one that attributes the statement to Cicero and one that denies it. In that situation, it seems arbitrary and irrational to defer to one of them just because it was subsequently copied twenty times.

A similar problem arises if we apply Condorcet's Jury Theorem to the majority opinion among experts. Many experts acquire their opinions from other experts in their discipline, especially those who taught them. Thus, the opinions of many experts are *not* independent of the opinions of other experts. This poses a problem for the application of Condorcet's Jury Theorem to resolve disagreements among experts. Of course, it would not be accurate to say that the opinions of experts are nothing more than copies of a single expert's opinion. Most experts exercise their own judgment, at least to some extent, in deciding what to believe. Nevertheless, it is doubtful that their opinions are *completely independent* of the opinions of other experts, especially the ones who taught them. With that said, it might be possible to use a version of Condorcet's Jury Theorem to support the opinion of the majority. If the opinions of most of the experts in an area are *at least partially independent of one another*, then we can still use a version of Condorcet's Jury Theorem. An example will illustrate this.

Imagine a group of ten meteorologists. On any given question about the weather, each of them is at least slightly better than chance. They are each more than 50 percent likely to be correct. Furthermore, suppose that nine of these ten meteorologists are influenced by the tenth one—call her Imani. The nine meteorologists are always influenced by Imani's opinion, but not decisively. To be more precise, suppose that they agree with Imani about 50 percent of the time. However, the other 50 percent of the time, their own reasoning leads them to *disagree* with Imani. Now, suppose that on a particular occasion, all ten of the meteorologists agree in their forecast. Does the agreement of all ten meteorologists *increase the probability* that they are right? Yes, it does. Their agreement does not raise the probability that they are right as much as it would if their opinions were completely independent of each other. However, it still increases the probability that they are correct. Moreover, if the number of experts who agree is in the thousands or in the tens of thousands, then as long as their opinions are *not completely dependent* on one another, their agreement still increases the probability that they are correct.

The existence of a consensus among the majority of the experts on some matter raises the probability that the majority opinion is correct. However, the consensus only raises that probability to the extent that the opinions of these experts are independent of one another. The more independent their opinions are of one another, the more their agreement raises the probability that they are correct. This leads us to a somewhat surprising conclusion. Arguably, the existence of dissenters in a discipline actually increases the probability that the opinion of the majority is correct. That is for multiple reasons. First of all, the existence of dissenters in an area of expertise shows that independent thought does occur in that area. If there are dissenting opinions in an area of expertise, then obviously, not every opinion in this area is a carbon copy of some other opinion. Second, the existence of dissenters in an area shows that independent thought is *tolerated* in that area, at least to some extent. Thus, it is *possible* for other experts in this area to dissent as well. And if it is possible for other experts to dissent, their agreement with the consensus cannot be explained by any enforced consensus. Finally, the existence of dissenters in an area of expertise implies that experts in this area are exposed to and aware of the reasons to doubt the consensus in their discipline. Consequently, if they accept the consensus in their discipline, it is *not* because they are unaware of the reasons that can be given for a dissenting opinion. Taken collectively, these facts raise the probability that the experts who accept the consensus in their area accept it because their own reasoning has led them to conclude that the consensus is correct. Thus, perhaps surprisingly, the existence of dissenters in an area of expertise actually increases the probability that the consensus opinion is correct.[24]

I now turn to the second reason for doubting an expert: cognitive bias. Research in psychology has found that all human beings are subject to cognitive biases, which distort our thinking. In Chapter 4, we will explore the subject of cognitive bias in depth and consider the extent to which our cognitive biases limit our ability to achieve knowledge. Here, we will focus on the relevance of cognitive bias to our trust in experts. As human beings, experts are subject to the same cognitive biases as the rest of us. Furthermore, experts seem vulnerable to some biases that result from their status as experts. One recent study found that self-perceptions of expertise contribute to a more close-minded or dogmatic cognitive style.[25] Another recent study found that professional traders and investment bankers showed a greater propensity for overconfidence than control groups of lay subjects, leading the authors to conclude that "expertise does not mitigate bias."[26] Several other studies have documented a systematic overconfidence among finance professionals and experts.[27]

---

24. John Beatty and Alfred Moore give additional arguments for this thesis in "Should We Aim for Consensus?" *Episteme* 7, no. 3 (2010): 198–214. Note: the presence of dissent in an expert community is not, by itself, sufficient to show that the community is a reliable community. However, in a community in which there is a majority consensus, the presence of some dissent is some evidence for that conclusion.

25. V. Ottati, E. D. Price, and C. Wilson, "When Self-Perceptions of Expertise Increase Closed-Minded Cognition: The Earned Dogmatism Effect," *Journal of Experimental Social Psychology* 61 (2015).

26. M. Glaser, T. Langer, and M. Weber, "True Overconfidence in Interval Estimates: Evidence Based on a New Measure of Miscalibration," *Journal of Behavioral Decision Making* 26 (2013): 405–417.

27. See the following: Michael S. Haigh and John A. List, "Do Professional Traders Exhibit Myopic Loss Aversion? An Experimental Analysis," *The Journal of Finance* 60 (2005): 523–534; and Richard Deaves, Erik Luders, and Michael Schroder, "The Dynamics of Overconfidence: Evidence from Stock Market Forecasters," *Journal of Economic Behavior and Organization* 75 (2010): 402–412.

Charles Manski found that policy experts frequently fail to express scientific uncertainty even when it exists and is significant, partly owing to misaligned incentives.[28] Finally, a recent study of bureaucratic expertise found that more experienced bureaucrats have higher levels of perceived expertise, and their self-perception tends to make them overconfident in their judgments.[29] The upshot of this research is that experts, like everyone else, are subject to cognitive biases that can distort their judgments.

Cognitive biases distort our judgment. If a person is under the influence of a cognitive bias, then they are less likely to form a true belief. This is also true of experts, and that is why the biases of experts are relevant to the rationality of deferring to them. The reason we should defer to experts is that they are more likely to have true beliefs in their area of expertise than we novices are. If an expert is under the influence of one or more cognitive biases, then they are less likely to form a true belief than they otherwise would be. The greater the influence of cognitive bias, the less likely they are to form true beliefs, and the less likely they are to form true beliefs, the less reason we have to defer to them. Thus, if we have reason to believe that an expert is under the influence of cognitive bias, we have less reason to defer to the opinion of that expert.

Return to Jimmy Carter's decision to defer to Paul Volcker with respect to the economy. Was Paul Volcker under the influence of cognitive biases? If so, then should that have altered Carter's deference to Volcker? There is some evidence that many economists suffer from specific cognitive biases. A recent study of economists found that strong ideological commitments among economists tend to produce overconfidence. According to the authors, the "results suggest that economists with ideologically patterned views report higher levels of certainty in their opinions than their less ideologically consistent

---

28. C. F. Manski, "Policy Analysis with Incredible Certitude," *The Economic Journal* 121 (2011): F261–F289; and "The Lure of Incredible Certitude," *Economics and Philosophy* 35 (2019): 1–30.

29. X. Liu, S. James, and V. Arnold, "Bureaucratic Expertise, Overconfidence, and Policy Choice," *Governance* 30 (2017): 705–725.

peers."[30] This is in addition to the other biases experts suffer from, such as a more closed-minded style of thinking and a tendency to overconfidence. Was Paul Volcker under the influence of some of these cognitive biases? Volcker was a lifelong advocate for cracking down on inflation. In his senior thesis at Princeton in 1949, he argued that the Federal Reserve should take stronger measures to crack down on inflation. He described inflation as "a grave threat to the economy." In graduate school at Harvard, Volcker recalled listening to one of his professors say that a little inflation is good for the economy. Volcker later recalled that in that moment, there was "a word flashing in my brain like a yellow caution sign: 'Bullshit.'"[31] It appears that Volcker formed these opinions relatively early in his education and retained them for decades after. If this was due to closed-mindedness, overconfidence, or an ideological bias, then Volcker would be less reliable. Thus, if Carter had been aware of any such biases in Volcker, he should have reduced his confidence in Volcker's judgment.

The third possible reason for a novice to doubt an expert is conflicting values. Sometimes, the opinions of experts presuppose certain value judgments. In some areas, this is unavoidable. A case in point is *welfare economics*, which is the use of economics to determine what is good for a society as a whole. As Daniel Hausman, Michael McPherson, and Debra Satz put it, "When welfare economists address policy questions, they purport to know how to make life better for people."[32] A judgment about how to make life better for people is a value judgment. When an economist recommends a certain public policy, the economist's recommendation must be based on value judgments about what is good for people. However, the economist, qua economist, cannot claim to be an expert on what constitutes a good human life.

---

30. Austin C. Kozlowski and Todd S. Van Gunten, "Are Economists Overconfident? Ideology and Uncertainty in Expert Opinion," *The British Journal of Sociology* 74 (2023): 476–500.

31. Appelbaum, *The Economists' Hour*, 76.

32. Daniel Hausman, Michael McPherson, and Debra Satz, *Economic Analysis, Moral Philosophy, and Public Policy*, 3rd ed. (New York: Cambridge University Press, 2017), 149.

Furthermore, public policy recommendations should be constrained by considerations of *justice*. When an economist recommends a public policy, that recommendation tacitly assumes that the policy in question would not be unjust. This, in turn, is based on some assumptions about what justice requires. However, the economist, qua economist, cannot claim to be an expert on matters of justice. Therefore, when economists make public policy recommendations, their opinions are based on value judgments outside the bounds of their expertise. Novices are entitled to disagree with those value judgments since the economist is no more of an expert in that area than the novice.

Return, at last, to President Jimmy Carter's decision to defer to Paul Volcker with respect to the economy. Recall the exchange that occurred between Wisconsin senator William Proxmire and Paul Volcker during Volcker's senate confirmation hearing in 1979. Senator Proxmire asked Volcker to assure him that he would not raise interest rates to a level that would be very difficult for small businesses, farmers, and working people. In his reply, Volcker made his intentions clear: "I don't think we have any substitute for seeking an answer to our problems in the context of monetary discipline."[33] In making this request to Volcker, Proxmire was expressing his conviction that raising interest rates to a level that would do severe harm to some people would be *unfair* to them and, hence, *unjust*. Thus, Proxmire's challenge to Volcker was based on his disagreement with Volcker's *value judgments*. This is a fair challenge for a novice to make to an expert. Paul Volcker was no more of an expert on justice than Senator Proxmire was. Thus, Proxmire's disagreement with Volcker's judgment was within his rights as a novice.[34]

---

33. Appelbaum, *The Economists' Hour*, 77.
34. Jennifer Lackey argues that we should not view experts as authorities whose opinions can never be questioned. Rather, we should view experts as *advisors* whose opinions provide some evidence that is defeasible. If this is correct, then it would explain why it is permissible for a layperson to reject expert opinion under certain conditions. See Jennifer Lackey, "Experts and Peer Disagreement," in *Knowledge, Belief, and God: New Insights in Religious Epistemology*, ed. Matthew A. Benton, John Hawthorne, and Dani Rabinowitz (New York: Oxford University Press, 2018), 228–245.

On September 8, 2023, the president of the Federal Reserve Bank of Chicago, Austan Goolsbee, delivered a policy speech in which he argued that reducing inflation without causing a recession is possible. According to Goolsbee, "Believing too strongly in the inevitability of a large trade-off between inflation and unemployment comes with the risk of a near-term policy error."[35] Did Paul Volcker believe too strongly in an inevitable trade-off between inflation and unemployment? Perhaps he did. Should Jimmy Carter have had less confidence in Volcker's judgment, given Volcker's apparent biases and the role of value judgments in Volcker's opinion? Perhaps he should have. Of course, in making these judgments, we have the benefit of twenty-twenty hindsight. The best that we can do, going forward, is to build reliable cognitive networks, get our information from those networks, and be aware of the role of cognitive biases and value judgments in shaping the opinions of experts.

---

35. Austan D. Goolsbee, "The 2023 Economy: Not Your Grandpa's Monetary Policy Moment," Federal Reserve Bank of Chicago, last updated September 28, 2023, https://www.chicagofed.org/publications/speeches/2023/september-28-peterson-institute.

Study Questions

1. What makes someone an expert? If you know that someone is an expert, then should you trust them? Why? Explain your answer.

2. Suppose you want to know if a certain person is an expert. What kinds of facts would constitute evidence that this person is an expert? Give an example to illustrate each kind of fact.

3. Suppose that you find out that your neighbor has a PhD in medical cosmetics from the Grigore T. Popa University of Medicine and Pharmacy. Does this give you good evidence that your neighbor is an expert? What problems does this raise? Explain your answer.

4. Suppose that a novice in psychology reads that the psychologist Roy Baumeister discovered the phenomenon known as *ego depletion*. Does the novice now have good evidence that Roy Baumeister is an expert in psychology? What problem does this raise? Explain your answer.

5. Suppose that you move to a new town just before the holiday season. In your first week there, you attend a party where people will wrap presents together. As you begin to wrap your presents, the people around you tell you that, when it comes to wrapping presents, Stephen knows how to do it best. Although you do not know these people, you decide to trust them, so you believe Stephen is an expert at wrapping presents. Unbeknownst to you, all of the people at the party have advanced degrees in packaging science, so they are all reliable judges of expertise in wrapping presents. Of course, you are unaware of this fact about the people in the room. According to the Reliable Network View, if you trust their testimony, then do you know that Stephen is an expert at wrapping presents?

For Further Reading

For an excellent introduction to the epistemology of expertise, see Jamie Carlin Watson's *Expertise: A Philosophical Introduction* (London: Bloomsbury Academic, 2020). For a defense of the Accessible Evidence View, see Elisabeth Anderson, "Democracy, Public Policy, and Lay Assessment of Scientific Testimony," *Episteme* 8 (2011): 144–164; and Alex Guerrero, "Living with Ignorance in a World of Experts," in *Perspectives on Ignorance from Moral and Political Philosophy*, ed. Rik Peels (New York: Routledge, 2017). For some further doubts about using track records to identify experts, see Alice C. W. Huang's article "Track Records: A Cautionary Tale," *British Journal for the Philosophy of Science* (forthcoming). For further discussion of the difference between internalism and externalism, especially with respect to testimony and expertise, see Mikkel Gerken's excellent essay, "Internalism and Externalism in the Epistemology of Testimony," *Philosophy and Phenomenological Research* 87 (2013): 532–557. Finally, for a thorough investigation of the role of values in scientific research, see Heather Douglas's excellent book *Science, Policy, and the Value-Free Ideal* (Pittsburgh: University of Pittsburgh Press, 2009).

CHAPTER THREE

Responding to Disagreement

In June 2010, the renowned journalist and social critic Christopher Hitchens was diagnosed with stage 4 esophageal cancer. And as Hitchens aptly put it, "There is no stage 5." After Hitchens announced his diagnosis, he was contacted by Francis Collins, the geneticist who led the Human Genome Project. Collins offered to use an experimental, new gene therapy to treat Hitchens. Hitchens agreed, and Collins proceeded to map Hitchens's genome by taking a sample of healthy tissue as well as a sample from his tumor. Upon careful examination, Collins found a mutation that enabled him to treat Hitchens. The treatment did not cure Hitchens's cancer, but it extended his life for many months. During this time, the friendship between Collins and Hitchens deepened. In an article in *Vanity Fair* in October 2010, Hitchens wrote:

> Dr. Francis Collins is one of the greatest living Americans. He is the man who brought the Human Genome Project to completion, ahead of time and under budget, and who now directs the National Institutes of Health. In his work on the genetic origins of disorder, he helped decode the "misprints" that cause such calamities as cystic fibrosis and Huntington's disease. He is working now on the amazing healing properties that are latent in stem cells and in "targeted" gene-based treatments. . . . I know Francis, too, from various public and private debates over religion. He has been kind enough to visit me in his own time and to discuss all sorts of novel treatments, only recently even imaginable, that might apply to my case.[1]

---

1. Christopher Hitchens, "Unanswerable Prayers," *Vanity Fair*, September 2, 2010, https://www.vanityfair.com/culture/2010/10/hitchens-201010.

In an interview many years later, Francis Collins expressed his admiration for Hitchens.

This was a guy who was intensely curious about everything. It was a guy who cared deeply about his wife and daughter. It was a guy who cherished the chance to develop a friendship, and especially with somebody who was very different from him.[2]

Unfortunately, Collins and Hitchens had little time to cultivate their friendship. Hitchens died in December 2011. At a memorial service for him, Francis Collins paid tribute to Hitchens with his own composition for piano, entitled "Hitchens Sonata."

The friendship between Francis Collins and Christopher Hitchens was remarkable. People around the world marveled at it. Why? To understand that, you have to understand who these men were. In addition to being a world-renowned geneticist, Francis Collins was (and is) a devout evangelical Christian and an outspoken defender of the Christian faith. In 2006, he published *The Language of God: A Scientist Presents Evidence for Belief*, in which he argued that there is evidence for the existence of God and that Christian faith is compatible with the acceptance of natural science, including Charles Darwin's theory of evolution by natural selection.[3] By contrast, Christopher Hitchens was a very outspoken atheist and a vehement critic of all religious beliefs. In 2007, just one year after Collins published *The Language of God*, Hitchens published his most famous book, *God Is Not Great: How Religion Poisons Everything*. The following passage from the book—one of Hitchens's most famous statements—sums it up. According to Hitchens, religion is

---

2. See Peter Wehner, "NIH Director: 'We're on an Exponential Curve': Francis Collins Speaks about the Coronavirus, His Faith, and an Unusual Friendship," *The Atlantic*, March 17, 2020.

3. Francis Collins, *The Language of God: A Scientist Presents Evidence for Belief* (New York: Simon & Schuster, 2006).

violent, irrational, intolerant, allied to racism and tribalism and bigotry, invested in ignorance and hostile to free inquiry, contemptuous of women and coercive toward children. . . .[4]

With respect to religion, the disagreement between Collins and Hitchens could not be much greater. In *The Language of God*, Collins recounts reading C. S. Lewis's *Mere Christianity* and finding Lewis's arguments very convincing. By contrast, in *God Is Not Great*, Hitchens's assessment is rather different: "Some religious apology is dreary and absurd—here one cannot avoid naming C. S. Lewis."[5] In *The Language of God*, Collins defends the rationality of believing in miracles, often referencing C. S. Lewis's defense of that belief. By contrast, chapter 10 of *God Is Not Great* is entitled "The Tawdriness of the Miraculous and the Decline of Hell." In the years prior to Hitchens's diagnosis, he and Collins engaged in public debates about science and religion. On at least one occasion, Collins described Hitchens's behavior toward him as "deeply insulting." Nevertheless, they slowly became friends, and by the end of Hitchens's life, they were very good friends.

What does any of this have to do with epistemology? The subject of this chapter is the epistemology of disagreement. The relationship between Francis Collins and Christopher Hitchens illustrates one such disagreement. In an interview with Dr. Jeremy Faust in 2022, Faust asked Collins if he and Hitchens tried to persuade each other that the other was wrong.

Faust: Did you try to convince him that he was wrong?

Collins: I did. I got nowhere.

Faust: Did he try to convince you that you were wrong?

Collins: Oh, yes, absolutely. And he didn't get anywhere either.[6]

---

4. Christopher Hitchens, *God Is Not Great: How Religion Poisons Everything* (New York: Hachette Book Group, 2007), 44.
5. Hitchens, *God Is Not Great*, 7.
6. Emily Hutto, "Faust Files: A Talk with Francis Collins, MD, Part 2," MedPage Today, July 3, 2022, https://www.medpagetoday.com/opinion/faustfiles/99544.

Francis Collins and Christopher Hitchens were both well-educated, well-informed, thoughtful people. Each of them had reasons for their beliefs. Over time, they became aware of each other's reasons for their beliefs. Each of them shared his evidence and arguments with the other. Nevertheless, at the end of that process, they still disagreed. What should they make of the fact that they still disagree?

Imagine that Francis Collins was to reflect on this today and imagine that, as he thinks about it, he finds himself reasoning in the following way.[7]

> Christopher Hitchens was a very intelligent, thoughtful, well-informed person. By the end of his life, after we had shared all of our reasons and arguments, he seemed to have been just as intelligent, thoughtful, and well-informed as I am, at least with respect to religion. Generally speaking, if one person is just as intelligent, thoughtful, and well-informed as another person, then they are equally likely to be right. After all, neither is in a *better* position to get the right answer than the other. If I apply that principle to myself and Hitchens, it follows that I am no more likely to be right than he is. But if I am no more likely to be right than he is, and he disagrees with me, then I should stop believing that I am the one who is right, and he is the one who is wrong. Of course, that means that I should stop holding my own beliefs about religion since that is just what we disagreed about. Instead, I should *suspend judgment* and say, "I have no belief one way or the other since I don't know whether I am right or Hitchens was right."

If this line of reasoning is correct, then Francis Collins should stop holding that his religious beliefs are true. Of course, if the facts are as we have described them, then *the very same reasoning applies to Hitchens as well.* Thus, if this line of reasoning is correct, then *both* Francis Collins *and* Christopher Hitchens should stop believing that they are

---

7. Note: in what follows, I *imagine* Francis Collins having these thoughts. There is no evidence that Collins himself has ever had these thoughts.

right and that the other is wrong. With respect to the subject of their disagreement, they should both *suspend judgment*—they should neither believe that they are right nor that they are wrong. They should just say, "I don't know." Is that correct? That is the question that we will explore in this chapter.

To explore this question and some possible answers to it, we need to define some terms. If two people are equally likely to get the right answer to some question, then we will say that they are *epistemic peers* with respect to that question. Two people are epistemic peers with respect to a question if they are in an equally good position to get the right answer to that question. By contrast, if one person is more likely to get the right answer to a question than another person, then the former person is an *epistemic superior* with respect to that question, and the latter person is an *epistemic inferior* with respect to that question. Here is an example to illustrate these concepts. Suppose that you and I have equally good eyesight. Moreover, we are equally observant and equally knowledgeable about the appearance of birds in North America. One day, we stand side by side and see a bird fly overhead. Each of us looks at the bird very attentively. Given the facts of this case, you and I are in an equally good position to identify the species of that bird. Since we were in an equally good position to identify the bird, we are each equally likely to be correct about it. In this situation, you and I are epistemic peers with respect to the question, "What kind of bird is that?" By contrast, suppose that I have very poor eyesight, and I forgot my glasses that morning. Then, in that situation, you would be an epistemic superior to me with respect to that question, and I would be an epistemic inferior to you. There are many other facts that could render one of us epistemically superior to the other. If one of us is a professional ornithologist who spends lots of time studying birds, while the other has never thought about birds at all, then the ornithologist will be epistemically superior to the novice with respect to the identification of the bird.

When two people disagree about something, the rational response to their disagreement depends on their comparative epistemic status—are they epistemic peers with respect to this question, or is one epistemically superior to the other? If one person is epistemically superior to another, then in cases of disagreement, it is rational for them to prefer their own judgment to their epistemic inferior. In the case above, if the ornithologist and the novice disagree about the identity of the bird they saw, then it would be rational for the ornithologist to trust their own judgment more than the judgment of the novice. In the very same way, if either Francis Collins or Christopher Hitchens was epistemically superior to the other, with respect to religious beliefs, then that person would be justified in retaining their belief despite the disagreement. Was either Collins or Hitchens epistemically superior to the other with respect to religion?

To answer this question, we need to consider how one person could be epistemically superior to another person with respect to these sorts of questions. In some cases, one person has more or better evidence, including background information, than the other person. In the case of the bird, the ornithologist has far more background information that is relevant to the identity of the bird, which is why the ornithologist is epistemically superior to the novice in that case. The ornithologist simply *knows more* that is relevant to the question. Did either Collins or Hitchens know more than the other with respect to religion? Let us consider each of them, starting with Collins. Collins certainly knew a lot more natural science than Hitchens knew. Collins was a trained physician and geneticist, whereas Hitchens never studied natural science. In his book, *The Language of God*, Collins appeals to scientific facts about the origin of the universe, the way in which the universe appears to be fine-tuned for life, and the difficulty of explaining human altruism in evolutionary terms. Does Collins's knowledge of natural science put him in a better position to interpret these scientific facts correctly? Does it make him epistemically superior to Hitchens in this respect? In his book, *God Is Not Great*, Christopher Hitchens discussed, at length, the facts and arguments that Collins adduced. Hitchens was well aware of all of these facts. The difference between Collins and Hitchens was that they made different *inferences* from the facts. They looked at the same set of facts, but then they each *interpreted* those facts differently. With respect to the relevant facts of natural science—the ones that are directly relevant to the debate over the existence of God—Hitchens appeared to be just as knowledgeable as Collins.

What about Hitchens? Could Hitchens claim to have more or better evidence than Collins with respect to matters of religion? Hitchens spent years studying the history of religions, including the apparent moral and political abuses of religious authority throughout history. He was extremely well informed on the history of religious doctrines, many of which seem very implausible to many people. It seems that Hitchens knew much more about the history of religious beliefs and practices than Collins. Did this background knowledge make Hitchens epistemically superior to Collins with respect to their religious beliefs? Collins was well aware of the fact that religious believers and religious institutions have believed in many absurdities and even committed many atrocities throughout history. In his book, *The Language of God*, Collins considers the relevance of this fact for the rationality of religious belief. Collins points out that no religious tradition—certainly not his own—claims that human beings are inherently good. On the contrary, traditional Christianity claims exactly the opposite. Thus, Collins contends that these facts do not contradict the content of his own religious beliefs. Here again, both Collins and Hitchens are aware of the relevant facts. Their disagreement arises because they interpret these facts differently. Thus, they possess the same evidence, but they interpret that evidence differently. In summary, then, it seems very doubtful that either Collins or Hitchens could claim that their evidence puts them in a better position to form a true belief than the other. That is because their evidence is not the source of their disagreement. Rather, their interpretation of the evidence—what they *infer* from it—leads them to different conclusions.

Another way one person can be epistemically superior to another is by having *superior cognitive ability that is relevant to the question at hand*. If you are much better at math than I am, then you would be my epistemic superior with respect to mathematical questions. If I am much better at interpreting the behavior of people than you are, then I would be epistemically superior to you with respect to questions about other people's thoughts and intentions. Did either Collins or Hitchens have superior cognitive ability to the other in the relevant respect? Let us consider each of them in turn. Francis

Collins excelled in scientific reasoning. His achievements attest to his cognitive ability in the natural sciences. Suppose, then, for the sake of argument, that Collins's cognitive ability in scientific reasoning was superior to Hitchens's ability in that respect. Does that make Collins epistemically superior to Hitchens with respect to their religious beliefs? No. Collins and Hitchens do not disagree about any facts of natural science. Their disagreement is not scientific but philosophical. Even if Collins is superior to Hitchens in scientific reasoning, it does not follow that he is superior to Hitchens in philosophical reasoning.

Christopher Hitchens studied philosophy at Oxford, as part of his program in philosophy, politics, and economics. Did Hitchens have superior cognitive ability in philosophy? Studying philosophy certainly improves one's ability to do good philosophical reasoning, and that might be some reason to believe that Hitchens was superior in this respect. However, it is clear that Collins studied philosophy on his own. His book is replete with quotations from philosophers, both past and present, on relevant subjects. Thus, it is possible, for all we know, that Collins managed to develop comparable skills of philosophical reasoning by studying on his own. When Collins debated Hitchens, he was able to present rational arguments for his beliefs and respond rationally to Hitchens's objections. In summary, then, it is hard to tell if either of them was cognitively superior to the other in this area.

One way a person can be epistemically *inferior* to another person is by being *more biased*. In the following chapter, we will examine the role of cognitive bias in shaping our beliefs. For present purposes, it will suffice to note that a cognitive bias makes a person less reliable— less likely to form true beliefs—than they otherwise would be. Thus, if one person is more biased than another person with respect to a certain question, then this bias will tend to make that person epistemically inferior with respect to that question. Consequently, if either Francis Collins or Christopher Hitchens were more biased than the other with respect to religion, then that person might be epistemically inferior to the other with respect to religion. A common suggestion, in this respect, is that most religious believers are biased because they were subjected to religious indoctrination when they were children.

Childhood indoctrination instills beliefs in a person at a time when they are less capable of thinking critically for themselves. People who acquired their religious beliefs in this way might retain those beliefs as adults, even if it is no longer rational to do so. Was Collins biased in this way? Did such a bias render him epistemically inferior to Hitchens with respect to religion?

As it happens, Francis Collins was not raised as a religious believer. Collins's parents were not serious about religion. When Collins joined an Episcopal boys' choir as a young man, his parents told him that the theology should not be taken too seriously.[8] As a college student, Collins was an agnostic, and by graduate school, he had decided that "no thinking scientist could seriously entertain the possibility of God."[9] It was only later in his life, as a student in medical school, that Collins became a religious believer. Thus, in the case of Collins, there was no childhood indoctrination to cause a cognitive bias. Of course, it is still possible that Collins suffered from some cognitive bias. However, that is also true of Hitchens. Thus, it is not obvious that either one was significantly more biased than the other.

One person can be epistemically superior to another person in other ways. If one of them has been more careful and attentive than the other, then that could make them epistemically superior. Alternatively, if one person has had more time to think about the question than the other person, that could also make them epistemically superior. However, there is no reason to think that either Collins or Hitchens was superior to the other in any of these respects. Each of them thought carefully enough, and for long enough, to write entire books on the subject and to participate in many public debates. Thus, it seems likely that they were comparable in these respects as well. At this point, we have considered the most salient ways in which one person can be epistemically superior to another. Neither Collins nor Hitchens appears to be superior to the other in any of these ways. Suppose that, in fact, neither Collins nor Hitchens was epistemically superior to the other with respect to their religious

---

8. Collins, *The Language of God*, 14.
9. Collins, *The Language of God*, 15–16.

beliefs. Then Collins and Hitchens were epistemic peers with respect to their religious beliefs. That is to say that they were in an equally good position to form true beliefs about religion, and thus, were equally likely to have formed true beliefs about religion. Now recall the line of reasoning that we imagined Collins's undertaking. If Hitchens is in just as good a position to form true beliefs about religion as Collins, then Hitchens is equally likely to have formed true beliefs as Collins. If Hitchens is just as likely to have formed true beliefs about religion as Collins, then Collins should not continue to believe that he is right and that Hitchens is wrong. After all, it is just as likely that Hitchens is right and Collins is wrong. Consequently, it seems that Collins should stop believing that he is correct. That means that Collins should stop holding his religious beliefs. Moreover, if this is correct, then this very same reasoning applies to Hitchens as well. In summary, it seems that both Collins and Hitchens should stop holding their prior beliefs about religion. In light of their disagreement, each of them should now suspend judgment with respect to religion—they should neither believe nor disbelieve that their prior beliefs are true. This view about disagreement between epistemic peers is called *The Equal Weight View*.

The Equal Weight View: If two people are epistemic peers, then they should give equal weight to each of their opinions on the matter. If they disagree, then they should each suspend judgment with respect to their prior belief.

To illustrate this view, consider the case of the Restaurant Check, originally due to David Christensen.[10] Suppose that you and I go out to dinner with a large group of people. At the end of our dinner, we want to split the check evenly, so you and I take turns looking at the check and calculate what each person owes. Suppose that you and I are equally good at simple arithmetic, and we are equally careful and attentive in doing our calculations. Nevertheless, upon doing our

---

10. David Christensen, "Epistemology of Disagreement: The Good News," *The Philosophical Review* 116 (2007): 193.

calculations, we get different results. Suppose that I say, "Well, obviously, you made a mistake and got the wrong result." In that situation, would it be rational? No, it seems not. I have no reason to think that it was you who made a mistake rather than me. At that moment, it seems that I should suspend judgment about whether it was you or I who made a mistake. That is the Equal Weight View.

To understand why some people find this view compelling, consider another example. Suppose that you are serving on a jury, hearing testimony from two expert witnesses. Each expert witness has excellent credentials, and each of them appears to be equally thoughtful and attentive. On reflection, neither of these experts seems to be more credible than the other. However, when they testify in court, they give opposing testimony. Who should you trust? If they have equally good credentials, and they seem to be equally thoughtful and attentive, etc., then it seems that you should trust them both equally. Under the circumstances, there is no reason to trust either one of them more than the other one. Thus, you should give each of their testimonies equal weight. That seems like the reasonable response. The reason is that those two people are in an equally good position to get the right answer. Well, by the very same reasoning, if you recognize that you and another person are both equally intelligent, well-informed, thoughtful, etc., with respect to some question, then you should give as much weight to their opinion as you give to your own. Consequently, if they disagree with you, then you should suspend judgment about who is right and who is wrong. That is what the Equal Weight View requires.

However, there appear to be cases where you should *not* give equal weight to someone else's opinion, even if they are your epistemic peer.[11] In the case of the restaurant check, suppose that I tell you that each person's share of the check is $23 million. It becomes clear to you that I am not joking, and I appear to be rational in every other respect. Should you give equal weight to my opinion? No. In this situation, it is more rational for you to believe that there

---

11. The following cases are introduced and discussed by Bryan Frances in part II of his book *Disagreement* (Cambridge: Polity, 2014).

is something wrong with me—I have suddenly become impaired in some way—than to believe that each person owes $23 million for dinner. Your overall evidence makes it more rational for you to retain your belief and infer that, although I am *usually* your epistemic peer, I am not really your epistemic peer *in this situation*.[12] This is an extreme case, but there are less extreme cases in which it seems that you should not give equal weight to another person's opinion. Suppose that I deny that smoking causes lung cancer, and I appear to be your epistemic peer with respect to issues like this. You should not give equal weight to my opinion. You know that the experts all agree that smoking causes lung cancer, which gives you good reason to retain your belief that this is so. In this situation, it is more rational for you to infer that, contrary to appearances, I am *not* really your epistemic peer in this particular situation.

In each of these cases, you should not give equal weight to the opinion of someone who appears to be an epistemic peer. Do these examples refute the Equal Weight View? Let's begin with the case of smoking and lung cancer. The Equal Weight View can be modified to accommodate this case without sacrificing the underlying principle of the view. In that case, you have one epistemic peer who disagrees with you, but you also have *many epistemic superiors who agree with you.* In that situation, you should defer to your epistemic superiors rather than give equal weight to your epistemic peer. The Equal Weight View can accommodate this fact by simply adding a clause that says that when your epistemic superiors disagree with one of your epistemic peers, then you should defer to your superiors. That is in keeping with the basic principle of the Equal Weight View: the weight that you give to each opinion should be proportionate to the probability that it is correct. Since the opinions of your epistemic superiors are more likely to be correct, you should give them more weight.

This modification of the Equal Weight View will only be relevant in cases where the majority of the experts agree. In many disagreements, there is no such consensus. Consider the disagreement

---

12. Frances, *Disagreement*, 125.

between Collins and Hitchens. In matters of religion, there is no consensus among philosophers who have studied these issues. There are philosophers who are religious believers, and there are philosophers who are unbelievers. The same is true of experts in the study of religion—psychologists of religion, sociologists of religion, historians of religion, etc. There are scholars of religion who are believers, and there are scholars of religion who are unbelievers. There is no consensus among recognized experts in matters of religion. Consequently, the modified Equal Weight View renders the very same verdict with respect to Collins and Hitchens as before—they should both give equal weight to each of their opinions.[13]

Now consider the case of the $23 million restaurant check. All of your life experience and the testimony of all the people you know tell you that no restaurant check would be as high as $23 million, much less that each person's share would be $23 million. Thus, your evidence against my belief is overwhelming. In that situation, it seems more rational for you to deny that I am your epistemic peer than to give equal weight to my opinion. Does this refute the Equal Weight View? Here again, it is possible to modify the Equal Weight View to accommodate this exception. According to the modified view, one should give equal weight to the opinion of an epistemic peer *unless* one has overwhelming evidence for one's own belief. But what counts as "overwhelming evidence," and how can we tell when we have it? Suppose that Francis Collins believes he has overwhelming evidence that his religious beliefs are true. Then is it rational for him to infer

---

13. The majority of philosophers today are atheists. According to the most recent survey, 67 percent of philosophers are atheists, while only 19 percent are theists. Consequently, one might argue that there is a consensus among experts that atheism is true. The question is whether these numbers merit using the term "consensus." When people speak of a consensus among climate scientists, they are referring to the fact that 97 percent of climate scientists believe in anthropogenic climate change. The percentage of philosophers who are atheists is certainly much smaller than that. Nevertheless, one might argue that the percentage is large enough to constitute a consensus. I will leave it to the reader to decide the matter. At the time of this writing, the most recent survey is the 2020 PhilPapers Survey, https://survey2020.philpeople.org/survey/results/all.

that Hitchens is not, after all, his epistemic peer in this regard? That seems too easy. A defender of the modified view can deny that Collins would be rational in doing this. Collins might *think* that he has overwhelming evidence for his religious beliefs, but that does not imply that he *does* have overwhelming evidence. According to the modified view, it is rational to deny that someone is an epistemic peer only when you really do have overwhelming evidence for your belief. Thus, the modified version of the Equal Weight View does not allow Collins to ignore his disagreement with Hitchens just because Collins *thinks* that he has overwhelming evidence for his beliefs. It is possible for a person to think that they have overwhelming evidence, even when they do not. Consequently, the modified version of the Equal Weight View does not license a free-for-all, in which anyone can ignore the disagreements with their epistemic peers simply by claiming that they have overwhelming evidence for their belief.

Unfortunately, the possibility of being mistaken about having overwhelming evidence makes it harder to apply the modified view to decide how to respond to actual disagreements. In some cases, it really does *seem* like I have overwhelming evidence for my belief. If it is *true* that I have overwhelming evidence, then the modified view says that I can ignore the fact that you disagree with me, even though you appear to be my epistemic peer in this matter. However, if I am mistaken about having overwhelming evidence—I think I have it, but I really don't—then I should give your belief equal weight. If I cannot tell whether I have overwhelming evidence, then I cannot use the modified version of the Equal Weight View to decide how to respond to our disagreement.

Fortunately, there is often a way to resolve this problem. Generally speaking, overwhelming evidence actually tends to overwhelm people, at least if they are rational. Thus, if my evidence is really overwhelming, then most of my epistemic peers and superiors will also find it overwhelming. In the case of the dinner check, suppose that you ask everyone else at the table if each person's share of the check could be $23 million. If everyone else agrees that they have overwhelming evidence against this, then that confirms, to some extent, that you really do have overwhelming evidence against my belief. By contrast, if Francis Collins were to ask a random sample of his epistemic peers if he has overwhelming evidence for his religious beliefs, they would not all say that he does. In fact, many of them would say that he does *not* have overwhelming evidence. In this way, it is often possible to test whether one has overwhelming evidence for a belief. In these cases, the modified version of the Equal Weight View can be applied to determine how to respond to a disagreement with an epistemic peer.

Even with this modification, some philosophers object to the Equal Weight View. One objection is that this view neglects the way things seem to each individual.[14] After Collins has listened to Hitchens's reasons and arguments, it still *seems* to Collins that his religious beliefs are true. Should Collins just ignore how things seem to him at that point? The Equal Weight View seems to require that he ignore it, but that doesn't seem right. In a similar vein, some philosophers argue that self-trust is indispensable to the pursuit of knowledge. However, self-trust requires that each person trust their own judgment, even when an epistemic peer disagrees.[15] Thus, the Equal Weight View is false.

However, just as it seems to Collins that the evidence supports his beliefs, *so it seems to Hitchens that the evidence supports the opposite beliefs*. Moreover, Collins is now aware that it seems to Hitchens that the evidence supports Hitchens's beliefs. The Equal Weight View does not prohibit Collins from attending to the way things seem to him. Rather, it requires that he recognize *both* the way it seems to him *and* the way it seems to Hitchens and give them equal weight. Likewise, the Equal Weight View does not deprive Collins of self-trust. Rather, it requires that Collins trust *both* himself *and* Hitchens to the

---

14. See, for example, Alvin Plantinga, "Pluralism: A Defense of Religious Exclusivism," in *The Philosophical Challenge of Religious Diversity*, ed. Philip L. Quinn and Kevin Meeker (New York: Oxford University Press, 2000), 172–192.

15. See Richard Foley, *Intellectual Trust in Oneself and Others* (Cambridge: Cambridge University Press, 2001).

degree that is appropriate to each of them. Collins has good reason to trust himself, and he also has good reason to trust Hitchens since Hitchens appears to be his epistemic peer. Thus, it is not clear that the Equal Weight View neglects the way things seem to each individual, nor that it runs afoul of the need for self-trust.

Here is a stronger objection to the Equal Weight View. Sometimes, the evidence we possess does not rationally compel us to adopt one particular conclusion. Two people with the very same evidence can form different and even opposing beliefs on the basis of the very same evidence. That seems to be possible. In fact, that seems to be what is happening in the case of Collins and Hitchens. They both possess the very same evidence, and they are both rational people, yet they form different beliefs on the basis of that evidence. Thus, it seems that there can be more than one rational response to the very same body of evidence. This view is sometimes called *permissivism*. According to permissivism, there can be more than one equally rational response to the very same evidence. It is possible for two people to form different and even opposing beliefs in response to the very same evidence. If permissivism is true, then perhaps Collins and Hitchens are equally rational in believing as they do, even though their beliefs are opposed. But if both of their responses to the evidence are equally rational, *then neither Collins nor Hitchens needs to give up their original beliefs, despite their disagreement.* Collins and Hitchens can each continue to hold their beliefs while conceding that the other's beliefs are just as rational. Consequently, if permissivism is true, then it seems that the Equal Weight View is false.[16] Is permissivism true?

To answer this question, we need to reflect on what it means to be rational. In the sense in which we are using that term here,

---

16. *Permissivism* is defended by Thomas Kelly, among others. See Kelly, "The Epistemic Significance of Disagreement," in *Oxford Studies in Epistemology*, vol. 1., ed. T. Gendler and J. Hawthorne (Oxford: Oxford University Press, 2005); and Kelly, "Can Evidence Be Permissive," in *Contemporary Debates in Epistemology*, 2nd ed., ed. Matthias Steup, John Turri, and Ernest Sosa (Hoboken, NJ: John Wiley & Sons, 2014), 298–312. The following exposition of *permissivism* is based on Kelly's presentation and defense in "Can Evidence Be Permissive?"

a rational person tries to believe what is true and to avoid believing what is false. As the American philosopher William James once pointed out, these two goals can actually pull us in opposite directions. To see that, imagine two unusual people, Bella and Dan. Bella's only goal, with respect to her beliefs, is to believe as many true things as possible. Bella doesn't care if she has false beliefs. She just wants to believe as many truths as she can. By contrast, Dan's only goal, with respect to his beliefs, is to avoid believing anything false. Dan hates being deceived. Dan doesn't care about having true beliefs. He just wants to avoid having false beliefs. Now, given their respective goals, what should each of these people believe? The answer is that Bella should believe *absolutely everything*, and Dan should believe *nothing at all*. By believing everything, Bella will achieve her goal of believing as many truths as possible, and that is her only goal. By believing nothing, Dan will achieve his goal of believing no falsehoods, and that is his only goal. This illustrates the fact that these two goals—believing what is true and not believing what is false—are separate goals, which can actually pull in opposite directions. Of course, most people have both of these goals. Most of us want to believe what is true *and* avoid believing what is false. However, we do not all value those two things to the very same degree. If it is rational for two people to differ at all in this respect, then that might lead to permissivism in the following way.

Suppose that, with respect to their religious beliefs, Collins and Hitchens differ in the following way. With respect to the existence of God, Collins values *having a true belief in God, if God exists* much more than he values *avoiding a false belief in God, if God does not exist*. To understand what this means, suppose that you ask Collins what he wants most with respect to his religious beliefs. Collins would say that what he wants most is to have a true belief in God, if God exists. His second favorite outcome would be to avoid believing in God, if God does not exist. Thus, for Collins, it would be much worse to *miss out on a true belief in God* than to *have a false belief that God exists*. By contrast, suppose that Hitchens has exactly the opposite priorities. Hitchens values *avoiding a false belief in God* much more than he values *having a true belief in God*. For Hitchens, having a false belief that

God exists would be much worse than missing out on a true belief in God. If Collins and Hitchens have different priorities, in this way, then their different responses to the evidence might both be completely rational.

Suppose that, given the evidence, the probability that God exists is exactly 0.5. Objectively speaking, the odds that God exists are fifty-fifty. Since Collins cares more about getting a true belief in God, if God exists, and cares less about avoiding a false belief in God, if God does not exist, it seems rational for Collins to believe that God exists. By contrast, since Hitchens cares more about avoiding a false belief in God than achieving a true belief in God, it seems rational for Hitchens to disbelieve in God. If that line of reasoning is correct, then neither Collins nor Hitchens is rationally required to give up their original beliefs despite their disagreement.

Is that correct? Here is one concern about this line of reasoning: Consider the case of Bella. Suppose that Bella follows through on her exclusive concern for true beliefs, and she believes absolutely everything. She believes in dragons, unicorns, and everything else. Is it rational for Bella to believe these things? No, it seems not. However, it seems that Bella can defend her beliefs in the very same way as we have defended Collins and Hitchens. Bella can say that since she cares only about having true beliefs, she can best achieve her goals by believing everything. In the case of Bella, this reasoning leads to an absurdity—that it is rational for Bella to believe everything. Therefore, there is something wrong with this line of reasoning.

Why are Bella's beliefs irrational? Her beliefs are irrational because rationality requires that we be concerned about *both* having true beliefs *and* avoiding false beliefs. If rationality requires that we be concerned about both of these things, then one might suspect that we should be *equally* concerned about both of these things. According to one view, we should have equal concern about believing what is true and not believing what is false. If that view is right, then it is not rational for Collins and Hitchens to have different values in that respect. However, it is not obvious that this view is correct. Even if rationality requires that we be concerned about both believing what is true and not believing what is false, it does not follow that we must be concerned about them to the very same degree. Thus, the case of Bella does not refute permissivism.

However, some philosophers remain unconvinced that permissivism is true. Thus, philosophers remain divided over whether we should accept the Equal Weight View or reject it in favor of permissivism. On reflection, that very disagreement poses an obstacle to accepting the Equal Weight View. According to the Equal Weight View, if an epistemic peer disagrees with me, then I should suspend judgment about the truth of the matter. As I have noted, not all philosophers accept the Equal Weight View. Some philosophers reject it. Moreover, these philosophers appear to be just as intelligent, thoughtful, and well-informed as anyone else on this matter. Consequently, we all have epistemic peers who reject the Equal Weight View. In that situation, the Equal Weight View *itself* requires us to suspend judgment about whether it is true. In other words, if we accept the Equal Weight View, then since some of our epistemic peers *reject* the Equal Weight View, we are led to the conclusion that *we should not accept the Equal Weight View*. Rather, we should suspend judgment about it. If that is correct, then in the current circumstances, in which there is peer disagreement about the Equal Weight View, the Equal Weight View is *self-defeating*.[17]

It is important to be clear about what this argument proves and what it does not prove. If this argument is right, then it shows that *in the current situation, in which we have epistemic peers who reject the Equal Weight View, we should not accept the Equal Weight View*. Notice: that does not prove that the Equal Weight View is *false*. It is still possible that the Equal Weight View is actually true and that some of our epistemic peers have made a mistake. In fact, in the interest of discovering the truth about this matter, it is rational to continue to

---

17. This objection is developed and defended by Brian Weatherson. See Weatherson, "Disagreements, Philosophical and Otherwise," in *The Epistemology of Disagreement: New Essays*, ed. Jennifer Lackey and David Christensen (New York: Oxford University Press, 2013).

examine the arguments for and against the Equal Weight View. By doing so, we might discover that those who have rejected the Equal Weight View have made a mistake.[18] However, with that said, the fact remains that, in the current circumstances, no one should actually *accept* the Equal Weight View as long as they have epistemic peers who reject it, and it appears that we all have epistemic peers who reject it.

One might defend the Equal Weight View by claiming that this is a case in which we have overwhelming evidence.[19] If there is overwhelming evidence for the Equal Weight View, then it is rational to believe it even if some epistemic peers disagree. However, if the evidence for the Equal Weight View were overwhelming, then it would be recognized as such by most rational people. That is not the case. There are many rational people who do not see the evidence for the Equal Weight View as overwhelming. That is some reason to doubt that the evidence for it really is overwhelming. Of course, this might change over time. At some point in the future, it is possible that everyone who thinks carefully about it accepts the Equal Weight View. However, in the meantime, it seems that the Equal Weight View itself requires that we suspend judgment about whether it is true or false.

If we should not accept the Equal Weight View in the present circumstances, then how should we respond to disagreements with our epistemic peers? If Collins and Hitchens need not give equal weight to each other's opinions, then how should they respond to their disagreement? There are at least two possibilities here. First, there is what is sometimes called *The Steadfast View*.

---

18. This point is developed and defended by Jonathan Matheson in "Are Conciliatory Views of Disagreement Self-Defeating?" *Social Epistemology* 29 (2015): 145–159.

19. In a similar vein, Tomas Bogardus has argued that the Equal Weight View is exempt from its own demand because it is *self-evidently true*. See Bogardus, "A Vindication of the Equal Weight View," *Episteme: A Journal of Social Epistemology* 6 (2009): 324–335.

The Steadfast View: *If two people are epistemic peers and they disagree, then it is permissible for each of them to retain their prior belief, with the very same degree of confidence.*

According to the Steadfast View, it is rationally permissible for Collins and Hitchens to retain their original beliefs despite their disagreement. By contrast, there is what I will call *Moderate Conciliationism*.

Moderate Conciliationism: *If two people are epistemic peers and they disagree, then it is permissible for each of them to retain their prior belief, but each of them should reduce their degree of confidence in their belief.*

According to Moderate Conciliationism, it is rational for Collins and Hitchens to retain their original beliefs, but not with the same degree of confidence that they had before. Rather, Collins and Hitchens should each have a lower degree of confidence in the truth of their beliefs after they become aware of their disagreement. The reason is that Collins and Hitchens should each give *some weight* to the other's opinion. They need not give it *equal weight*, but they should certainly give it some weight. Moderate Conciliationism is, as the name suggests, a more moderate version of the Equal Weight View. Which of these views is correct? Is it rational for Collins and Hitchens to retain their original beliefs with the very same degree of confidence they had before, or should they each be less confident that their beliefs are true?[20]

---

20. Both the Steadfast View and Moderate Conciliationism are types of *permissivism*. Both the Steadfast View and Moderate Conciliationism hold that it is rationally permissible for two people to hold different beliefs on the basis of the same evidence. The Steadfast View says that it is permissible for two people to hold their original beliefs *with the very same degree of confidence*, even after they are aware of the disagreement. By contrast, Moderate Conciliationism says that it is permissible for two people to hold their original beliefs, but *they should reduce their confidence in the truth of their beliefs* after they have discovered their disagreement.

Moderate Conciliationism is not undermined by the fact that we have epistemic peers who reject it. If we accept Moderate Conciliationism, then the fact that some of our epistemic peers reject it requires that we reduce our confidence in it, but it does not require that we stop believing it altogether. Thus, we can consistently accept Moderate Conciliationism despite disagreement about it. Second, Moderate Conciliationism is consistent with permissivism. Even if Collins and Hitchens should reduce their confidence in their original beliefs, they can continue to have different beliefs. Thus, a Moderate Conciliationist can accept some degree of permissivism. Consequently, Moderate Conciliationism is not vulnerable to the very same problems as the Equal Weight View.

Throughout this chapter, we have asked how we should respond to disagreement with respect to our *beliefs*. However, an equally important question is how we should respond to disagreement with respect to our *actions*. Our intellectual life involves not just our beliefs but also our actions. Actions like gathering evidence, listening to other points of view, and reflecting critically on our beliefs are all part of our intellectual life. When we discover that some of our epistemic peers disagree with us about something, how should this affect our actions? On the face of it, it seems that we should listen to our epistemic peers and take their opinions into account. We should reflect on their reasons and arguments with an open mind and reconsider our own opinions. As long as some of our epistemic peers disagree with us, it seems that we should continue to respond in this way. Thus, as long as Collins and Hitchens disagree with each other, they should continue to listen to each other's reasons and arguments. They should continue to reflect critically on their own beliefs and their evidence for them.

If that is correct, then it might support Moderate Conciliationism as opposed to the Steadfast View. Suppose that it is rational for Collins to continue to believe that he is right and to believe it with the very same degree of confidence as before. If this was a very high level of confidence, then even after his disagreement with Hitchens, Collins is justified in having a very high level of confidence that his religious beliefs are true. If Collins is justified in being very confident that his religious beliefs are true, then he is also justified in believing, very confidently, that Hitchens is wrong. But if Collins is justified in believing, very confidently, that Hitchens is wrong, then it seems that Collins *should not* listen to Hitchens or take his reasons into account. After all, Collins is justified in believing, very confidently, that Hitchens is *wrong*. To listen carefully to someone, when you have good reason to believe that they are mistaken, is not rational. Thus, the Steadfast View seems to imply that Collins would be rational in ignoring Hitchens's reasons and arguments. If that seems like a mistaken conclusion, then it shows that the Steadfast View is, itself, mistaken.

However, a defender of the Steadfast View need not accept this line of reasoning. First, even very confident belief is not the same as *certainty*. A person who believes something very confidently can still recognize that they might be mistaken, even if they think that is unlikely. The mere possibility of error, on any matter, gives a person some reason to listen to epistemic peers who disagree. Second, a person who is very confident in her beliefs might be committed to pursuing the truth *together with other people in a community*.[21] If we see ourselves as part of a community of truth-seekers with common goals, then we have reason to pursue the truth together, as a community. In order to do that in a meaningful way, we must listen to our epistemic peers in the community and take their reasons and arguments seriously. This is something that a person can be committed to doing, even if they continue to hold their beliefs very confidently in the face of disagreement. Thus, the Steadfast View does not preclude a person from continuing to listen to her peers and think with an open mind.

Moreover, for the purposes of communal inquiry, retaining confident beliefs might have a distinct advantage for the whole community. Recent studies have found that groups of people working together are better at discovering the truth than individuals working alone.[22] In fact,

---

21. This idea is developed and defended by Heather Rabenberg in "Knowing With," *Ratio* 37, no. 2–3 (2024): 112–122.
22. See Emmanuel Trouche, Emmanuel Sander, and Hugo Mercier, "Arguments, More Than Confidence, Explain the Good Performance of Reasoning Groups," *Journal of Experimental Psychology* 143 (2014): 1958–1971.

a group of people working together to solve a problem even outperforms the most intelligent member of the group, working alone. Most importantly, for our purposes, is how this works. When members of a group listen to each other's reasons, they are often persuaded by the very best reasons that are offered. Thus, the member of the group who has the best reasons is often able to persuade the other members of the group. In this way, the person who is right—whoever that is—convinces the other members of the group, and they also arrive at the truth. Over time, a group that functions this way will outperform even the smartest individuals. However, in order for this process to work, each member of the group must share their reasons for their beliefs. People who hold their beliefs confidently might be more likely to share their reasons in a way that will persuade the other members of the group than people who reduce their confidence in the face of disagreement. If that is true, then for the purposes of collective inquiry, the Steadfast View would have a distinct advantage since confident belief will facilitate the process that leads to the truth more often. Of course, it is possible for people who reduce their confidence to continue to share their reasons. The question is whether they will actually do so.

In conclusion, what should we say about the disagreement between Francis Collins and Christopher Hitchens? In the current circumstances, it seems they need not give equal weight to each other's opinions. As long as there is disagreement among epistemic peers about the Equal Weight View, neither Collins nor Hitchens is required to accept it. Thus, it seems rational for each of them to retain their original beliefs despite the disagreement between them. The question is whether it is rational for each of them to continue to hold their beliefs with just as much confidence as they did prior to their disagreement. The Steadfast View says that it is, while Modest Conciliationism says that it is not. One thing that seems clear is that Collins and Hitchens should continue to share their reasons for their beliefs, listen to the reasons of their epistemic peers, and reflect on the matter with an open mind. The degree of confidence that best facilitates that process is probably the right one to have.

Study Questions

1. Think of a topic on which you know someone who disagrees with you. Suppose that you want to know if this person is your epistemic peer with respect to this topic. What facts do you need to know about yourself and this person in order to know if the two of you are epistemic peers?
2. According to the Equal Weight View, if someone who is your epistemic peer disagrees with you, then you should give equal weight to their view. What does this mean, and what is the argument for it? Explain this in your own words.
3. Are there intelligent, thoughtful people who reject the Equal Weight View? Do some of them appear to be epistemic peers of those who accept the Equal Weight View? How does this pose a problem for the Equal Weight View?
4. Two horses, Lightning Speed and Photo Finish, are each given a 50 percent chance of winning the Kentucky Derby. All of the experts agree that they each have an equal chance of winning. According to permissivism, what is the rational position to take on which horse will win? Explain your answer.
5. Imagine that you disagree with someone who seems to be your epistemic peer on the subject. According to Moderate Conciliationism, what should you do? According to the Steadfast View, what should you do?

For Further Reading

There are two excellent introductions to the epistemology of disagreement: Bryan Frances's book *Disagreement* (Cambridge: Polity Press, 2014); and Jonathan Matheson, *The Epistemic Significance of Disagreement* (London: Palgrave, 2015). For a careful examination of the charge that the Equal Weight View is self-defeating, see Jonathan Matheson's essay "Are Conciliatory Views of Disagreement Self-Defeating?" *Social Epistemology* 29 (2015): 145–159. For a critique of the arguments for permissivism, see Nathan Ballantyne, "Is Epistemic

Permissivism Intuitive," *American Philosophical Quarterly* 55 (2018): 365–378. For a defense of something close to the Steadfast View, see David Enoch's essay "Not Just a Truthometer: Taking Oneself Seriously (but not Too Seriously) in Cases of Peer Disagreement," *Mind* 119 (2010): 953–977. Finally, Thomas Mulligan applies the principles of Bayesian epistemology to disagreement, with interesting results, in his essay "The Epistemology of Disagreement: Why Not Bayesianism?," *Episteme* 18 (2021): 587–602.

CHAPTER FOUR

Acknowledging Bias

On February 25, 2000, Kathy Thompson married Robert Miles in Eau Claire, Wisconsin. At 1:50 a.m. the next morning, Thompson and Miles got into a fight, in which Thompson hit and bloodied Miles. The police were called, and Thompson was arrested. Miles was also arrested on charges relating to outstanding warrants. After signing a prepared statement, Thompson was released from jail at 3:00 a.m. and began walking toward home. At 5:40 a.m. that morning, a 911 caller reported that a woman was lying face down on the sidewalk, wearing very few clothes. It was Kathy Thompson. It appeared that Thompson had been strangled to death. It also appeared that her hair had been brushed.[1]

Thompson's husband, Robert Miles, had been in jail at the time of the murder, so he could not have killed Thompson. Consequently, the police immediately turned their attention to Thompson's ex-boyfriend, Evan Zimmerman. Zimmerman dated Thompson from November 1998 to May 1999, and he lived just one and one-half blocks from her. Moreover, there were at least two reports that Zimmerman was obsessed with Thompson. On February 27, police searched Zimmerman's van, finding a telephone cord and a hairbrush. The medical examiner who performed the autopsy on Thompson stated it was possible that the telephone cord had been used to strangle Thompson. DNA tests also revealed that the hair in the brush belonged to Thompson. In the minds of the police investigators, this confirmed that Zimmerman was guilty. According to Zimmerman, on the night of the murder, he was at the VFW until it closed at 2:00 a.m., at

---

1. The facts of the case are stated in Zimmerman v. City of Eau Claire, 06-C-85-S (W.D. Wis. September 12, 2006). The following summary is based on that source.

which time he purchased a six-pack of beer from the bartender, and proceeded to walk home. He stopped at the houses of two friends on the way home, but neither one answered the door. On March 3, the police conducted a polygraph of Zimmerman, and they interpreted his scores on the polygraph chart as indicating deception.

In the following months, the police continued to search for evidence that Zimmerman killed Thompson. They interviewed Zimmerman's friend, Jim Stefanic. Stefanic reported being in Thompson's house on the day before the murder, but this was not documented by the police. The investigators found a witness who remembered seeing a white van on the morning of the murder. According to the witness, there was a woman in the passenger's seat of the van who appeared to be either asleep or passed out. When the investigators showed the witness a picture of Zimmerman's van, the witness was not certain that it was the van he saw. The police subsequently sent the witness to Madison, Wisconsin, to undergo hypnosis to see if he could recall any more details of what he saw. Under hypnosis, the witness could not recall anything more. Another witness testified to the police that Zimmerman had spoken to her on the morning after the murder and reported that Kathy Thompson had been strangled to death. The fact that Thompson had been murdered by strangulation had not been revealed to the public at that time.

On February 2, 2001, Evan Zimmerman was charged with the murder of Kathy Thompson. In the months leading up to his trial, investigators continued to gather evidence. On May 8, 2001, a forensic scientist at the State of Wisconsin Crime Lab reported that the injured area of Kathy Thompson's neck contained very short fiber fragments of blue and black cotton. This was inconsistent with the belief that Zimmerman's telephone cord was the murder weapon. At Zimmerman's trial in May 2001, a police officer testified that he had located cigarette butts in the vicinity of Thompson's body. The officer testified that testing was done on the cigarettes, but it produced no evidence relevant to the crime. Based on the evidence, the jury convicted Evan Zimmerman of murder. However, on August 12, 2003, the Wisconsin Court of Appeals found that Zimmerman's defense had failed him since the attorney did not present DNA evidence that exculpated Zimmerman. DNA taken from the cigarette butts, as well as hair found on Thompson's clothing and scrapings under her fingernails could not belong to Zimmerman. Moreover, that DNA could all belong to another male. In June 2004, Zimmerman was released from prison, pending a retrial. He was tried again in August, but the trial was suspended for lack of sufficient evidence. In 2006, Zimmerman sued the city of Eau Claire, Wisconsin, for violating his right to due process. He died of cancer in 2007.

From the very beginning of this investigation, the police officers believed that Evan Zimmerman committed the crime. From that time forward, they searched for evidence that Zimmerman was guilty. They did not seriously consider any other possibilities. In the process, they found what appeared to be very strong evidence that Zimmerman was guilty. At that point, were the officers rationally justified in believing that Zimmerman was guilty? If it turned out that Zimmerman committed the crime, would we even say that the officers *knew* that he did it? Based on the evidence alone, one might answer these questions in the affirmative. However, the officers' conviction that Zimmerman was guilty heavily influenced their investigation and their reasoning throughout the process. Moreover, studies have shown that this sort of bias often leads to false beliefs. As we will see, this case is no exception.

The subject of this chapter is *cognitive bias*. It is common knowledge that people are biased. As far back as 1623, Francis Bacon identified what he called "idols of the mind." These idols of the mind are

> the deepest fallacies of the human mind: For they do not deceive in particulars, as the other [fallacies] do, by clouding and snaring the judgment; but by a corrupt and ill-ordered predisposition of mind, which as it were perverts and infects all the anticipations of the intellect.[2]

---

2. Francis Bacon, *The Works of Francis Bacon*, vol. 4, ed. James Spedding, Robert Leslie Ellis, and Douglas Denon Heath (Boston, MA: Houghton Mifflin, 1901), 431.

The idols of the mind are not just mistakes of reasoning. They are deeply embedded dispositions to reason and act in ways that lead us to error. These dispositions are now known as cognitive biases, and psychologists have discovered an astonishing array of them. In fact, the influence of cognitive bias on human reason is so pervasive that it poses a significant threat to human knowledge. If many of our beliefs are strongly influenced by cognitive biases, then how can we know that they are true? That is the question that we will explore in this chapter.

To understand the problem posed by cognitive bias, it is necessary to have some knowledge of the nature and effects of our cognitive biases. Thus, I will begin with some examples of the cognitive biases that have been discovered by empirical psychologists. In their seminal work on cognitive biases, Amos Tversky and Daniel Kahneman first identified the *anchoring bias*.[3] The anchoring bias is a tendency to use the first piece of information we receive about something as an "anchor"—it exerts an undue influence on our subsequent thinking about the subject. In their original experiment, Tversky and Kahneman first spun a wheel to choose a number randomly. Subjects in the experiment observed them spin the wheel to select the number. They then asked each subject whether the percentage of African countries in the United Nations was higher or lower than that number. After the subject answered that question, they then asked the subject to guess the actual percentage of African countries in the United Nations. The subject's answer to the second question depended on the number that had been arbitrarily selected by spinning the wheel prior to the first question. The higher the number that was randomly selected by the wheel, the higher the estimate the subject then gave in answer to the second question. If the wheel landed on a high number, then the subject guessed a relatively high percentage, whereas if the wheel landed on a low number, then the subject guessed a relatively low percentage. Even though the number was selected randomly by spinning a wheel, it still influenced the subject's own estimate.

---

3. Amos Tversky and Daniel Kahneman, "Judgment under Uncertainty: Heuristics and Biases," *Science* 185 (1974): 1124–1131.

Subsequent experiments have confirmed the existence and prevalence of the anchoring bias.[4]

Next, consider the *framing effect*. The framing effect occurs when the way in which something is framed—in positive or negative terms—influences our judgment. For example, when beef is described as 75 percent lean, it is given a higher rating than if it is described as 25 percent fat.[5] Another study found that research and development teams are given more money when their results are stated in terms of their rate of success than if the very same results are stated in terms of their rate of failure.[6] Subsequent research has confirmed that the framing effect is also a prevalent bias in human reasoning.[7]

One of the most prevalent cognitive biases is *confirmation bias*, which is "the seeking or interpreting of evidence in ways that are partial to existing beliefs, expectations, or a hypothesis in hand."[8] Scott Plous conducted a study involving two groups of people—one group supported nuclear energy, while the other group opposed it. Both groups were asked to read the very same literature on the potential benefits and harms of nuclear energy. After reading the literature, each group took it to support their own view. Those who favored nuclear energy took the literature to confirm that they were right,

---

4. See Adrian Furnham and Huan Chu Boo, "A Literature Review of the Anchoring Effect," *Journal of Socio-Economics* 40 (2011): 35–42; and P. Teovanović, "Individual Differences in Anchoring Effect: Evidence for the Role of Insufficient Adjustment," *European Journal of Psychology* 15 (2019): 8–24.

5. See I. P. Levin and G. J. Gaeth, "How Consumers Are Affected by the Framing of Attribute Information before and after Consuming the Product," *Journal of Consumer Research* 15 (1988): 374–378.

6. D. Duchon, K. J. Dunegan, and S. L. Barton, "Framing the Problem and Making Decisions: The Facts Are Not Enough," *IEEE Transactions on Engineering Management* (February 1989): 25–27.

7. Christina Chick, Valerie Reyna, and Jonathan Corbin, "Framing Effects Are Robust to Linguistic Disambiguation: A Critical Test of Contemporary Theory," *Journal of Experimental Psychology: Learning, Memory, Cognition* 42 (2016): 238–256.

8. Raymond Nickerson, "Confirmation Bias: A Ubiquitous Phenomenon in Many Guises," *Review of General Psychology* 2 (1998): 175.

while those who opposed nuclear energy took the literature to confirm that *they* were right.⁹ In another study, Deanna Kuhn asked people to state their position on some social issue. After they stated their position on the issue, Kuhn then asked them to give their reasons for holding that position. The subjects in the study offered many reasons for their position. Then Kuhn asked them to state some arguments *against* their position. Only 14 percent of them could consistently state arguments against their view.¹⁰ Other studies have confirmed this tendency—people are aware of reasons supporting their opinion, but they are unaware of the reasons for opposing positions.¹¹

If we were aware of our own biases, then we might be able to overcome them. Unfortunately, one of our biases is the *bias blind spot*—we are often unaware of our own cognitive biases. In fact, everyone thinks that they are less biased than other people.¹² This mistake results from the fact that we use two different methods to detect biases—one for ourselves and one for other people. To see if we are biased, we use *introspection*—we look within ourselves to see if there are any biases. Not finding any, we infer that we are not biased or not very biased. To determine if other people are biased, we observe their behavior, and we see that their behavior manifests bias. Thus, we infer that we are less biased than other people. Unfortunately, this is a mistake. Our own cognitive biases are not always transparent to us—they

---

9. Scott Plous, "Biases in the Assimilation of Technological Breakdowns: Do Accidents Make Us Safer?" *Journal of Applied Social Psychology* 21 (1991): 1058–1082.

10. Deanna Kuhn, *The Skills of Arguments* (Cambridge: Cambridge University Press, 1991), 142. Hugo Mercier and Dan Sperber identify this implication of Kuhn's study in *The Enigma of Reason: A New Theory of Human Understanding* (Cambridge, MA: Harvard University Press, 2017), 213–214.

11. See Charles Taber and Milton Lodge, "Motivated Skepticism in the Evaluation of Political Beliefs," *American Journal of Political Science* 50 (2006): 755–769; and Charles Taber, *The Rationalizing Voter* (Cambridge: Cambridge University Press, 2013).

12. See Emily Pronin, Daniel Y. Lin, and Lee Ross, "The Bias Blind Spot: Perceptions of Bias in Self versus Others," *Personality and Social Psychology Bulletin* 28 (2002): 369–381.

are often hidden below the surface of our conscious thought. That is why we do not see them when we introspect. Thus, we mistakenly infer that we are less biased than other people.[13]

Since we find ways to confirm our own opinions, and we are unaware of our own cognitive biases, it is probably no surprise that we are prone to the *overconfidence bias*. We overestimate our ability to get things right. In one experiment, subjects were asked to answer random questions, like "Does Corsica belong to France or Italy?" and then were asked to state their confidence in their answers. Their confidence in their answers far exceeded their accuracy.[14] The overconfidence bias is just one member of a family of self-serving biases. We tend to overrate ourselves in comparison with other people in a multitude of ways.[15] In one study, 83 percent of college students predicted that they themselves would purchase a flower to raise money for a charity. The same students predicted that only 56 percent of their peers would do so. However, only 46 percent of the students actually bought a flower.[16]

This is just a small sample of the cognitive biases discovered in recent decades. Taken together, these discoveries raise skeptical doubts about much of our everyday reasoning. In any situation where a person has an "anchor," where a question has been framed in either positive or negative terms, or where they already have a belief that they would like to confirm, it is likely that their reasoning will be

---

13. This explanation of the bias blind spot is developed and supported by Nathan Cheek and Emily Pronin in "I'm Right, You're Biased: How We Understand Ourselves and Others," in *Reason, Bias, and Inquiry: The Crossroads of Epistemology and Psychology*, ed. Nathan Ballantyne and David Dunning (New York: Oxford University Press, 2022).

14. A. Koriat, B. Lichtenstein, and B. Fischhoff, "Reasons for Confidence," *Journal of Experimental Psychology: Learning, Memory, Cognition* 6 (1980): 107–118.

15. Mark D. Alicke, M. L. Klotz, David L. Breitenbecher, Tricia Yurak, and Debbie S. Vredenburg, "Personal Contact, Individuation, and the Better-Than-Average Effect," *Journal of Personality and Social Psychology* 68 (1995): 804–825.

16. Nicholas Epley and David Dunning, "Feeling 'Holier than Thou': Are Self-Serving Assessments Produced by Errors in Self- or Social Perception?" *Journal of Personality and Social Psychology* 79 (2000): 861–875.

influenced by one of the relevant biases noted above. Moreover, this is true for each of the many other cognitive biases that have been discovered. Consequently, in any such situation, the person's reasoning will be driven toward a certain conclusion—based on their anchor, the framing of the question, or their prior belief, and they will be driven toward that conclusion *even if the conclusion is false*. That is why cognitive bias seems to prevent us from acquiring knowledge. To understand this, we need to return to a basic principle concerning knowledge.

Knowledge requires more than just true belief. A true belief that is true just by accident, as a matter of luck, is not knowledge. This point has been made by philosophers as far back as Plato in the *Theaetetus*, and it can be illustrated with an example from Bertrand Russell.[17] Suppose that I use an old analog watch to tell the time when I am at work. One morning, after I get to work, I look at my watch to tell the time, and the watch reads 8:00 a.m. On that basis, I form the belief that it is 8:00 a.m. Suppose that when I look at my watch, it is, in fact, 8:00 a.m. However, unbeknownst to me, my watch stopped working at precisely 8:00 a.m. the previous day, and I simply failed to notice. I have not looked at my watch since then, and it has read "8:00 a.m." for the last twenty-four hours. I was simply unaware of it. When I now look at my watch to tell the time, I happen to form a true belief since I just happen to look at the watch at 8:00 a.m. As they say, "Even a stopped clock is right twice a day." Since I happen to look at my watch at 8:00 a.m., my belief that it is 8:00 a.m. is true. However, I don't *know* that it's 8:00 a.m. Since I could easily have looked at the watch at a different time, I was just lucky to have looked at it when I did. Consequently, I was just lucky to have formed a true belief rather than a false belief. Knowledge is true belief that is not just true as a matter of luck. Since I was just lucky to have formed a true belief, I don't really know that it's 8:00 a.m.

---

17. Bertrand Russell, *Human Knowledge: It's Scope and Limits* (London: Allen and Unwin, 1948), 170.

This example illustrates a certain principle concerning knowledge, *The Safety Principle*.[18] The Safety Principle says that in order to have knowledge, *you must form your belief in a way that could not easily have led to a false belief*. In the case of the watch, I formed my belief about the time by looking at my watch, which had stopped working. Forming a belief about the time by looking at a watch that has stopped could very easily lead to a false belief. I could easily have looked at it at a time when it would have led to a false belief. Thus, even though I happen to form a true belief by looking at my watch, I don't get knowledge because I formed my belief in a way that could easily have led to a false belief. If the Safety Principle is correct, then the existence of cognitive bias threatens our pursuit of knowledge. That is because cognitive biases could just as easily lead us to false beliefs as to true beliefs. In sum, the Safety Principle seems to lead to *Bias Skepticism*—where there is bias, there is no knowledge. Is that correct?[19]

To explore this question carefully, we will examine the role of cognitive bias in the investigation of Kathy Thompson's murder. Specifically, we will focus on the influence of two biases—the anchoring

---

18. Versions of the Safety Principle have been developed and defended by Ernest Sosa, Timothy Williamson, and Duncan Pritchard. See, for example, Sosa, "How to Defeat Opposition to Moore," *Philosophical Perspectives* 13 (1999): 141–154; Williamson, *Knowledge and Its Limits* (Oxford: Oxford University Press, 2000); and Pritchard, *Epistemic Luck* (Oxford: Oxford University Press, 2005).

19. Versions of Bias Skepticism have been defended by Jennifer Saul, Mark Alfano, and Robert Pasnau. See the following: Saul, "Skepticism and Implicit Bias," *Disputatio* 5 (2013): 243–263; Alfano, "Expanding the Situationist Challenge to Reliabilism about Inference," in *Virtue Epistemology Naturalized*, ed. A. Fairweather (Dordrecht, Holland: Springer, 2014), 103–122; and Pasnau, "Bias and Interpersonal Skepticism," *Nous* 56 (2020): 154–175. In their recent discussion of bias, Thomas Kelly and Sarah McGrath reject Bias Skepticism because, as they see it, it is based on the Sensitivity Principle, which is now widely rejected. See Kelly and McGrath, "Bias: Some Conceptual Geography," in *Reason, Bias, and Inquiry: The Crossroads of Epistemology and Psychology*, ed. Nathan Ballantyne and David Dunning (Oxford: Oxford University Press, 2022), 11–34. Unfortunately, Kelly and McGrath do not consider the possibility that the Safety Principle can also be used to support Bias Skepticism. That is the question that we will consider here.

effect and confirmation bias. Several studies have found that both the anchoring effect and confirmation bias exert a strong influence on criminal investigations. A study in 2015 found that "the order in which evidence was presented influenced guilt beliefs. When police officers encountered exculpatory evidence prior to inculpatory evidence, guilt belief scores decreased, suggesting their final decisions were influenced by their initial impressions."[20] In other words, if officers were first presented with evidence of innocence, and then presented with evidence of guilt, they were less likely to believe that the accused person was guilty than if the very same evidence was presented in the opposite order. This is the anchoring effect—the first piece of information that the officers receive exerts an undue influence on their subsequent thinking. Likewise, studies have found that confirmation bias also exerts a strong influence on criminal investigations. A study in 2007 found that "when experienced criminal investigators read a vignette that implied a suspect's guilt (but left room for an alternative explanation), they rated subsequent guilt consistent evidence as more credible and reliable than evidence that was inconsistent with their theory of guilt."[21] A study in 2008 found that "police recruits discredited or supported the same exact evidence . . . depending on whether it was consistent or inconsistent with their hypothesis of a suspect's guilt."[22] Finally, in 2017, a study found that "police officers' initial beliefs about the innocence or guilt of a suspect in a fictional criminal case predicted their evaluation of subsequent ambiguous evidence, which in turn predicted their final beliefs about the suspect's innocence or guilt."[23] Additional studies have confirmed these results. Both the

---

20. See Vanessa Meterko and Glinda Cooper, "Cognitive Biases in Criminal Case Evaluation: A Review of the Research," *Journal of Police and Criminal Psychology* 37 (2022): 107. The other studies cited here are also summarized in the review by Meterko and Cooper.
21. Meterko and Cooper, "Cognitive Biases in Criminal Case Evaluation," 106.
22. Meterko and Cooper, "Cognitive Biases in Criminal Case Evaluation," 106.
23. S. D. Charman, M. Kavetski, and D. H. Mueller, "Cognitive Bias in the Legal System: Police Officers Evaluate Ambiguous Evidence in a Belief-Consistent Manner," *Journal of Applied Research in Memory and Cognition* 6 (2017): 193–202.

anchoring effect and confirmation bias exert a powerful influence on the beliefs of criminal investigators. Once they have decided the guilt or innocence of a suspect, they tend to interpret subsequent evidence as confirming their belief.

This is exactly what happened in the investigation of Kathy Thompson's murder. From the very beginning of the investigation, the police interpreted all the evidence in a way that confirmed their initial belief that Evan Zimmerman was the perpetrator. Kathy Thompson had a history of volatile relationships. In the time leading up to her death, she had been corresponding with several prison inmates, and she was known to have had relationships with some of them. Nevertheless, the police focused exclusively on Evan Zimmerman from the very beginning. In his diary, they found entries that showed that Zimmerman had struggled to get over his relationship with Thompson. The police took this as evidence that Zimmerman was obsessed with Thompson. However, those entries in Zimmerman's diary ended five months before Thompson's murder. Moreover, there was independent evidence that Zimmerman had gotten over Thompson well before her murder. When another man started dating Thompson in 1999, he reported that Zimmerman was not angry about it but simply asked him to treat Thompson well.

Even the physical evidence that the police discovered was merely circumstantial. Kathy Thompson was known to have borrowed Zimmerman's van on many occasions, so the hairbrush with her hair in it could easily have belonged to her. Finally, the officers' confirmation bias is especially clear in their reaction to evidence that appeared to contradict their initial belief. At the scene of the murder, investigators found cigarette butts, and the DNA recovered from them excluded Zimmerman definitively. They also found hair on Thompson's body, and the DNA recovered from that also excluded Zimmerman. The DNA came from a male, so this evidence suggested another perpetrator. Nevertheless, the police persisted in their belief that Zimmerman was guilty. At every step of the investigation, the police interpreted the evidence in ways that confirmed their initial belief that Zimmerman was guilty.

Suppose, for the sake of argument, that the officers' initial belief was true—that Evan Zimmerman killed Kathy Thompson. Even if that were true, these officers did not know it was true. Given the role of confirmation bias in forming their belief, they could easily have been led to a false belief about this. Even if Zimmerman had *not* committed the crime, the officers' confirmation bias could easily have led them to believe that he did. Thus, even if the officers' belief was true, they were just *lucky* that their belief was true. They didn't know.

This example illustrates a general problem. These police officers are not the only people who suffer from confirmation bias. Research has found that *we all* suffer from confirmation bias, even if we do so to different degrees on different occasions. If these officers' confirmation bias undermines their pursuit of knowledge in this case, then the same bias would seem to undermine everyone's pursuit of knowledge. Thus, the problem of cognitive bias isn't just a problem for criminal investigators. It is a problem for all of us. Moreover, as I have noted, confirmation bias is just one of many cognitive biases that afflict us. The list is quite long. What does this imply? The Bias Skeptic infers that cognitive bias undermines many of our claims to knowledge on a very wide scale. Is that correct? There are at least three possible replies to Bias Skepticism, which I will call *Responsibilism*, *Evidentialism*, and *Social Interactionism*. Each of these theories implies that, under certain conditions, the presence of cognitive bias does not prevent us from achieving knowledge. In the remainder of this chapter, we will consider each reply, starting with Responsibilism.

Responsibilism is a theory of knowledge that emphasizes the importance of forming our beliefs in a responsible way. When we form a belief about something, we can either be attentive or inattentive, honest or dishonest, open-minded or closed-minded. If we form a belief by being attentive, honest, and open-minded, then we will have done our best to form a true belief. According to Responsibilism, if a person does their best to form a true belief, then they have done everything in their power to achieve knowledge. Moreover, if their belief turns out to be true, it will not be a complete accident that their belief is true. After all, beliefs formed in a responsible way are more likely to be true than beliefs formed in an irresponsible way. In summary, then, the Responsibilist says that if a person forms a true belief in a responsible way—by being attentive, honest, and open-minded, then, practically speaking, they have knowledge. There might be unusual circumstances in which they would still fail to achieve knowledge, but that is beyond their control, and thus it is practically irrelevant.[24]

How is Responsibilism relevant to Bias Skepticism? Responsibilism becomes relevant when it is combined with a particular theory of human rationality—*The Theory of Bounded Rationality*. In the mid-1950s, the Nobel Prize–winning economist Herbert Simon pioneered a new approach to human rationality. Simon argued that the prevailing approaches to human reason were unrealistic in their expectations. The human mind is limited in its ability to process information. In a complex world riddled with uncertainty, human beings have evolved to use simple strategies to process complex information. Such simple strategies are now called *heuristics*. Heuristics are fast, efficient ways of processing information. They require less time, energy, and cognitive capacity. Moreover, in most of the environments in which we use them, heuristics are reliable enough for the practical purposes of everyday life. They are not perfectly reliable in all environments, but they are good enough for most purposes.

In recent decades, this idea of Bounded Rationality has been developed and defended by Gerd Gigerenzer and his colleagues at the Centre for Adaptive Behavior and Cognition. The basic idea of

---

24. Responsibilism is often stated as a theory of *epistemic justification* rather than a theory of knowledge. However, the concept of epistemic justification is a technical term of art in epistemology, and I fear that introducing it will cause more confusion than clarification. Thus, I have decided to state this theory in terms of knowledge. With that said, I am careful in the text to state the theory accurately—the Responsibilist does not claim that responsible true belief is sufficient for knowledge, but only that it is the best a person can do to pursue knowledge responsibly. Versions of Responsibilism have been developed and defended by Lorraine Code and James Montmarquet. See Code, *Epistemic Responsibility* (Hanover, NH: University Press of New England, 1987); and Montmarquet, *Epistemic Virtue and Doxastic Responsibility* (Lanham, MD: Rowman & Littlefield, 1993).

Bounded Rationality is that, in a complex world with limited time and resources, it is rational for human beings to use heuristics since they are fast and efficient, and reliable enough for most purposes. The gain in speed and efficiency provided by heuristics compensates for the loss of perfect reliability across all contexts. This explains why human beings have evolved to use heuristics. Moreover, several studies support the claim that this is how people actually reason. Whether they are doctors prescribing blood pressure medicine, judges making bail decisions, or psychiatrists prescribing antidepressants, people use fast and efficient heuristics to make their decisions.[25]

The theory of Bounded Rationality casts our cognitive biases in a more positive light. What we have been calling cognitive biases are by-products of our use of heuristics. In order to process large quantities of complex information, we use heuristics that simplify the process. This saves us time and energy and is usually good enough for practical purposes. However, it increases the risk of error. Defenders of Bounded Rationality say that the increase in efficiency is worth the risk of error. When we see our cognitive biases as side effects of our use of heuristics, we are forced to see them as part of a larger package that is well adapted to our needs. Consequently, one might say that when we use heuristics, with their attendant biases, we are *doing the best we can*, under the circumstances, to form true beliefs. Now recall that, according to Responsibilism, if we do the best we can to form true beliefs, then we have done everything in our power to achieve knowledge, and that is all that can be asked of us. Thus, if we combine Responsibilism with the theory of Bounded Rationality, it follows that using heuristics, with their attendant biases, is actually doing the best we can to achieve knowledge, and that is all that can be asked of us. Is this a good reply to Bias Skepticism?

To explore this question, let us return to the role of confirmation bias in criminal investigations. In an article published in 2008, Brent Snook and Richard Cullen appeal to the theory of Bounded

---

25. See Gerd Gigerenzer and Reinhard Selten, *Bounded Rationality: The Adaptive Toolbox* (Cambridge, MA: MIT Press, 2001).

Rationality to defend the role of confirmation bias in criminal investigations. According to Snook and Cullen,

> it is unrealistic to expect police officers to investigate *all* possible suspects, collect evidence on *all* of those suspects, explore *all* possible avenues concerning the circumstances surrounding a crime, search for disconfirming and confirming evidence of guilt for every suspect, and integrate all of this information to make an "optimal" decision.[26]

Throughout their article, Snook and Cullen identify the many limitations that police officers face in the course of an investigation—limitations of time, money, personnel, and cognitive ability. They also point out that confirmation bias might lead to correct convictions that would not otherwise occur. By doggedly pursuing evidence that confirms their suspicion, investigators might find the evidence that leads to a legitimate conviction. However, as Snook and Cullen wryly note,

> officers who build a *successful case* by searching for evidence that supports their belief while ignoring evidence that contradicts their belief would likely be applauded for being persistent, focused, determined, and dedicated. Those who use the same strategy in *a case that ends in a wrongful conviction*, on the other hand, might be accused of using confirmation bias . . . as though they neglected to properly fulfill their duties.[27]

Finally, Snook and Cullen point out that confirmation bias is seldom a conscious choice. Rather, confirmation bias is usually an unconscious tendency of which the subject is unaware. Thus, it is doubtful that criminal investigators could simply "turn off" their confirmation

---

26. Brent Snook and Richard M. Cullen, "Bounded Rationality and Criminal Investigations: Has Tunnel Vision Been Wrongfully Convicted?" in *Criminal Investigative Failures*, ed. D. Kim Rossmo (New York: Routledge, 2008), 2.
27. Snook and Cullen, "Bounded Rationality and Criminal Investigations," 31.

bias by a simple act of will, even if they wanted to. If that is correct, then perhaps it is unreasonable to demand that criminal investigators stop succumbing to their confirmation bias since that is not in their control. Moreover, it might be unfair to *blame* criminal investigators for following their confirmation bias since they cannot help doing so.

Does Responsibilism, together with the theory of Bounded Rationality, rescue knowledge from cognitive bias? Have Snook and Cullen vindicated the role of confirmation bias in good criminal investigations? The following claims seem to be true. Our cognitive biases are by-products of heuristics—rules of thumb that can be applied easily. These heuristics are fast, efficient ways of processing large amounts of complex information. Moreover, in many contexts, these heuristics are reliable enough for everyday purposes. Finally, our use of these heuristics and their attendant biases is typically an unconscious process that is not in our direct control. Consequently, we are not always blameworthy for succumbing to these biases since we cannot always help it. Thus, a person who is under the influence of cognitive bias might still be *doing the best they can* to form a true belief. If so, then a person who is influenced by cognitive bias might have done everything in their power to form a true belief. In that case, Responsibilism implies that they have done everything a person can do to achieve knowledge, and that is all we can ask of them. To demand anything more is unreasonable.

According to the critics of Responsibilism, forming a belief responsibly is nowhere near sufficient for knowledge. Moreover, sometimes we really need knowledge, not just responsibly formed beliefs. I will begin with the first point—that a responsible belief is not sufficient for knowledge. Under the influence of cognitive bias, people form beliefs that are not adequately supported by the evidence. In the case of Evan Zimmerman, the evidence that he was guilty was entirely circumstantial. However, the influence of confirmation bias led the investigators to interpret the evidence as proof of Zimmerman's guilt. That is no surprise since confirmation bias often leads people to overestimate the strength of the evidence for their belief. However, if a person's belief is based on insufficient evidence, then they do not *know* that their belief is true. Insufficient evidence does not give you knowledge. Now here is the problem for Responsibilism. People who are under the influence of cognitive bias are usually unaware of their bias. Thus, they are doing *the best they can* to form true beliefs. Nevertheless, their bias leads them to form beliefs that are not adequately supported by the evidence. When a person holds a belief on the basis of insufficient evidence, they do not have knowledge. Responsible belief is simply insufficient for knowledge.

Of course, the Responsibilist did not say that responsible belief was sufficient for knowledge in all circumstances. The Responsibilist only claims that responsible belief is the best that we can do to achieve knowledge. However, according to the critic, sometimes we need more than merely responsible belief. We need knowledge, and we should not settle for anything less. Arguably, the context of a criminal investigation is one such context. To be indicted for murder changes a person's life in profound ways. Even if they are not convicted, they might live the rest of their lives under a cloud of suspicion. Moreover, simply being indicted greatly increases the probability that a person will be convicted and spend many years in prison. If the person in question is actually innocent, then this is a grave injustice. Thus, pursuing an indictment of a person for a serious crime like murder is acting in a way that risks causing a grave injustice. In that context, it might be reasonable to demand that a criminal investigator *knows* that a person is guilty before they proceed with an indictment. Otherwise, the investigator risks causing a very grave injustice to be done to an innocent person. That might be what happened to Evan Zimmerman. Thus, one might argue that the standard for indicting a person for murder must be higher than merely responsible belief. Those who indict a person for murder should *know* that the accused person is guilty. I will leave it to the reader to consider whether that is true.

The second reply to Bias Skepticism is Evidentialism. According to Evidentialism, a true belief constitutes knowledge only if it is sufficiently well-supported by the evidence. Moreover, if a true belief is sufficiently well-supported by the evidence, then it will usually constitute knowledge. Only in very unusual circumstances will a true belief that is supported by the evidence fail to constitute knowledge. Thus, according to the Evidentialist, when we ask if a person knows, we should focus on whether the person's belief is sufficiently well-supported by the evidence that she possesses. Most importantly, according to Evidentialism, it does not matter how or why a person acquired the evidence that they possess. If the evidence that they possess supports their belief sufficiently, and their belief is true, then in ordinary circumstances, this person will *know* that their belief is true.[28]

According to the Evidentialist, the reason that the investigators did not know Evan Zimmerman was guilty was that their belief was not adequately supported by the evidence. However, suppose they *had* found evidence that clearly indicated that Zimmerman was guilty. Then, according to the Evidentialist, the investigators would know that he was guilty. Even if the investigators' bias prevents them from looking for any evidence that Zimmerman is innocent, the Evidentialist says that their evidence of guilt can be sufficient to give them knowledge. The fact that cognitive bias prevented them from finding any evidence to the contrary is simply irrelevant. Thus, according to the Evidentialist, the presence of cognitive bias does not always prevent us from achieving knowledge. If cognitive bias leads us to find evidence that supports our belief, and if our belief is true, then we can know that it is true.[29]

To understand this position, consider the following analogy. Suppose I am a paranoid person who believes that everyone is conspiring against me. This is an extreme case of cognitive bias. As a result of my bias, I constantly look for evidence that people are conspiring against

---

28. Like Responsibilism, Evidentialism is often stated as a theory of *epistemic justification* rather than a theory of knowledge. However, epistemic justification is a technical term of art in epistemology, and I fear introducing it will cause more confusion than clarification. Thus, I have decided to state this theory in terms of knowledge. With that said, I am careful in the text to state the theory accurately—the Evidentialist does not claim that true belief supported by evidence is always sufficient for knowledge, but only that it is sufficient for knowledge in ordinary circumstances. Evidentialism has been developed and defended by Earl Conee and Richard Feldman in *Evidentialism: Essays in Epistemology* (New York: Oxford University Press, 2004).

29. This position is developed and defended by Thomas Kelly in "Disagreement, Dogmatism, and Belief Polarization," *Journal of Philosophy* 105 (2008): 611–633.

me. It even leads me to spy on people to discover how they are conspiring against me. On one particular occasion, I am spying on my neighbor, and I hear him tell his partner how he plans to harm me in some way. Suppose that my neighbor is being sincere—he really does plan to harm me in this way. In this situation, it seems clear that I *know* that my neighbor is conspiring against me. I know it because I have good evidence for it, and it is true. Of course, I acquired this evidence as a result of my cognitive bias—my paranoia. Thus, it would be accurate to say that my cognitive bias caused me to form this belief. However, that does not change the fact that I *know* that my neighbor is conspiring against me. My cognitive bias led me to *good evidence* for my belief, which is sufficient for me to *know* that my belief is true. This example shows that the influence of cognitive bias does not necessarily prevent us from achieving knowledge. If our cognitive bias leads us to find evidence that supports our belief adequately, then we can still know that our belief is true.

Critics of Evidentialism will say that this story ignores the most pernicious effect of a cognitive bias, such as confirmation bias. Under the influence of confirmation bias, a person might find evidence that supports their belief, *but they will not find evidence against their belief, even if such evidence exists.* Suppose the investigators had found very strong evidence that Evan Zimmerman was guilty. Then the Evidentialist says they can know that Zimmerman is guilty. However, suppose there was, in fact, *even stronger evidence* that Zimmerman was innocent, but the investigators did not find that evidence because they did not look for it. And they did not look for it because they were under the influence of their cognitive bias. Then, it seems that forming a belief in this way could easily have led them to a false belief. If their bias leads them to find only evidence that supports their belief when even stronger evidence exists that contradicts their belief, then they could easily be led to a false belief. Thus, even if they happen to be led to the truth in this way, it seems that they were just lucky. They don't really *know* that their belief is true. Thus, the critic of Evidentialism says that cognitive bias deprives us of knowledge, even if it leads to evidence that supports our belief. I will leave it to the reader to consider the merits of this objection.

The third reply to Bias Skepticism is Social Interactionism. Although cognitive biases are useful as shortcuts, some psychologists are still puzzled by the extent to which human reason is infected with them. If human reason is so saturated with cognitive biases, then why did it evolve in the first place? What is it good for? That question is explored in depth by Dan Sperber and Hugo Mercier in their influential book, *The Enigma of Reason*.[30] As the title indicates, Sperber and Mercier propose an answer to that question. After surveying what psychology tells us about our cognitive biases, Sperber and Mercier propose a novel theory of the function of human reason. As they see it,

> whereas reason is commonly viewed as a superior means to think better on one's own, we argue that it is mainly used in our interactions with others. We produce reasons in order to justify our thoughts and actions to others and to produce arguments to convince others to think and act as we suggest. We also use reason to evaluate not so much our own thoughts as the reasons others produce to justify themselves or to convince us.[31]

According to Sperber and Mercier, the function of human reason is essentially *social*. Moreover, it is not aimed directly at discovering the truth. Rather, the purpose of human reason is to justify ourselves to others and persuade them to think and act as we want. The principal advantage of this theory is that it explains exactly why we have cognitive biases like the confirmation bias. If the function of reason is to persuade other people to believe what I want them to believe, then reason will serve me best if it helps me to find evidence that supports my own beliefs. Finding evidence for my own beliefs will help me to persuade other people that I am right. Thus, once we understand the true function of human reason, we can see that confirmation bias is not really a failure of reason at all. On the contrary, it aids human reason in achieving its true purpose, which is to persuade others to accept what we want them to accept.

---

30. Sperber and Mercier, *The Enigma of Reason*.
31. Sperber and Mercier, *The Enigma of Reason*, 7.

At this point, one might wonder how this will help us avoid Bias Skepticism. If anything, it seems like grist for the Bias Skeptic's mill. If the very function of human reason is not to find the truth but only to persuade others, then that is just one more reason to doubt that our biases can lead to genuine knowledge. However, that is not the end of the story. If Sperber and Mercier are right, then human reason was built to function in a social context. It was built for social interaction in a community of other people. Thus, when we consider the effects of cognitive bias on our pursuit of knowledge, we should take into account the social context in which our biases occur. When we take this into account, Sperber and Mercier maintain that

> in the right interactive context, *reason works*. It allows people to change each other's minds so they end up endorsing better beliefs and making better decisions.[32]

According to Sperber and Mercier, the social context in which our biases occur ameliorates their negative effect on us. If that is correct, then cognitive bias might not prevent us from achieving knowledge.

A large body of research has found that groups of people working together consistently outperform individuals on a wide variety of intellectual tasks.[33] In some tasks, groups even outperform the very

---

32. Sperber and Mercier, *The Enigma of Reason*, 264.
33. See the following: R. S. Baron, N. L. Kerr, and N. Miller, *Group Process, Group Decision, Group Action* (Buckingham, UK: Open University Press, 1992); J. H. Davis, "Some Compelling Intuitions about Group Consensus Decisions, Theoretical and Empirical Research, and Interpersonal Aggregation Phenomena: Selected Examples, 1950–1990," *Organizational Behavior and Human Decision Processes* 52 (1992): 3–38; D. R. Forsyth, *Group Dynamics*, 3rd ed. (New York: Brooks/Cole, 1999); V. B. Hinsz, R. S. Tindale, and D. A. Vollrath, "The Emerging Conceptualization of Groups as Information Processors," *Psychological Bulletin* 121 (1997): 43–64; J. Levine and R. L. Moreland, "Small Groups," in *The Handbook of Social Psychology*, vol. 2, ed. D. T. Gilbert, S. T. Fiske, and G. Lindzey (New York: McGraw-Hill, 1998), 415–467; and G. Stasser and B. Dietz-Uhler, "Collective Choice, Judgment and Problem Solving," in *Blackwell Handbook of Social Psychology*, vol. 3, *Group Processes*, ed. M. A. Hogg and R. S. Tindale (Oxford: Blackwell, 2001), 31–55.

best individuals acting alone. In the following passage, Sperber and Mercier describe one of the experiments in which this was discovered.

> For more than twenty years, Dave Moshman, psychologist and educational researcher, had asked his students to solve the Wason four-card selection task . . . individually and then in small groups. While individual performance was its usual low—around 15 percent correct—something extraordinary was happening in the course of group discussions. More than half of the groups were getting it right. When Moshman teamed with Molly Geil to conduct a controlled version of this informal experiment, groups reached 80 percent of correct answers. It may be difficult for someone who hasn't read article after article showing pitiful performance on the Wason four-card selection task to realize just how staggering this result is. No sample of participants had ever reached anywhere close to 80 percent correct answers on the standard version of the task. Students at the best American universities barely reach 20 or 25 percent of correct answers when solving the task on their own.[34]

In this case, groups of students working together performed far better than even the very best individuals working alone.

Why do groups of people working together outperform individuals? Hugo Mercier and his colleagues devised an experiment to test competing answers to that question. They found that *argumentation* played a key role in leading the group to the right answer. That is because

> a single participant with the correct answer can convince a group that unanimously embraces the wrong answer, even if she is initially less confident than the other group members.[35]

---

34. Sperber and Mercier, *The Enigma of Reason*, 264.
35. E. Trouche, E. Sander, and H. Mercier, "Arguments, More than Confidence, Explain the Good Performance of Reasoning Groups," *Journal of Experimental Psychology* 5 (2014): 1958–1971, quoted in Sperber and Mercier, *The Enigma of Reason*, 265.

Notice what has happened here. Since confirmation bias is very widespread, it is reasonable to assume that the members of this group who embrace the wrong answer are under the influence of confirmation bias. As a result, they will tend to interpret the evidence in a way that confirms their initial belief. Nevertheless, a single member of the group with the right answer is able to overcome their confirmation bias and convince them that they are wrong. Thus, it appears that when people reason together in a group, the effects of their cognitive biases can be overcome by the reasoning of other members of the group. When that happens, people can arrive at the correct answer to a question despite the influence of their cognitive biases.

Collective reasoning can correct our cognitive biases. Even when the individual members of a group are biased, the interactions between them can constitute a process of collective reasoning that is *unbiased*. Stated abstractly, we could say that although the parts of this system are biased, the whole system is unbiased. In a recent article on the nature of bias, Thomas Kelly and Sarah McGrath develop this point.

> A whole might be unbiased even if its constituent parts are biased to a high degree. Perhaps the most obvious possibility here is when the biases of the parts offset or counteract one another in such a way as to produce a lack of bias at the level of the whole. This could even be due to intentional design—for example, someone could deliberately design an organization or institution to be unbiased in spite of, or even because of, the biases of its constituent parts or members. As a rough comparison, think of the idea behind adversarial systems of justice. In the American legal system, there is no ideal according to which the defense attorney is supposed to be scrupulously neutral between their client and the prosecution; nor is there any ideal to the effect that the prosecution is supposed to be scrupulously neutral. . . . a procedure which deliberately incorporates biased parts, even heavily biased parts, might score better when we evaluate the whole.[36]

---

36. Kelly and McGrath, "Bias: Some Conceptual Geography," 20.

This suggests a general solution to the problem of cognitive bias. If we situate ourselves in diverse groups of people and participate in collective reasoning with them, then our biases can be overcome in the process. The interaction between the members of the group generates a process that is reliable despite the biases of the individual members of the group. In this kind of situation, the members of the group can achieve knowledge.

Can we achieve something like this in the context of a criminal investigation? Some people believe that we can. In 2004, it was revealed that a miscarriage of justice had occurred in the Netherlands. Four years earlier, a child was killed in a park in the Dutch town of Schiedam. The police quickly focused on a man named Kees Borsboom, who was present nearby. Borsboom was convicted and sentenced to eighteen years in prison. Then, in 2004, the real killer confessed, and DNA evidence confirmed his confession.[37] Consequently, in 2006, the Dutch government instituted a new critical review procedure for criminal investigations. This process includes embedding a "contrarian" in the investigation—a person who questions and challenges the investigators. The role of the contrarian is precisely to counteract the biases of the investigators, including their confirmation bias. The implementation of this idea is difficult, and it is still a work in progress. However, it holds some promise of a solution to the problem of cognitive bias in criminal investigations.[38]

In summary, then, the most promising solution to the threat of Bias Skepticism is to mitigate the effects of our cognitive biases through social interaction with people who challenge us. If human reason evolved to be used in a social context, with other people who have their own, separate interests and cognitive biases, then human reason will function best when used in that way. Moreover, we can incorporate this insight into our design of social institutions, like law

---

37. The facts of this case are detailed in Peter J. van Koppen, "Blundering Justice: The Schiedam Park Murder," in *Serial Murder and the Psychology of Violent Crimes*, ed. R. N. Kocsis (Totowa, NJ: Humanities Press, 2008), 207–228.
38. See R. Salet and J. Terpstra, "Critical Review in Criminal Investigation: Evaluation of a Measure to Prevent Tunnel Vision," *Policing* 8 (2014): 43–50.

enforcement, in order to reduce the harmful effects of cognitive bias. In academic research, this idea has been implemented recently in what is called *adversarial collaboration*. In adversarial collaboration, ideologically opposed academics are paired together in the same research project. These solutions are all a work in progress, but they seem to give us our best prospects for overcoming our cognitive biases.[39]

---

39. Jack Grove, "Adversarial Collaboration Makes Feuding Scholars Work Together," *Inside Higher Ed*, September 27, 2023, https://www.insidehighered.com/news/global/us-colleges-world/2023/09/28/adversarial-collaboration-makes-feuding-scholars-work.

Study Questions

1. In the investigation of Kathy Thompson's murder, how did confirmation bias influence the investigators? Which aspects of their investigation indicate that they were influenced by confirmation bias? Be specific.
2. How does the example of the stopped watch illustrate the Safety Principle? Explain it in your own words. Construct your own example to illustrate the Safety Principle and explain exactly how it illustrates the principle.
3. If the Safety Principle is true, then cognitive bias seems to threaten our claims to knowledge in many cases. Explain, in detail, why this is true. Feel free to use one of the examples from the previous question to illustrate it.
4. Suppose someone in our neighborhood has been letting their dog defecate on everyone's lawn. The culprit has not been identified, but I suspect it is my neighbor Ted. To confirm my suspicion, I begin to look for evidence that Ted did it, and I find some evidence that he did. If it happens to be true that Ted did it, then do I *know* that Ted did it? What would a Responsibilist say about this case? What would an Evidentialist say about this case?
5. In the example described in the previous question, what could I do to counteract the influence of confirmation bias on my beliefs? What sort of activity might offset my bias?

For Further Reading

For a general introduction to the nature of bias, see Thomas Kelly's book *Bias: A Philosophical Study* (New York: Oxford University Press, 2022). For an excellent overview of the epistemological problem of bias, see Nathan Ballantyne's essay "Debunking Biased Thinkers (Including Ourselves)," *Journal of the American Philosophical Association* 1 (2015): 141–162. For a trenchant critique of Bias Skepticism, see Louise Antony's essay, "Bias: Friend or Foe? Reflections on Saulish Skepticism," in *Implicit Bias and Philosophy*, vol. 1: *Metaphysics and*

Epistemology, ed. Michael Brownstein and Jennifer Saul (New York: Oxford University Press, 2016). J. Adam Carter and Robin McKenna defend a moderate form of Bias Skepticism in "Skepticism Motivated: On the Skeptical Import of Motivated Reasoning," *Canadian Journal of Philosophy* 50 (2020): 702–718. Finally, for a fascinating discussion of how much evidence is required to justify a criminal conviction, see Martin Smith's excellent essay "When Does Evidence Suffice for Conviction?" *Mind* 127 (2018): 1193–1218.

CHAPTER FIVE

The Threat of Polarization

In 1960, Republicans and Democrats were asked how they would feel if their son or daughter married someone outside their political party. Only 5 percent of Republicans and 4 percent of Democrats said that they would be "displeased" if that happened. From 1960 to 2008, those numbers rose to 27 percent of Republicans and 20 percent of Democrats.[1] Then, in the next two years, they rose again to 49 percent of Republicans and 33 percent of Democrats.[2] By 2016, 63 percent of Republicans and 60 percent of Democrats said that they would be displeased if their son or daughter married someone outside their political party.[3] This is just one instance of the rise of political polarization in recent years.

The members of each political party now see each other in increasingly negative terms. In 2016, more than 55 percent of Democrats and Republicans described their feelings toward the opposing party as "very unfavorable."[4] By 2019,

---

1. Shanto Iyengar, Gaurav Sood, and Yphtach Lelkes, "Affect, Not Ideology: A Social Identity Perspective on Polarization," *Public Opinion Quarterly* 76 (2012): 405–431.
2. Ezra Klein and Alvin Chang, "'Political Identity Is Fair Game for Hatred': How Republicans and Democrats Discriminate," *Vox*, December 7, 2015, https://www.vox.com/2015/12/7/9790764/partisan-discrimination.
3. Yascha Mounk, "The Doom Spiral of Pernicious Polarization," *The Atlantic*, May 21, 2022, https://www.theatlantic.com/ideas/archive/2022/05/us-democrat-republican-partisan-polarization/629925/.
4. "Partisanship and Political Animosity in 2016," Pew Research Center, June 22, 2016.

wide majorities in both parties—three-quarters of Democrats (75%) and 64% of Republicans—say those in the other party are more closed-minded than other Americans. And 55% of Republicans and 47% of Democrats view members of the other party as more immoral than other Americans. In both parties, the share saying those in the other political camp are closed-minded or immoral has increased since these questions were last asked in 2016.[5]

Scholars have a term for the growing animosity between members of opposing political parties—they call it *affective polarization*. Affective polarization has risen to an alarming level.

What caused the sudden rise of affective polarization? One possible answer is that the rise of affective polarization is due to a corresponding rise in *ideological polarization*. Over the last few decades, the ideologies of the two major parties have grown further and further apart.[6] There is now very little overlap between them, and there are very few "centrist" representatives left in Congress. Moreover, the rise of ideological polarization has been accompanied by yet another type of polarization—*factual belief polarization*. Factual belief polarization occurs when there is a factual answer to a question, but people's beliefs are better correlated with their political affiliation than with the facts.[7] When factual belief polarization occurs, it is as if people are living in two different worlds. As of August 2022, 53 percent of

---

5. "How Partisans View Each Other," Pew Research Center, October 10, 2019.
6. For the historical details of how this happened, see each of the following: Nolan McCarty, "What We Know and Don't Know about Our Polarized Politics," *Washington Post*, December 7, 2021; Nolan McCarty, Keith T. Poole, and Howard Rosenthal, "Does Gerrymandering Cause Polarization?" *American Journal of Political Science* 53 (2009): 666–680; and Michael Barber and Nolan McCarty, "Causes and Consequences of Polarization," in *Political Negotiation: A Handbook*, ed. Jane Mansbridge and Cathie J. Martin (Washington DC: Brookings Institution Press, 2015), 37–90.
7. R. Rekker, "Political Polarization over Factual Beliefs," in *Knowledge Resistance in High-Choice Information Environments*, ed. J. Strömbäck, A. Wikforss, K. Glüer, T. Lindholm, and H. Oscarsson (Thames, UK: Routledge, 2022).

Americans believe that there is an "invasion" at the southern border, while 46 percent deny that claim or say they don't know. At the same time, almost half of Americans say that "Democrats are working to open our borders to more immigrants," while the other half doubts or denies this.[8] As of September 2023, 49 percent of Americans say that gun ownership does more to increase safety than to reduce safety, while 49 percent say exactly the opposite.[9] These are just a few examples of factual belief polarization in the United States in recent years. Americans from opposing political parties hold opposing beliefs on basic matters of fact.

Political polarization is not restricted to the United States. In recent years, it has occurred in multiple countries throughout the world. The first study to focus specifically on factual belief polarization was conducted in the Netherlands in 2021.[10] Using data from the Dutch Parliamentary Election Study (DPES) of 2021, Roderick Rekker and Eelco Harteveld investigated the extent of factual belief polarization among Dutch voters. In the DPES, Dutch voters were asked the following questions about inequality, immigration, and climate change:

---

8. "A Majority of Americans See an 'Invasion' at the Southern Border, NPR Poll Finds," *NPR Morning Edition*, August 18, 2022. As one reviewer pointed out, the use of the term "invasion" implies more than just a factual claim—it is also an *evaluation* of the facts, implying that they are *bad*. I agree. However, the claim that there is an invasion at the border is at least *partly* factual. For example, it implies that what is happening at the border is *unprecedented*, or at least *unusual*, and that is a factual claim. Nevertheless, the reviewer is right. The disagreement over this claim is partly factual and partly evaluative. In fact, many disagreements that seem to be factual disagreements are, on reflection, at least partly evaluative disagreements. I will leave it to the reader to think of examples of this. Thanks to Jeff Dean for helpful comments on this.
9. Katherine Schaeffer, "Key Facts about Americans and Guns," Pew Research Center, September 13, 2023.
10. Roderick Rekker and Eelco Harteveld, "Understanding Factual Belief Polarization: The Role of Trust, Political Sophistication, and Affective Polarization," *Acta Politica* (October 20, 2022): 1–28.

1. "How many times more do you think the 10% households with the highest incomes earn compared to the 10% households with the lowest incomes? This is about the amount of money that a family can spend after taxes (disposable household income)." The response scale ranged from 1× to 15×. Based on data from the 'Organization for Economic Co-operation and Development' (OECD, the true value of this indicator is '7×').

2. "What do you think is currently the share of immigrants in the Netherlands? By immigrants, we mean people who were born in another country (first-generation immigrants) as well as their children (second-generation immigrants)." The response scale ranged from 0 to 100%. Based on census data, Statistics Netherlands reports that the true share of first- and second-generation immigrants is 25% of the Dutch population.

3. "How convinced are you that climate change is mainly caused by human activity? Please place yourself on a scale from 0 to 100% where 0% means that you think it is extremely unlikely that climate change is caused mainly by human activity, 100% means that you are sure that climate change is caused mainly by human activity, and 50% means that you are unsure whether or not climate change is caused mainly by human activity." The response scale ranged from 0 to 100%. Based on reports from the Intergovernmental Panel on Climate Change, any answer between about 95% and 100% confidence can be considered in line with the scientific consensus.[11]

The answers to these questions revealed that Dutch voters often have factually incorrect beliefs. Moreover, on close inspection, it turns out that voters' misperceptions are driven by their political partisanship. Voters who supported the redistribution of wealth overestimated

---

11. Rekker and Harteveld, "Understanding Factual Belief Polarization." For the Dutch Parliamentary Election Study, see K. Jacobs, M. Lubbers, T. Sipma, N. Spierings, and T. W. G. Van der Meer, *Dutch Parliamentary Election Study 2021 (DPES/NKO 2021)* (Nijmegen, Netherlands: SKON, 2021).

the amount of economic inequality in the Netherlands, whereas voters who opposed redistribution gave lower estimates, which were closer to the truth.[12] Voters who favored restricting immigration overestimated the percentage of people in the Netherlands who are immigrants, while those who support immigration gave estimates that sometimes underestimated that number. Finally, voters who favor policies to combat climate change were much more confident that climate change is caused by human activity than those less committed to combatting it.[13] On each of these issues, at least one group of voters held false beliefs that correlated with their political affiliation and preferences. Moreover, these misperceptions were not restricted to voters on the right. Voters on the left held misperceptions, too, and those misperceptions were correlated with their political party.

What does any of this have to do with epistemology? Factual belief polarization poses an epistemological problem. In one way, this problem is akin to the problem of disagreement, which we explored in Chapter 3. If I hold a belief on one side of a polarized issue, then how do I know that my belief is correct rather than my opponents' belief? Why should I think that I am more likely to be right than the people on the other side of the divide? However, this is just the beginning of the problem. As we will see, the epistemological problem of polarization is also akin to the problem of cognitive bias, which we explored in the last chapter. On close inspection, the way in which polarized beliefs are formed appears to be a form of cognitive bias or a combination of several biases. Thus, the epistemological problem of polarization combines elements of both the problem of disagreement and the problem of cognitive bias. To understand this, we need to examine how polarized beliefs are actually formed. In what follows, I will summarize some recent research in political psychology concerning

---

12. Somewhat surprisingly, *all* Dutch voters overestimated the degree of economic inequality in the Netherlands. Voters on the left overestimated it by much more than voters on the right, but both groups overestimated it. Rekker and Harteveld point out that this is easy to do since the Netherlands is an unusually egalitarian society.

13. Rekker and Harteveld, "Understanding Factual Belief Polarization."

the etiology of *polarized political beliefs*.[14] Once we understand how polarized political beliefs are formed, we will be in a better position to determine if they are rationally justified or if they ever constitute knowledge.

To understand the process that leads to polarized beliefs, we must begin with the concept of *social identity*. As Bert Klandermans explains, "Social identity . . . is a characteristic of a person. It is that part of a person's self-image that is derived from the groups of which he or she is a member. . . . [Social identity is] an awareness of similarity, in-group identity, and shared fate with others who belong to the same category."[15] As Leonie Huddy puts it, "A social identity involves a subjective sense of belonging to a group that is internalized to varying degrees, . . . a desire to positively distinguish the group from others, and the development of in-group bias.[16] A person's social identity can be based on their race, gender, religion, class, or ideology, among other things. Once a person consciously identifies with a particular group in this way, then they become motivated to protect and advance the interests of that group. Moreover, "This motivation to protect and advance group status . . . is the psychological foundation for the development of in-group bias."[17] According to Lilliana Mason and Julie Wronski,

> because group identification is driven by an innate desire to positively distinguish one's ingroup, the most prominent effect generated by this process is ingroup bias, in which strongly identified group members reliably privilege and judge the members

---

14. The etiology of a belief is the *causal history* of that belief—the series of causes that led to it.

15. Bert Klandermans, "Identity Politics and Politicized Identities: Identity Processes and the Dynamics of Protest," *Political Psychology* 35 (2014): 1–22.

16. Leonie Huddy, L. Mason, and L. Aarøe, "Expressive Partisanship: Campaign Involvement, Political Emotion, and Partisan Identity," *American Political Science Review* 109 (2015): 3.

17. Huddy, Mason, and Aarøe, "Expressive Partisanship," 3.

of their own group as superior to members of the outgroup, without regard to the constraints of reality.[18]

Thus, a strong sense of group identity leads to in-group bias—favoring the members of one's in-group and disfavoring members of out-groups. The next stage of the process occurs when social identities become politically relevant. As Mason and Wronski put it, "Social identities translate into political ones when group identities are associated with explicit, political demands."[19] At this stage of the process, a person's political identity begins to function as a social identity. As Leonie Huddy explains, "Once identified with . . . a political party, members are motivated to protect and advance the party's status and electoral dominance, as a way to maintain their party's positive distinctiveness.[20] Moreover, at this stage, a person's political identity begins to affect their cognition as well. According to Roderick Rekker, citizens often base their factual perceptions on their political attitudes.[21] For instance, people's attitudes toward immigration tend to steer their interpretation of factual information about immigration.[22] More generally, there is some evidence that people use their political attitudes as heuristics (cognitive shortcuts) to fill in gaps in their knowledge.[23] In summary, when people identify with a political party, their political identity begins to shape their thinking about matters of fact.

The final step in the process is political polarization itself. Polarization amplifies the effects of social and political identities.

---

18. Lilliana Mason and Julie Wronski, "One Tribe to Bind Them All: How Our Social Group Attachments Strengthen Partisanship," *Advances in Political Psychology* 39 (2018): 259.
19. Mason and Wronski, "One Tribe to Bind Them All," 259.
20. Huddy, Mason, and Aarøe, "Expressive Partisanship," 3.
21. Rekker, "Political Polarization over Factual Beliefs."
22. K. Glinitzer, T. Gummer, and M. Wagner, "Learning Facts about Migration: Politically Motivated Learning of Polarizing Information about Refugees," *Political Psychology* 42 (2021): 1053–1069
23. D. Herda, "Too Many Immigrants? Examining Alternative Forms of Immigrant Population Innumeracy," *Sociological Perspectives* 56 (2013): 213–240.

As Bert Klandermans explains, when polarization happens, each group identifies itself in opposition to the other group.[24] Each group feels threatened by what the other group stands for. As the conflict escalates, the members of each group feel that their very identity is threatened by the other group. Each group begins to aim their actions at the other group. At this point, the attitudes and actions of each group reinforce each other, and the conflict escalates. In this process, the feelings of in-group identity strengthen. Members of each group favor their own group more strongly in order to deflect criticisms from the other group. Each group thinks, "We are good, and they are evil." This process of affective polarization leads to motivated cognition—it leads to biased reasoning. That is because "affectively polarized partisans feel a need to signal their partisan identity, distinguishing themselves from the other party. This leads to directional motivated cognition and more partisan cue-taking."[25]

At this stage of the process, the pressure on individuals to identify completely with their in-group sometimes develops into a rigid intolerance of dissent within the group. If a member of the in-group happens to dissent from the majority by holding one opinion of the out-group, then the animus felt by the in-group toward the out-group is sometimes redirected toward the dissenting member of the in-group. In this way, dissent within the group is discouraged, and those who dissent are sometimes excluded from the group. As a result, the in-group is effectively purged of dissent, and group membership alone determines opinion. At this point, the in-group becomes what C. Thi Nguyen calls an *echo chamber*, in which only the opinions of the in-group have a voice.[26]

---

24. Klandermans, "Identity Politics and Politicized Identities," 17.
25. Jon Kingzette, James N. Druckman, Samar Klar, Yanna Krupnikov, Matthew Levendusky, and John Barry Ryan, "How Affective Polarization Undermines Support for Democratic Norms," *Public Opinion Quarterly* 85 (2021): 663–677.
26. See C. Thi Nguyen, "Echo Chambers and Epistemic Bubbles," *Episteme* 17, no. 2 (2020): 141–161.

In the final stage of the process, the strengthened political identity of partisans leads them to trust members of their political in-group *exclusively*. As Roderick Rekker explains,

> when citizens become more emotionally invested in their political identity and more hostile toward opponents, they may develop a stronger tendency to exclusively trust identity-consistent information from in-group members, while disregarding identity-incongruent information from out-groups.[27]

Several recent studies support this hypothesis. When Israeli Jews were presented with a draft of a peace proposal and told that it was authored by Palestinians, they were less favorable toward it than when they were shown the very same proposal and told that it was authored by Jews. An experiment with Palestinians showed exactly the opposite bias.[28] In another experiment, information about whether House Republicans or House Democrats supported certain welfare policies predicted people's attitudes to them better than the actual content of the policies.[29] More recently, endorsements by Donald Trump influenced Republican attitudes toward policies. Liberal policies that Trump allegedly supported were more likely to be supported by Republicans.[30]

Polarization leads people to trust only in-group sources and to distrust any out-group sources. Moreover, affective polarization, in particular, makes people more susceptible to misinformation that favors their in-group. In a study published in 2023, Libby Jenke found that "citizens with higher levels of affective polarization are

---

27. Rekker, "Political Polarization over Factual Beliefs."

28. I. Maoz, A. Ward, M. Katz, and I. Ross, "Reactive Devaluation of an 'Israeli' vs. 'Palestinian' Peace Proposal," *Journal of Conflict Resolution* 46 (2002): 515–546.

29. G. L. Cohen, "Party over Policy: The Dominating Impact of Group Influence on Political Beliefs," *Journal of Personality and Social Psychology* 85 (2003): 808–822.

30. M. Barber and J. C. Pope, "Does Party Trump Ideology? Disentangling Party and Ideology in America," *American Political Science Review* 113 (2019): 38–54.

more likely to believe in-party-congruent-misinformation and less likely to believe out-party-congruent-misinformation."[31] This is further confirmed by the study of Dutch voters conducted by Rekker and Harteveld. In that study, Rekker and Harteveld found that the affective polarization of Dutch voters was positively correlated with in-group-favoring beliefs, even when those beliefs were mistaken. Thus, affective polarization made Dutch voters more prone to misinformation that favored their own political party.[32]

We are now in a position to describe the causal process that leads to polarized political beliefs. First, a person identifies with one or more groups of people on the basis of shared characteristics, like race, gender, religion, class, or ideology. This is their social identity. When a person's social identity becomes politically relevant, then they also form a political identity. Moreover, their political identity begins to function as a social identity. Consequently, their political identity leads to in-group bias, in which they favor the members of their own group over the members of out-groups. They only trust members of their own political party. Moreover, their political attitudes begin to steer their beliefs about matters of fact. They use their political attitudes as cognitive shortcuts to fill in gaps in their information. Finally, the process of political polarization amplifies these effects and adds another one. Polarization causes people's identification with their political party to increase, and their in-group bias also increases. Moreover, as affective polarization increases, people become more likely to accept misinformation that favors their in-group. As a result, they form beliefs opposite to their political opponents, even on factual matters.

This explanation of polarized belief is somewhat surprising. One might have thought that the process went like this: people first form beliefs about matters of fact, and then they form a political ideology, followed by a political identity and an attachment to a political party. However, the evidence suggests that the order of events goes

---

31. L. Jenke, "Affective Polarization and Misinformation Belief," *Political Behavior* (2023).
32. Rekker and Harteveld, "Understanding Factual Belief Polarization."

in exactly the opposite direction. People first form a social and political identity. Their political identity then leads them to favor members of their political in-group and disfavor members of out-groups. Polarization strengthens this attachment and preference. Finally, at the end of the process, they form their beliefs about politically relevant matters of fact. At that final stage of the process, they form many of their beliefs by exclusively trusting members of their political in-group. Their attachment to their political in-group leads them to form beliefs that favor their in-group and makes them more likely to accept misinformation that favors their in-group.

This explanation is hypothetical, but it is not *merely* hypothetical. It is supported by empirical evidence. However, it would be premature to say that the evidence is conclusive. This is an area of ongoing research, and, as such, it is subject to change. With that said, there is some reason to think that this is how polarized political beliefs are formed. Thus, in the rest of this chapter, we will consider the following question: If this is how polarized political beliefs are formed, then are such beliefs rationally justified? Could such beliefs ever constitute knowledge? On the face of it, that seems very doubtful. However, as we will soon see, matters are not so simple.

We will begin by considering the case for skepticism about polarized political beliefs. The skeptic says that polarized political beliefs are never rationally justified, nor could they ever constitute knowledge. Here is an argument for that conclusion. As we have described them, the processes that lead to polarized beliefs are not aimed at truth. They are aimed at supporting and favoring a person's political in-group. The subject of polarized beliefs might not be aware of this fact. He might see himself as believing what is true. However, the real, underlying cause of his polarized beliefs is the desire to support his political in-group. Thus, the process that actually causes polarized beliefs is not aimed at truth. Consequently, even if a polarized belief turns out to be true, it will be *just an accident* that it is true. However, as we have seen in previous chapters, a true belief that is true just by accident, as a matter of luck, is not knowledge. Therefore, polarized political beliefs never constitute knowledge. No one who has a polarized belief ever *knows* that their belief is true.

We can make this argument more precise by stating it in terms of the Safety Principle, which was introduced in the previous chapter. The Safety Principle says that in order to have knowledge, *you must form your belief in a way that could not easily have led to a false belief.* To apply this principle to polarized political beliefs, we need to ask this question: Could the process that leads to polarized political beliefs easily lead to a false belief? The answer seems to be *yes.* In fact, we have seen cases in which that actually happens. Dutch voters whose affective polarization influenced their beliefs were led to false beliefs about inequality, immigration, and climate change. More generally, it seems that believing something because it favors my political in-group is a process that could easily lead me to a false belief. If this is the process that is actually causing my polarized beliefs, then if a particular belief favored my political in-group, I would tend to accept it whether or not it was true. That could easily lead to a false belief. Thus, given how polarized beliefs are actually formed, they cannot constitute knowledge.

Moreover, as we saw in the previous chapter, once I become aware of this fact—that my beliefs were formed in a way that could easily lead to a false belief, I now have a *defeater* for my polarized beliefs. I have a reason to doubt that my belief is true—one that requires me to stop holding this belief. Once I become aware of this fact about my belief, I should suspend judgment about whether this belief is true or false. The belief is no longer rationally justified for me. Thus, for anyone who becomes aware of how their polarized beliefs were formed, those polarized beliefs are no longer rationally justified.

Here is a second argument for skepticism about polarized political beliefs. According to one conception of knowledge, a belief constitutes knowledge only if it is produced by a reliable cognitive process. A reliable cognitive process is a process that produces mostly true beliefs. For example, in a typical human being, *vision* is a reliable cognitive process—it produces mostly true beliefs. It is not infallible, of course, but it is generally reliable. Most of the time, vision leads to a true belief. By contrast, *wishful thinking*—believing something just because you want it to be true—is not a reliable cognitive process because it leads to as many false beliefs as true beliefs. Suppose, for the sake of argument, that a belief constitutes knowledge only if it is produced by a process that leads to mostly true beliefs.[33] Then it seems that polarized political beliefs do not constitute knowledge. The reason is that *the very same process that produces polarized beliefs on one side of the political divide produces exactly the opposite belief on the other side of the political divide*. Thus, the very same cognitive process—forming beliefs that favor a person's political in-group—leads people to form one belief about half the time and to exactly the opposite belief about half the time. Thus, it seems that this cognitive process leads to false beliefs just about as often as it leads to true beliefs. If so, then this is not a reliable cognitive process. The result, once again, is that polarized political beliefs do not constitute knowledge.

In addition, if a person becomes aware that her polarized belief was produced by an unreliable process, then it seems that she has a defeater for all of her polarized beliefs. To see this, consider the following analogy. Suppose I discover, through self-examination or psychotherapy, that some of my beliefs were caused solely by wishful thinking. I discover that I formed these beliefs just because I wanted them to be true. Since I know that wishful thinking is not a reliable process, I now have reason to doubt these beliefs. Under these circumstances, it would not be rational for me to continue to hold these beliefs, knowing that they were just the product of wishful thinking. In the same way, if a person discovers that their polarized beliefs were formed by a process that is unreliable because the very same process leads to false beliefs almost as often as true beliefs, then they have a reason to doubt their polarized beliefs. It would not be rational for them to continue to hold these beliefs. Thus, once a person becomes aware of the fact that their polarized beliefs were formed by an unreliable process, their polarized beliefs are no longer rationally justified.

---

33. This conception of knowledge is called *process reliabilism*. According to process reliabilism, a true belief constitutes knowledge if and only if it is produced by a reliable cognitive process. Here, we are only considering one of these two claims—that a belief constitutes knowledge only if it is produced by a reliable cognitive process.

Those are the arguments for skepticism about polarized political beliefs. Are they good arguments? Is the skeptic correct? Let us begin with the last argument—the argument from unreliability. That argument assumes that the people on each side of the political divide use the same cognitive process to form their beliefs. However, one might deny that assumption. For convenience, I will refer to the two sides of the political divide as A and B. One might say that the members of A and B form their beliefs through different cognitive processes. The members of A form their beliefs through the process of *favoring and trusting only members of A*, while the members of B form their beliefs through the process of *favoring and trusting members of B*. These are clearly two different processes. Moreover, suppose that one of these two groups, A, has mostly true beliefs. Then the cognitive process of favoring and trusting only members of A is actually a reliable cognitive process. Consequently, the members of A actually know that their beliefs are true. The fact that the members of B use a very similar process to arrive at mostly false beliefs is simply irrelevant.

To consider this reply to the skeptic, we must make a distinction. The term "cognitive process" is ambiguous. When we speak of a cognitive process, we could be speaking of a general *type* of process, or we could be speaking of a particular instance or *token* process. For example, *vision* is a general type of process, whereas *my seeing the computer screen in front of me right now* is a particular instance or *token* of that process type. A process type is something general—there can be many particular instances or cases of it. By contrast, a process token is an individual instance, which occurs at a particular time and place. When we ask if a particular belief was produced by a reliable cognitive process, we are asking a question about the particular process that produced this belief. What are we asking about that particular process? We are asking if that particular process is an instance of a general process type that is reliable. Although we are asking a question about a particular process, what we want to know is whether that particular process is an instance of a general process type that is reliable.

However, at this point, we encounter a problem. On reflection, it turns out that every particular cognitive process is an instance of many, many different process types. Moreover, these different process types are not all equally reliable. To see this, consider the following example. Suppose you read a news report in which a man reported a bear in his backyard. Suppose you want to know if his belief was produced by a reliable cognitive process. Since the man reported seeing the bear, you can infer that his belief was produced by a reliable cognitive process since *vision* is a reliable cognitive process. However, as you read on, you discover that this man had very poor eyesight, and he was looking out his window right at dusk without his glasses. Here is what you have now learned. The particular process that produced this man's belief was an instance of the type *vision*, but it was *also* an instance of the following type: *vision in a man with poor eyesight, without his glasses, when it is getting dark*. Whereas the first type of process, vision, is generally reliable, this second process is not so reliable. Now here is the problem. To determine whether this man's belief was produced by a reliable process, we need to determine whether the particular process that caused his belief is a token of a reliable process type. However, the particular process that produced this man's belief is a token of *two different process types*. Moreover, one of these process types is generally reliable, but the other one is much less reliable or even unreliable. Which of these two process types is relevant?[34]

Here is how this problem arises in the case of polarized belief. Imagine the following hypothetical example. Imagine two soccer fans, both of whom grew up on the west side of London.[35] Emily is a fan of Fulham, while Claire is a fan of Chelsea. Suppose that Emily and Claire each acquire their beliefs about soccer from their fellow fans, and so they each form beliefs that favor their own team. Thus, Emily forms beliefs that favor Fulham, while Claire forms beliefs that favor Chelsea. Now let us suppose, for the sake of the example, that the beliefs that favor Fulham are usually true, while beliefs that favor Chelsea are usually false. Now suppose Emily forms the belief that

---

34. This is called *The Problem of Generality*. See Earl Conee and Richard Feldman, "The Generality Problem for Reliabilism," *Philosophical Studies* 89 (1998): 1–29.
35. My apologies to British and European fans of The Beautiful Game for using the American term "soccer."

Fulham's striker is a much better striker than Chelsea's striker. Then let us ask this question: *What type of process caused Emily's belief?* The answer is that the process that caused her belief belongs to two distinct types. First, it belongs to the general type, *forming beliefs that favor my favorite team.*[36] Second, it belongs to the more specific type, *forming beliefs that favor Fulham.* If we want to know if this belief was produced by a reliable process, then which of these two types is relevant? The answer matters. Recall that Fulham fans form mostly true beliefs. Thus, the process type *forming beliefs that favor Fulham* is a very reliable process. Thus, if that is the process that caused Emily's belief, then her belief was produced by a reliable process. However, it is also true to say that Emily's belief was formed by the more general process, *forming beliefs that favor my favorite team in West London.* Is that a reliable process? Unfortunately, no, that is *not* a reliable process. Half of the fans in this example are Chelsea fans, and Chelsea fans form mostly false beliefs. Thus, if we consider all the beliefs that are formed by this process—forming beliefs that favor my favorite team, then 50 percent of those beliefs are false. Thus, if we say that Emily's belief was formed by the process *favoring her favorite team,* then we have to say that her belief was formed by an *unreliable* process.

We can now explain what this means for the skeptical argument from unreliability. If the process that produces polarized beliefs in a reliable group is best described as *forming beliefs that favor that group—the reliable group*—then the beliefs of people in a reliable group are produced by a reliable process. However, if the process that produced their beliefs is better described as *forming beliefs that favor my in-group, whichever group that happens to be*, then their beliefs are *not* produced by a reliable process *since that same process leads to false beliefs about half of the time.* The skeptic's point is that, under conditions of polarization, the members of the reliable group and the members of the unreliable group use the very same process to form their beliefs, which is *forming beliefs that favor your in-group,* and that is not a reliable process since it leads to false beliefs about half the

---

36. For the sake of this example, I am restricting the relevant teams to these two—Fulham and Chelsea. Imagine that they are the only teams.

time. The reply to this argument is that one of these two groups is actually following a more specific process, and the more specific process is reliable. Is there any principled way to decide who is right in this debate?

When we ask whether a belief was produced by a reliable process, we want to know whether the process that *actually caused the belief* is a reliable type of process. Thus, we are looking for the correct causal explanation of a person's belief.[37] With that in mind, consider this question: Are polarized political beliefs caused by the same process on both sides of the political divide? If we put the question in that way, then the answer seems to be yes. The members of both groups form their polarized beliefs by favoring their own in-group. That is what causes their beliefs. If that is correct, then the process type that produces polarized beliefs is the more general type, *forming beliefs that favor my in-group*, and that is not a reliable cognitive process. Thus, the skeptical argument seems to withstand this particular challenge.[38]

However, there is a much better reply to the skeptic's argument from unreliability. In the case in which one polarized group is reliable, while the other group is unreliable, the members of both groups form their beliefs in the same way, but one group forms mostly true beliefs, while the other group forms mostly false beliefs. This example illustrates an important fact about reliable processes—*the reliability of a cognitive process is relative to the environment in which it is used*. The very same cognitive process can be reliable in one environment but unreliable in another environment. For example, vision in a typical human being is very reliable in broad daylight but unreliable in the dark or in a blinding snowstorm. Moreover, in order for a process to generate knowledge, it only needs to be reliable in some environments.

---

37. This idea has been developed and defended by several philosophers. See, for example, William Alston, "How to Think about Reliability," *Philosophical Topics* 23 (1995): 1–29; and James Beebe, "The Generality Problem, Statistical Relevance and the Tri-Level Hypothesis," *Noûs* 38 (2004): 177–195.

38. Note: people can be mistaken about what actually favors their in-group. Thus, it is more accurate to say that, under conditions of polarization, people tend to form beliefs that *they think* favor their in-group. When I use the phrase "favors their in-group," it should be understood in this way.

Since vision is a reliable process in broad daylight, it generates knowledge under those conditions. The fact that vision is not reliable in the dark does not prevent me from getting knowledge through vision in the daylight.

With that in mind, here is another way to rebut the skeptic's argument. The process type, *forming beliefs that favor my in-group*, is reliable in the right environment, such as a group of people who have mostly true beliefs. If this process is used in that environment, then it is actually a reliable cognitive process. Thus, if a person forms polarized beliefs by favoring their in-group, *and their in-group has mostly true beliefs*, then they are using a process that is reliable in that particular environment. The fact that this process is unreliable in another environment, such as that of the opposing group, does not prevent a person from using it to get knowledge in the environment in which it is reliable. Thus, if a person belongs to a group that has mostly true beliefs, then forming beliefs that favor their in-group is actually a way of getting knowledge.

Suppose that the skeptic's argument from unreliability can be rebutted. Now we must consider the skeptic's other argument—the argument based on the Safety Condition. The Safety Condition says that in order for a belief to constitute knowledge, it must be formed in a way that could not easily have led to a false belief. The skeptic applies this principle to polarized belief in the following way. Polarized beliefs are caused by the process of *forming beliefs that favor your in-group*. In our society today, that process leads to many false polarized beliefs. Consequently, a person who is led to a polarized belief through this process could easily have been led to a false belief by this process. After all, that is what is happening right next door, so to speak. Thus, polarized beliefs are formed by a process that could easily lead to a false belief.

Is the skeptic right? It is true that people in our environment form their polarized beliefs in the same way as we do, and many of them are thereby led to false beliefs. However, it does not automatically follow that any given person could easily have formed a false belief in this way. Suppose, again, that Fulham fans have mostly true beliefs while Chelsea fans have mostly false beliefs. The skeptic is saying that, by forming beliefs that favor their in-group, the Fulham fans could easily have formed a false belief. But how could that happen? If the idea is that Fulham fans could easily form beliefs that favor Chelsea, then that is clearly false. Polarization between Fulham fans and Chelsea fans guarantees that Fulham fans will *not* form beliefs that favor Chelsea. Thus, there is no danger of Fulham fans suddenly forming false beliefs by forming beliefs that favor Chelsea. That is not likely to happen.

In order to use the Safety Condition to support skepticism about polarized belief, the skeptic needs to explain exactly how a Fulham fan, whose fellow fans have mostly true beliefs, could easily form a false belief. To answer this question, the skeptic will say that the polarized beliefs of *the entire group* are caused by the very same process—the process of forming beliefs that favor Fulham. Moreover, *that process* could easily lead to a false belief. That is because this process is not aimed at the truth, and so it could easily lead to false beliefs. In fact, it will lead to false beliefs whenever the beliefs that favor this group are false. Remember—the skeptic is not saying that this is true of *all* beliefs held by this group. The skeptic is only referring to the polarized political beliefs of this group. With respect to those beliefs, the skeptic says that they are produced by a process aimed at favoring the group. Consequently, these beliefs are formed in a way that could easily lead to false beliefs.

At this point, one might begin to wonder if the skeptic's argument is based on an undue amount of cynicism. Surely most people are also concerned about believing what is true and disbelieving what is false. After all, no one believes obvious falsehoods just because they would favor their in-group. However, that is not what the skeptic is saying. Polarized beliefs are usually about subjects that are far from obvious. There are exceptions, of course, but they are not very common. The skeptic need not say that human beings are extremely irrational, to the point of believing obvious falsehoods. The skeptic is only saying that when the truth is not obvious, then the mechanisms of social identity, political identity, and in-group bias take over. That is not implausible.

At this point, one might object that the skeptic is ignoring the fact that some polarized beliefs are based on *good evidence*. One reply to the skeptic is that true beliefs that are based on good evidence can constitute knowledge, even if they were produced by a process that was not aimed at truth. This is the theory known as *Evidentialism*, which was introduced in the last chapter. According to Evidentialism, a true belief constitutes knowledge only if it is sufficiently well-supported by the evidence. Moreover, if a true belief is sufficiently well-supported by the evidence, then it will usually constitute knowledge. Only in very unusual circumstances will a true belief that is supported by the evidence fail to constitute knowledge. Thus, according to the evidentialist, when we ask if a person knows, we should focus on whether the person's belief is sufficiently well-supported by the evidence that she possesses. Most importantly, according to Evidentialism, it does not matter how or why a person acquired the evidence that they possess. If the evidence that they possess supports their belief sufficiently, and their belief is true, then in ordinary circumstances, this person will *know* that their belief is true.

According to the Evidentialist, even if polarized beliefs were caused by in-group bias, that does not necessarily prevent them from constituting knowledge. If in-group bias leads a person to acquire evidence that adequately supports their belief, then they might know that this belief is true despite the influence of their bias. If they discover good evidence for their belief, then the influence of in-group bias in leading them to this evidence is simply irrelevant. Thus, according to the Evidentialist, the presence of in-group bias in causing polarized beliefs does not always prevent us from achieving knowledge. What matters is whether our in-group bias leads us to good evidence for our beliefs.

The critic of Evidentialism will say that this story ignores the most pernicious effect of in-group bias. Under the influence of in-group bias, a person might find evidence that supports their belief, *but they will not find evidence against their belief, even if such evidence exists*. Suppose that a member of one political group acquires very strong evidence for one of their polarized beliefs. Then, the Evidentialist says that they can know this belief is true. However, suppose that there is, in fact, even stronger evidence *against* this polarized belief, but this person never heard that evidence because they did not listen to any out-group sources. And they did not listen to any out-group sources because they were under the influence of their in-group bias. Then it seems that forming their belief in this way could easily have led them to a false belief. If their bias leads them to find only evidence that supports their polarized belief and prevents them from hearing any evidence that contradicts their belief, then they could easily be led to a false belief. Thus, even if they happen to be led to a true belief in this way, it seems that they were just lucky. They don't really *know* that their belief is true.

Furthermore, there is yet another way in which in-group bias seems to undermine knowledge, even when a person has good evidence. Like confirmation bias, in-group bias causes people to believe that their evidence is good evidence, even when it is not good evidence. Now imagine someone under the influence of in-group bias who happens to possess good evidence for her belief. Given the influence of her bias, this person would see her evidence as good evidence even if it was not good evidence. Thus, there is a sense in which she is just lucky to form a true belief, despite having good evidence, since she would see her evidence as good evidence, even if it was not good evidence. Once again, it seems to follow that a person under the influence of in-group bias is just lucky to have a true belief, even when she has good evidence for her belief. In summary, then, the critic of Evidentialism says that in-group bias deprives us of knowledge with respect to our polarized beliefs, even if it leads us to evidence that supports our belief. I will leave it to the reader to consider the merits of these objections.

With respect to at least one type of belief, it appears that many people *are* being led to false beliefs as a result of their in-group bias. According to the most recent research, at the time of this writing, most political partisans hold false beliefs on one particular subject, namely, *the beliefs of the people on the other side*. As it turns out,

> most partisans hold major misbeliefs about the other party's preferences that lead them to think there is far less shared policy

belief. This perception gap is highest among progressive activists, followed closely by extreme conservatives: in other words, the people who are most involved in civic and political life hold the least accurate views of the other side's beliefs.[39]

On a wide range of issues, from gun control to immigration to climate change, members of each political party have many false beliefs about what the other party believes. Notably, these misperceptions are most prevalent at the extreme ends of the political spectrum.

However, political partisans are *not* mistaken about the beliefs of their representatives. At least in the United States, American politicians are just as polarized in their beliefs and policy preferences as they appear to be. That is one reason that most partisans misperceive the beliefs of partisans on the other side—they assume that the representatives on the other side really represent the beliefs and attitudes of the partisans on the other side. If citizens are not as polarized in their beliefs as they think they are, then why do they elect extremely polarized representatives? According to Rachel Kleinfeld,

> it is easy to assume that polarized voters are selecting more polarized leaders—and that theory may hold true for recent primary elections. However, that is not the main story. The process begins long before voters get a choice: more ideologically extreme politicians have been running for office since the 1980s. Among the pool of people wishing to run, party chairs more often select and support extreme candidates, especially on the right. (In 2013, Republican party chairs at the county level selected ten extreme candidates for every one moderate; the ratio was two to one for Democrats.) . . . Parties and candidates clearly believe that more polarizing candidates are more likely to win elections. This may be a self-fulfilling prophecy: voters

---

39. Rachel Kleinfeld, "Polarization, Democracy, and Political Violence in the United States: What the Research Says," Carnegie Endowment for International Peace, September 5, 2023, https://carnegieendowment.org/2023/09/05/polarization-democracy-and-political-violence-in-united-states-what-research-says-pub-90457.

exposed to more polarizing rhetoric from leaders who share their partisan identity are likely to alter their preferences based on their understanding of what their group believes and has normalized—particularly among primary voters whose identity is more tied to their party. However, only about 20 percent of each party votes in primaries, and 41 percent of Americans are independents who may not have strong party identity and are barred from voting in some states' primaries. That leaves the majority of voters with a relatively low ability to pick a less polarizing candidate of their party. Philanthropists and prodemocracy organizations attempting to reduce polarization often assume that the problem they must grapple with is polarized voters, but their interventions should also take into account the fact that some of the ideological extremism and polarization since the 1980s is candidate- and party-driven. While at this point, candidates and parties may be responding to polarized primary voters, candidates and parties have been driving the polarization, and not all voters are ideologically polarized.[40]

Here is the important point for our purposes. Political partisans' beliefs about the opinions of partisans on the other side are caused by a political process aimed at the promotion of candidates and their parties. The political process in the United States leads to the election of representatives who hold views that are more extreme than the people they represent. Moreover, these politicians have a vested interest in misrepresenting the members of the opposing party. They then succeed in persuading the average voter to accept false beliefs about the opinions of partisans on the other side. It is no surprise that this process leads to many false beliefs since the process was never aimed at truth in the first place. According to the skeptic about polarized belief, this example illustrates how all polarized beliefs are formed. The processes that lead to polarized beliefs are not aimed at truth, so even when they do happen to cause a true belief, it is just by accident.

---

40. Kleinfeld, "Polarization, Democracy, and Political Violence."

Thus, polarized beliefs never amount to knowledge. No one knows that their polarized beliefs are true.

However, even if the skeptic is right about partisans' beliefs about each other, it does not follow that this is also true about other polarized beliefs. In order to show that, the skeptic would have to show that other polarized beliefs are also produced by processes that are not aimed at truth. It is an empirical question whether that is true of all or even most polarized beliefs. We have seen some evidence that the processes that produce polarized beliefs are not aimed at truth. However, the research on this question is ongoing, and it would be premature to draw a conclusion with too much confidence. One can hope that, even with respect to polarized beliefs, good reasoning can still guide us to the truth.

Study Questions

1. Imagine two people, Randy and Delia. Randy is a registered Republican, and Delia is a registered Democrat. Randy believes that allowing people to own guns makes most people safer, while Delia believes that allowing people to own guns makes most people less safe. Neither Randy nor Delia has done extensive research on this question. According to the psychological research described in this chapter, what factors led each to form their belief on this subject? Pick either Randy or Delia and describe, in detail, the factors that caused them to form their belief.
2. What is the Safety Principle—what does it say? If you apply the Safety Principle to the way in which polarized beliefs are formed, then what follows about polarized beliefs? Explain your answer.
3. A cognitive process is a way of forming beliefs. A reliable cognitive process is a process that leads to mostly true beliefs. Can a cognitive process be reliable in one environment but unreliable in another environment? Think of an example of a cognitive process to illustrate your answer, and explain how it illustrates your answer.
4. What is Evidentialism—what does it say? According to Evidentialism, how could a polarized belief still constitute knowledge? What is one objection to this view?
5. According to recent research, what are most political partisans mistaken about? What causes most partisans to have these mistaken beliefs?

For Further Reading

For an in-depth discussion of the epistemological problem of polarization, see Robin McKenna, "Asymmetrical Irrationality: Are Only Other People Stupid?" in *The Routledge Handbook of Political Epistemology*, ed. Michael Hannon and Jeroen de Ridder (New York: Routledge, 2021). For an argument against pure partisanship on epistemological grounds, see Hrishikesh Joshi, "What Are the Chances

You're Right about Everything? An Epistemic Challenge for Modern Partisanship," *Politics, Philosophy and Economics* 19 (2020): 36–61. On the epistemology of political partisanship, also see Elise Woodard's essay "What's Wrong with Partisan Deference?" in *Oxford Studies in Epistemology*, vol. 8, ed. Alex Worsnip (Oxford: Oxford University Press, forthcoming). For a defense of the Evidentialist response to the problem of belief polarization, see Thomas Kelly, "Disagreement, Dogmatism, and Belief Polarization," *Journal of Philosophy* 105 (2008): 611–633. For a critique of Kelly, see Emily McWilliams, "Evidentialism and Belief Polarization," *Synthese* 198 (2021): 7165–7196. Finally, for a review of the empirical evidence that one side of political polarization is more rational than the other, see Keith Stanovich, "The Irrational Attempt to Impute Irrationality to One's Political Opponents," in *The Routledge Handbook of Political Epistemology*, ed. Michael Hannon and Jeroen de Ridder (New York: Routledge, 2021).

CHAPTER SIX

Propaganda, Nudging, and Big Data

On August 24, 2022, NBC News reported that

> Facebook and Twitter cracked down on a series of covert influence campaigns designed to spread pro–U.S. sentiment abroad, researchers announced Wednesday. A report, jointly published by Stanford University and Graphika, a social media analytics company that works with Facebook and Twitter, found hundreds of inauthentic accounts designed to spread pro–U.S. views on current events to users in the Middle East and central Asia.[1]

The *New York Times* reported the same story, in the same terms, speaking of a "pro–U.S. Influence Campaign."[2] Two days later, the BBC also reported the story. However, the BBC used a term that neither NBC nor the *New York Times* had used. In the BBC version of the story, the headline read "Twitter and Meta Take Down Pro–U.S. Propaganda Campaign." Quoting from the original source of the story, the BBC reported that "Twitter and Meta have removed from their platforms an online propaganda campaign aimed at promoting U.S. interests abroad, researchers say. . . . This is the first major covert pro–U.S. propaganda operation taken down by the tech giants."[3]

---

1. Kevin Collier, "Researchers Discover Sprawling Pro–U.S. Social Media Influence Campaign," NBC News, August 24, 2022.

2. "Facebook, Twitter, and Others Remove Pro–U.S. Influence Campaign," *New York Times*, August 24, 2022.

3. "Twitter and Meta Take Down Pro–U.S. Propaganda Campaign," BBC News, August 26, 2022.

In reporting the story, the BBC used a term that neither NBC nor the *New York Times* used—*propaganda*. Why did NBC and the *New York Times* refrain from using the word *propaganda*? Perhaps it is because the word "propaganda" is pejorative. As Étienne Brown explains,

> like many political buzzwords, . . . propaganda is notoriously difficult to define. This can be explained by the fact that it mostly functions as a rhetorical weapon rather than a precise analytical tool. If we accuse someone of engaging in propaganda, the implied judgment is usually that this person intends to achieve questionable political ends by misleading the masses.[4]

NBC and the *New York Times* are based in the United States, whereas the BBC is based in Great Britain. Perhaps that made NBC and the *Times* more reluctant to use a pejorative term. On the other hand, perhaps NBC and the *Times* were just being more cautious. Be that as it may, this raises the questions that we will explore in this chapter. What is propaganda? Is it always bad? When it is bad, what makes it bad? To answer these questions, we will begin by taking a closer look at the facts of this case.

These news stories are based on a study that was published by the Stanford Internet Observatory (SIO) and Graphika. The SIO is a policy research center at Stanford University, and Graphika is a social media analytics firm. In the Executive Summary of that study, the authors summarize their findings as follows:

> In July and August 2022, Twitter and Meta removed two overlapping sets of accounts for violating their platforms' terms of service. Twitter said the accounts fell afoul of its policies on "platform manipulation and spam," while Meta said the assets on its platforms engaged in "coordinated inauthentic behavior." After taking down the assets, both platforms provided

---

4. Étienne Brown, "Propaganda, Misinformation, and the Epistemic Value of Democracy," *Critical Review* 30 (2018): 194–218.

portions of the activity to Graphika and the Stanford Internet Observatory (SIO) for further analysis. Our joint investigation found an interconnected web of accounts on Twitter, Facebook, Instagram, and five other social media platforms that used deceptive tactics to promote pro-Western narratives in the Middle East and Central Asia. The platforms' datasets appear to cover a series of covert campaigns over a period of almost five years rather than one homogeneous operation. These campaigns consistently advanced narratives promoting the interests of the United States and its allies while opposing countries including Russia, China, and Iran. . . . To promote this and other narratives, the accounts sometimes shared news articles from U.S. government-funded media outlets, such as Voice of America and Radio Free Europe, and links to websites sponsored by the U.S. military.[5]

According to the report, the dataset from Twitter contained 299,566 tweets by 146 accounts between March 2012 and February 2022, while the dataset from Meta included 39 Facebook profiles, 16 pages, two groups, and 26 Instagram accounts active from 2017 to July 2022. The source of these accounts was somewhere in the continental United States, but they were aimed at people in several countries in the Middle East and central Asia. According to the study, "The Central Asia group was the most active campaign, with posting/tweeting volumes peaking at almost 200 a day in the months leading up to and immediately after Russia's invasion of Ukraine in February this year." In what follows, I will focus on two aspects of this activity—the *methods* that were used, which involved various kinds of deception, and the *goal* of their activity, which was *political persuasion*. These accounts deceived people in various ways in order to persuade them to accept certain political claims.

---

5. "Unheard Voice: Evaluating Five Years of Pro-Western Covert Influence Operations," Graphika and the Stanford Internet Observatory Cyber Policy Center, August 24, 2022.

According to the study, these online accounts "created fake personas with GAN-generated faces, posed as independent media outlets, leveraged memes and short-form videos, attempted to start hashtag campaigns, and launched online petitions."[6] In the group of accounts based in central Asia,

> fake personas created by the actors were typically linked to one of 10 sham media outlets, which posed as independent news entities covering events in Central Asia. These fake personas posed as individuals living in Europe and Central Asia, were listed as administrators for the sham media outlets, and posted content from the campaign to different social media groups.[7]

At the very core, these online accounts were based on deception. One of the accounts used a doctored photo of Puerto Rican actor Valeria Menendez. Other accounts used pictures stolen from dating websites. These fake people were represented as citizens of countries in Europe and central Asia.

The accounts also created fake news media outlets and posted content that allegedly came from these outlets. The content that they posted was clearly intended to convince readers that these media outlets were real and that they were trustworthy. One example from the study illustrates this tactic.

> The sham media outlet Intergazeta repeatedly copied news material with and without credit from reputable Western and pro-Western sources in Russian, such as Meduza.io and the BBC Russian Service. The sham outlet often made minor changes to the copied texts in a likely effort to pass them off as original content. Intergazeta also produced articles in Russian compiled from sections of different English-language sources. . . . At least half of the assets interspersed their posts with content promoting the cultures and natural beauty of

---

6. "Unheard Voice," 3.
7. "Unheard Voice," 11.

Central Asia, possibly in an attempt to appear authentic and obscure their politically motivated activity.[8]

Even when these fake media outlets posted something true, the post was designed to convince the reader of a lie—that the source was a real media outlet. Likewise, the posts about beauty and culture, even when true, were designed to disguise the political motivations of these accounts. In short, these accounts used deception to earn the trust of their readers.

If the method of these accounts was deception, then the purpose was political persuasion. The central Asia group of accounts

> heavily promoted narratives supportive of the U.S. . . . . These posts primarily focused on U.S. support for Central Asian countries and their people, presenting Washington as a reliable economic partner that would curb the region's dependence on Russia. Other posts argued that the U.S. was the main guarantor of Central Asia's sovereignty against Russia, frequently citing the war in Ukraine as evidence of the Kremlin's "imperial" ambitions. Interestingly, the assets also promoted U.S. humanitarian efforts, mentioning the United States Agency for International Development 94 times on Twitter and 384 times on Facebook in the respective datasets.[9]

While praising and promoting the United States, the accounts in the central Asia group "consistently portrayed Russia as a threat to Central Asian countries. A recurring narrative claimed that Russia is abusing Russian-Central Asian partnerships, namely the CSTO [Collective Security Treaty Organization] and, to a lesser extent, the Commonwealth of Independent States (CIS), to extract one-sided benefits."

After promoting a pro–U.S. point of view, these online accounts proceeded to recommend specific courses of action to their readers. After describing the CTSO as a "hazardous tool that Russia

---

8. "Unheard Voice," 14.
9. "Unheard Voice," 20.

could use," they argued that "Central Asian countries must leave these organizations if they wish to retake their full sovereignty from Russia." Moreover, the accounts advocated for specific political petitions. Specifically,

> the assets pushed at least four petitions on Facebook, Twitter, and Instagram. One called for Kazakhstan to leave the Collective Security Treaty Organization (CSTO) and the Eurasian Economic Union (EEU). A second demanded that Kyrgyzstan curb Chinese influence in the country. The last two called on the Kazakh government to ban Russian TV channels.[10]

The goal of these activities was to persuade readers to accept pro–U.S. political beliefs and to act on those beliefs. Ironically, the accounts often took time to decry Russian propaganda. For example, they

> criticized Russia's use of propaganda to spread anti-West and pro-Russia narratives in Central Asia, depicting Russia as a nefarious actor working to undermine independent democracies. In January 2022, for example, the accounts covered mass protests that followed a sudden increase in fuel prices in Kazakhstan, but mainly through the lens of debunking Russian allegations of "foreign interference."[11]

Once again, the goal was to persuade readers to adopt a pro–U.S. and anti-Russian point of view in political matters.

Those are the facts of the case. Let us begin with this question: *Was this propaganda?* To answer this question, we must determine what constitutes propaganda. The first answer that comes to mind is that propaganda is simply a collection of *lies*. The terms "propaganda" and "lies" are sometimes used together as near-synonyms. If propaganda is a set of false statements, then the statements of the online accounts would certainly count as propaganda. However, these accounts also

---

10. "Unheard Voice," 18–19.
11. "Unheard Voice," 21.

made many true statements. When they described U.S. aid to countries in central Asia, those statements were true. When they described China's mistreatment of some Chinese Muslim minorities, some of those statements were true. And when they described Russia's actions in Ukraine, some of those statements were also true. Nevertheless, these true statements were also instances of propaganda, and it is important to understand exactly why they constituted propaganda. These statements were intended to cause their readers to form certain beliefs about the United States, China, and Russia and to form those beliefs *on the basis of these statements alone.*[12] When the intended audience read these statements, they were supposed to form an impression of the United States, China, and Russia that would guide their subsequent thinking about those nations. Now notice something. If a person in central Asia wanted to decide for themselves what to think about the United States, China, and Russia, they would not form their opinion solely on the basis of these facts alone. Moreover, they would not form their opinion by consulting only sources that were favorable to one party in an ongoing dispute between these nations. If a person wanted to decide for themselves what to think about these nations, they would consult multiple sources and gather lots of relevant information. Thus, even the true statements made by these accounts were intended to cause readers to form their beliefs in a very different way from how they would form them on their own. These statements—even the true ones—were designed to cause these people to form opinions *without thinking for themselves*, and that is what makes them instances of propaganda.

According to Randal Marlin, propaganda is "the organized attempt, through communication, to affect belief or action, or

---

12. As one reviewer pointed out, people often make statements with the intention of inducing others to accept what they are saying without being guilty of propaganda. Thus, the fact that a speaker intends to induce acceptance is not sufficient for propaganda. That is correct. The distinctive feature of propaganda is that propaganda aims to prevent, impede, or impair the victim's future reasoning on the subject. The propagandist aims to induce acceptance by impairing the victim's ability to think in ways that might lead to a different conclusion from the one the propagandist favors.

inculcate attitudes in a large audience in ways that circumvent an individual's adequately informed, rational, reflective judgment."[13] The essence of propaganda is that it aims to circumvent a person's ability to form their own opinions and choose their own actions in a way that is rational and fully informed. This can be achieved with false statements, but it can also be achieved with true statements. Any statement that is designed to affect a person's actions or opinions in a way that circumvents their ability to think for themselves in a rational way is an instance of propaganda. With that in mind, it becomes clear that a statement need not be false to be an instance of propaganda. For example, one way to circumvent a person's ability to think for themselves in a rational way is to manipulate their emotions. Some statements are designed to cause people to feel fear, anger, or disgust in a way that will short-circuit their ability to think rationally about something. If those statements are also intended to influence people's actions or opinions, then they are also instances of propaganda. As Jason Stanley notes, the statement "There are Muslims among us" can be used in this way—to instill fear and thereby short-circuit people's ability to think for themselves in a rationally. When it is used in this way, this statement is propaganda, even if the statement is true.[14]

Based on such examples, Stanley takes the manipulation of people's emotions to be essential to propaganda. According to Stanley, propaganda aims to cut off rational debate by appealing to people's affective states and exploiting an ideal.[15] However, just as making false statements is just one possible method of propaganda, among many, so manipulating people's emotions is just one possible method of propaganda, among many. As Brian and Samuel Leiter point out, "Much of the propaganda that mobilized support in America for the 2003 invasion of Iraq . . . involved simple falsehoods or misleading

---

13. Randal Marlin, *Propaganda and the Ethics of Persuasion*, 2nd ed. (Peterborough, ON: Broadview Press, 2013).
14. Jason Stanley, *How Propaganda Works* (Princeton, NJ: Princeton University Press, 2015), 42.
15. Stanley's account of propaganda is developed in *How Propaganda Works*, chaps. 5 and 6.

statements." These statements did not appeal to people's emotions, nor did they reference an ideal of any sort. Nevertheless, they were instances of propaganda.[16] They constituted propaganda simply because they aimed to influence people's opinions in a way that circumvented their ability to think for themselves in a rational and fully informed way.

As noted above, the term "propaganda" is a pejorative term. The very meaning of the term implies that there is something wrong with propaganda. There are many objections to propaganda, some of which are moral or political in nature. However, here we will focus on the epistemology of propaganda. From an epistemological point of view, what is wrong with propaganda? It is not that propaganda always leads to *false beliefs*, for we have seen that even true statements can constitute propaganda. As a first approximation, we might say that the problem with propaganda is that even when it leads to true beliefs, it is just an accident that those beliefs are true. As we have seen, accidentally true beliefs do not constitute knowledge. Thus, propaganda leads to beliefs that do not constitute knowledge. Why does propaganda lead to beliefs that are only accidentally true? Propaganda is not aimed at truth. That is not the goal or purpose of propaganda, as such. The goal of propaganda is to produce beliefs that the propagandist wants the recipient to hold, regardless of whether those beliefs are true or false. Thus, if those beliefs happen to be true, it is just an accident that they are true.

We can make this idea more precise in terms of the Safety Principle, which was introduced in Chapters 4 and 5. The Safety Principle says that in order to have knowledge, you must form your belief in a way that could not easily have led to a false belief. To apply this principle to propaganda, we need to ask this question: Could propaganda easily lead to a false belief? The answer seems to be *yes*. The online accounts that spread pro–U.S. propaganda aimed to cause their readers to form beliefs that favored the United States, and disfavored Russia and China. If false beliefs would serve those ends, then the

---

16. Brian Leiter and Samuel Leiter, "Not Your Grandfather's Propaganda," *The New Rambler: An Online Review of Books,* October 12, 2015.

propagandists would happily promote false beliefs. Thus, even if the beliefs they promoted were true, they could just as well have been false. Thus, the process that led those readers to form their beliefs—being influenced by pro–U.S. propaganda—could easily have led to false beliefs. Consequently, they do not know that their beliefs are true, even if they are.

That is not the only negative effect of propaganda on human knowledge. When propaganda becomes widespread, it threatens to deprive people of knowledge in other ways as well. To see this, consider the following example.[17] Imagine that a man is driving out in the country, and he sees a barn out in a field. Naturally, he believes that he is seeing a barn, and in fact, he is. However, unbeknownst to him, there are many fake barn facades in the country all around him. These fake barn facades have been erected to attract tourists to the region, since the tourists like the view of barns in the country around them. Then, even though this man is seeing a real barn, he could easily have been looking at one of the fake barn facades. Since he could easily have seen one of the fake barn facades, he does not *know* that he is seeing a real barn, even though he is. The presence of the many fake barn facades makes it very easy for the man to form a false belief in these circumstances, and that fact deprives him of knowledge, even when he sees a real barn. In much the same way, if propaganda becomes very widespread, then even when a person listens to a reliable source, they could easily have been listening to propaganda. Consequently, even when they listen to a reliable source, they do not know that what they hear is true. In this way, when propaganda becomes widespread in a society, it deprives many people of knowledge, even when they are actually listening to a reliable source.

That problem will only occur in societies in which propaganda is very widespread. However, the existence of any propaganda at all can have a similar effect, even when it occurs less frequently. To see this, consider a variation on the case of the fake barns. Imagine again that a man is driving out in the country. However, rather than seeing

---

17. This example was originally stated by Alvin Goldman in "Discrimination and Perceptual Knowledge," *Journal of Philosophy* 73 (1976): 771–791.

a barn, he sees a sign that announces that he is in "Fake Barn Country." The sign says that there are fake barn facades in the vicinity. The sign does not say just how many fake barns there are. It just says that there are fake barns in the vicinity. As the man continues driving, he sees what looks like a barn in a field. In fact, he is seeing a real barn. Moreover, the fact of the matter is that there are very few fake barn facades in this county. Most of the barns are real. However, all this man knows is that there are fake barns in the vicinity, and he does not know *how many* fake barns there are. In that context, does this man know that he is seeing a real barn? It seems that he does not. The reason is that he has a *defeater* for his belief that he is seeing a real barn. As the term suggests, a defeater for a belief is something that defeats a person's reason for holding their belief. In this case, the driver's reason for believing that he is seeing a real barn is that he sees something that *looks like* a real barn. However, the sign has told him that there are fake barn facades in the vicinity, so the driver now knows that he could be seeing a fake barn facade. Moreover, if he were seeing a fake barn facade, it would look exactly like a real barn. Thus, the fact that he sees something that looks like a real barn no longer gives him a reason to believe that he is seeing a real barn. He now has reason to believe that he could just as well be seeing a fake barn facade. Consequently, the driver does not know that he is seeing a real barn, even though he is.

When people become aware of the existence of propaganda in their society, then that knowledge has an effect similar to the effect of the sign that says "Fake Barn Country." They now know some sources that appear to be reliable sources of information are actually sources of propaganda. Moreover, they do not know *how many* sources are actually sources of propaganda. In that situation, they have some reason to doubt even those sources that are actually reliable. This threatens to deprive people of knowledge they could have gained from reliable sources if it were not for the existence of propaganda in their society. In this way, the awareness of any propaganda at all threatens to deprive people of knowledge that would otherwise be acquired from reliable sources.

But perhaps our situation is not as dire as this analogy suggests. In a society in which propaganda is relatively rare, the mere occurrence of one or two instances does not deprive people of knowledge acquired from reliable sources. A person who stops trusting most sources of information simply because there are a few sources of propaganda would be guilty of an overgeneralization. With that said, the effect of propaganda on knowledge in a society depends on two factors: (1) Does propaganda occur very frequently in this society? (2) Is there reason for people to believe that, for all they know, propaganda might be very common in their society? If the answer to either of these questions is yes, then many people in that society will be deprived of knowledge that they otherwise would have acquired from reliable sources.

Up to this point, I have made two crucial assumptions. First, I have assumed that the recipients of propaganda would have formed their opinions in a rational, well-informed way if they had not been under the influence of propaganda. Second, I have assumed that the producers of propaganda are not concerned about the truth. It is now time to consider situations in which these assumptions are false. First, people often form beliefs and perform actions that they, themselves, on reflection, judge to be irrational. For example, people sometimes have an unhealthy diet, even though they would rather have a healthy diet. Likewise, people tend to discount or disregard the distant future, and thus, they fail to save enough money for retirement. In these cases, people think and act in ways that they, themselves, ultimately judge to be irrational. In cases like these, it is possible to change the circumstances of people's choices in such a way as to *nudge* them to make better choices. If healthier foods are placed at eye level, then people tend to choose them more frequently, relative to less healthy foods.[18] Likewise, if the default choice that is offered to new employees is one that puts more money into a retirement savings account,

---

18. T. Bucher, C. Collins, M. E. Rollo, T. A. McCaffrey, N. De Vlieger, D. Van der Bend, H. Truby, and F. J. A. Perez-Cueto, "Nudging Consumers towards Healthier Choices: A Systematic Review of Positional Influences on Food Choice," *British Journal of Nutrition* 115 (2016): 2252–2263.

people tend to save more money for retirement.[19] In these cases, the people who are nudged would *not* have believed or acted in a rational, well-informed way if they were not influenced by these nudges.[20] Second, those who would do the nudging in these cases *are* concerned about the truth—that these people would be better off if they chose healthier foods and saved more money. Under these conditions, is this activity—nudging—just as objectionable as propaganda?

In these cases, it is people's *actions* that are influenced rather than their beliefs. However, for present purposes, we can imagine they are caused to believe that the choices they make are better for them. Furthermore, I will suppose that these beliefs are true—it really would be better for these people to eat healthier diets and save more money for retirement. Finally, imagine that those who nudge these people to form these beliefs are concerned about the truth, and they nudge these people to form beliefs *because* these beliefs are true. Then, under those conditions, the objection to propaganda does not apply in these cases. The objection to propaganda was that forming a belief by trusting propaganda was a process that could easily lead to a false belief. However, in these cases, the motivation for nudging is to get people to form true beliefs about what is best for them. As long as that is the motivation for nudging, nudging is not a process that could easily lead to a false belief. Moreover, since the recipients of nudging would have formed false beliefs about what is best for them if they had not been nudged, the process of nudging actually produces true beliefs in cases where people otherwise would have formed false beliefs. In sum, nudging that is performed by people who reliably aim at the

---

19. N. C. Smith, D. G. Goldstein, and E. J. Johnson, "Choice without Awareness: Ethical and Policy Implications of Defaults," *Journal of Public Policy and Marketing* 32 (2013): 159–172.

20. The concept of nudging was popularized by Richard Thaler and Cass Sunstein in their book *Nudge* (London: Penguin Books, 2008). Thaler and Sunstein define a nudge as "a form of choice architecture that alters people's behavior in a predictable way without forbidding any options or significantly changing their economic incentives" (6).

truth seems to generate knowledge where there would have been ignorance.[21]

Critics will object that this defense of nudging conveniently overlooks what it has in common with propaganda. In both nudging and propaganda, one person circumvents the other person's ability to decide for themselves, in a rational and well-informed way, what to think or how to act. The first problem with this objection is that, as we have noted, in these circumstances, people do not seem to have the ability to choose in a rational way. Consequently, the nudger is not circumventing their ability to think rationally in these cases since they do not have that ability. One might reply that people do have the ability to think rationally in these cases, and they simply fail to use that ability. However, even in that case, the nudger has not deprived the recipient of a rational process of thought since the recipient would not have used a rational process anyway. Thus, nudging does not deprive a person of a reliable cognitive process since the person being nudged would not have used a reliable process to form their belief. Thus, nudging does not deprive a person of knowledge that they otherwise would have had since, in the absence of nudging, they would not have acquired knowledge.[22]

Even if nudging does not deprive a person of knowledge they otherwise would have had, one might still deny that nudging *gives* people knowledge. One reason to deny that nudging gives people knowledge is that beliefs caused by nudging are not based on *good evidence*. If a person's belief that a food item is best for them was

---

21. I am imagining that, in these cases, people do form false beliefs on the occasions when they act irrationally. It is not just that they *act* irrationally. In the moment, before they act, they also form false beliefs about what would be best for them. But perhaps that is not the case. Perhaps people have true beliefs or no beliefs at all, and they just *act* irrationally. If that is what happens, then this defense of nudging *beliefs* does not really justify it. Nudging *actions* might still be justified, but that is a different matter. I will leave it to the reader to consider this question further.

22. Of course, one might object to nudging on *moral* grounds, namely, that it violates a person's autonomy. However, here we are only concerned with the epistemology of nudging.

caused simply by the fact that the item was at eye level, then their belief is not based on any good evidence. Likewise, if a new employee's belief that financial plan A is the best plan for them is caused solely by the fact that it is the default option, then their belief is not based on good evidence. According to some theories of knowledge, knowledge requires that a person's belief be based on good evidence. If that is correct, and nudging produces beliefs that are not based on good evidence, then nudging does not generate knowledge.

However, Neil Levy has argued that nudging *does* give people evidence for their resulting beliefs. That is because nudging is actually a way of giving implicit recommendations to people.[23] Empirical evidence shows that people understand default options as a kind of communication.[24] They understand that the default choice they are offered is thereby being recommended to them. Thus, nudging is actually an instance of *testimony*, and testimony can constitute good evidence. Consequently, nudging can be seen as part of a rational process in which a person is given testimonial evidence, through the nudge, that they take into account in deciding what to think and how to act. If knowledge requires that the subject of a belief have good evidence for her belief, then nudging can generate knowledge.

Nudging can produce knowledge, but only if those who do the nudging reliably produce true beliefs through their nudges. Under those conditions, nudging can transmit knowledge from one person to another in much the same way that testimony transmits knowledge. However, the reliability of this process depends on the intentions and reliability of those who give the nudges.

This brings us to the third and final subject of this chapter: *Big Data*. As Karen Yeung explains, "Big Data is shorthand for the combination

---

23. Neil Levy, "Nudge, Nudge, Wink, Wink: Nudging Is Giving Reasons," *Ergo: An Open Access Journal of Philosophy* 6 (2019): 10.
24. S. A. Fisher, "Meaning and Framing: The Semantic Implications of Psychological Framing Effects," *Inquiry* (2020); and "Rationalizing Framing Effects: At Least One Task for Empirically Informed Philosophy," *Critica: Revista Hispanoamericana de Filosofía* 52 (156): 5–30.

of a technology and a process."[25] The technology involved in Big Data is the ability to find patterns in enormous quantities of data that could not be found by human analysis alone. The subsequent process involved in Big Data is to use this information to give what Yeung calls *hypernudges*. As Yeung uses the term, a hypernudge is a series of nudges in which each nudge is informed by the users' prior choices, together with other background information, to direct the user in the way the choice architect wishes to direct her. Throughout the process, the user feels completely free to choose what to do next, but her choices are influenced by the options that she is offered at each point.

This is precisely how the Google search engine works.[26] The user enters a search term, and Google offers a list of pages to look at. At this point in the process, the user has already been nudged. The user is completely free to choose which of these pages to look at. However, the pages are presented in a particular order, and the user is thereby nudged to look at the pages presented first. Moreover, the user's searches are saved by Google and then used to refine future nudges. Thus, there is a *feedback loop*, in which Google uses the information gathered from the user's prior choices to nudge again the next time. This is hypernudging and as Yeung points out,

> for Google, this entails driving web traffic in directions that promote greater use of Google applications (thereby increasing the value of Google's sponsored advertising space).[27]

Hypernudging raises moral and political concerns about manipulation. However, we will focus on the effects of hypernudging on human knowledge. Many people get most of their information online, and they get to that information through platforms like Google and Facebook. Thus, the ability to hypernudge their users, many of whom

---

25. Karen Yeung, "'Hypernudge': Big Data as a Mode of Regulation by Design," *Information, Communication & Society* 20 (2017): 118–136.
26. I will use Google and Facebook to illustrate these points, but the very same points apply mutatis mutandis to other platforms, like TikTok and X.
27. Yeung, "Hypernudge," 121.

get most of their information from these sources, gives Google and Facebook an enormous amount of power over the information that people receive. This, in itself, does not undermine our ability to get knowledge through Google and Facebook. If those firms hypernudge in ways that lead people to form true beliefs, at least as often as they would through other means, then Google and Facebook are at least as reliable sources of knowledge as people would otherwise use. However, there is a potential threat to knowledge here. The source of the threat is aptly described by Karen Yeung:

> Hypernudging entails the use of "soft" power . . . but it is extraordinarily strong. And where power lies, there also lies the potential for overreaching, exploitation and abuse. . . . the massive power asymmetry between global digital service providers, particularly Google and Facebook, and individual service users cannot be ignored, especially given that the scale of corporate economic surveillance via Big Data tracking dwarfs the surveillance conducted by national intelligence agencies. . . . a single algorithmic hypernudge initiated by Facebook can directly affect millions of users simultaneously.[28]

Big Data gives firms like Google and Facebook the power to shape the opinions of millions of people. To see what that looks like, consider the following experiments. On November 2, 2010, Facebook conducted an experiment on sixty million people. The goal of the experiment was to find out if Facebook could get people to vote in an election when they otherwise would not have voted. To find out the answer,

> millions of Facebook users were shown a graphic within their news feeds with a link to find their polling place, a button to click to say that they'd voted, and the profile pictures of up to six of their friends who had indicated they'd already voted. Other users weren't shown the graphic. Then, in an awesome feat of

---

28. Yeung, "Hypernudge," 122.

data-crunching, the researchers cross-referenced everyone's name with the day's actual voting records from precincts across the country. That way they could see if, on average, someone in the group receiving the voting prompt was more likely to mark a ballot than someone with an untouched news feed.[29]

The answer was yes. Roughly 340,000 people turned out to vote in the 2010 congressional elections because they received this nudge from Facebook.[30]

This shows that Big Data can influence people's actions. Another experiment illustrates exactly how Big Data can influence people—by manipulating their emotions. In January 2012, Facebook conducted another experiment.

> The experiment manipulated the extent to which people (689,000 of them) were exposed to emotional expressions in their News Feed. This tested whether exposure to emotions led people to change their own posting behaviors, in particular whether exposure to emotional content led people to post content that was consistent with the exposure—thereby testing whether exposure to verbal affective expressions leads to similar verbal expressions, a form of emotional contagion. . . . Two parallel experiments were conducted for positive and negative emotion: One in which exposure to friends' positive emotional content in their News Feed was reduced, and one in which exposure to negative emotional content in their News Feed was reduced. . . . It is important to note that this content was always available by viewing a friend's content directly by going to that friend's "wall" or "timeline," rather than via the News

---

29. Jonathan Zittrain, "Engineering an Election: Digital Gerrymandering Poses a Threat to Democracy," *Harvard Law Review* 127, no. 8 (2014): 335.
30. Zoe Corbyn, "Facebook Experiment Boosts US Voter Turnout," *Nature*, September 12, 2012.

Feed. Further, the omitted content may have appeared on prior or subsequent views of the News Feed.[31]

This experiment was conducted for one week, from January 11 to January 18, 2012. The results were striking. When Facebook users were exposed to fewer positive posts in their News Feed, their own posts became less positive and more negative. And when they were exposed to fewer negative posts in their News Feed, their own posts became less negative and more positive. As the researchers put it, this intervention in their News Feed caused a kind of "emotional contagion," in which Facebook could manipulate their user's positive and negative emotions.[32]

These experiments show that Big Data can influence people's actions and emotions. The final set of experiments shows that Big Data can also influence people's beliefs and preferences. In 2015, Robert Epstein and Ronald Robertson published the results of five experiments they conducted to determine the effects of search engine manipulation on voters' beliefs and preferences. In these experiments,

> subjects were asked for their opinions and voting preferences both before and after they were allowed to conduct research on candidates using a mock search engine we had created for this purpose. Subjects were randomly assigned to groups in which the search results they were shown were biased in favor of one candidate or another, or, in a control condition, in favor of neither candidate.[33]

Epstein and Robertson first conducted three experiments in the lab, with 102 people in each experiment. In all three of these experiments,

---

31. A. D. I. Kramer, J. E. Guilloy, and J. T. Hancock, "Experimental Evidence of Massive-Scale Emotional Contagion through Social Networks," *Proceedings of the National Academy of Sciences* 11 (2014): 8788–8790.
32. Kramer, Guilloy, and Hancock, "Experimental Evidence."
33. Robert Epstein and Ronald E. Robertson, "The Search Engine Manipulation Effect (SEME) and Its Possible Impact on the Outcome of Elections," *PNAS* 112 (2015): E 4512–4521.

the result was the same: "Following the Web research, all candidate ratings in the bias groups shifted in the predicted directions compared with candidate ratings in the control group."[34] After conducting these experiments in the lab, Epstein and Robertson conducted a large-scale, online replication of the experiment. They used a sample of 2,100 people taken from all fifty states. In this large replication of the experiment, the result was the same. After doing Web research on the manipulated search engine, all the candidate ratings in the bias groups shifted in the predicted directions compared with candidate ratings in the control group.[35] Finally, Epstein and Robertson conducted one more experiment, this time with real voters in an actual election. They conducted the same experiment with undecided voters in India prior to the election there. Once again, they got the same result. Voters who did research on the biased search engine changed their beliefs and preferences in favor of the relevant candidates. Epstein and Robertson conclude that manipulated search engines can change the beliefs and preferences of voters.

How does this pose a threat to human knowledge? It appears that Big Data has the power to manipulate our actions, our emotions, and our beliefs. This raises two questions. First, are there situations in which Google or Facebook *would* manipulate our beliefs? Second, how likely is it that such a situation will actually occur? It is important to remember that Google and Facebook have goals distinct from the goal of causing people to have true beliefs. These goals include things like marketing their brand and making a profit. I will refer to these goals as their *commercial goals*. When Google and Facebook pursue their commercial goals, they can do it in a way that also causes people to have true beliefs. In fact, sometimes, an activity that causes people to have true beliefs will also be the best way for them to achieve their commercial goals. If customers get accurate information from Google and Facebook, then that will motivate them to use them more, which will help Google and Facebook achieve their commercial goals. In that situation, Google and Facebook will perform actions, like hypernudging, in a way that

---

34. Epstein and Robertson, "The Search Engine Manipulation Effect," 4514.
35. Epstein and Robertson, "The Search Engine Manipulation Effect," 4515.

produces knowledge. However, it is easy to imagine situations in which the commercial goals of Google and Facebook would *not* be best served by causing customers to form true beliefs. Imagine a situation in which there are facts that, if known, would severely damage both of these brands. If many people came to recognize these facts, then Google and Facebook would lose the bulk of their market share. Further, suppose that, through hypernudging, Google and Facebook could direct their users to websites that cast doubt on these facts and thereby prevent the loss of their market share. If they were to do this, then tens of millions of people would be deprived of the knowledge of these facts.

Perhaps it is unlikely that either Google or Facebook would attempt such a plan. However, there are other ways in which the data collected by Google and Facebook can be gathered and used to misinform people. After all, it would only take one whistleblower to expose the whole enterprise. In 2018, Christopher Wylie, a former employee of Cambridge Analytica, revealed that his former employer had illicitly gathered the personal data of millions of Facebook users and used that data to interfere in multiple political campaigns.[36] Cambridge Analytica hired Aleksandr Kogan, a data scientist at Cambridge University, to develop an app that would be used, with consent, by Facebook users. However, Facebook allowed the app to collect personal data from the Facebook friends of these users as well, without their consent. Kogan told Facebook that the data would be used for academic purposes. However, Cambridge Analytica proceeded to use the data to interfere in political campaigns in multifarious ways. This illustrates one way malevolent actors have acquired data from large platforms and used it for political purposes. However, this case also shows the difficulty of sustaining such a project for very long. It only took one whistleblower, Christopher Wylie, to expose the entire operation.

Unfortunately, such diabolical plans are not the only way, or even the principal way that Google and Facebook threaten human

---

36. Rosalie Chan, "The Cambridge Analytica Whistleblower Explains How the Firm Used Facebook Data to Sway Elections," *Business Insider*, October 5, 2019.

knowledge. The deeper threat that they pose to human knowledge lies in a different direction. For any knowable fact, Google and Facebook can either nudge people *toward* knowledge of that fact or they can nudge people *away* from knowledge of that fact. For any given fact, what will determine whether Facebook or Google nudge people toward knowledge of that fact or nudge people away from knowledge of that fact? If knowledge of this fact will promote Google and Facebook's commercial interests, then their algorithms will nudge people toward knowledge of this fact. However, if knowledge of this fact is detrimental to their commercial interests, then they will nudge people away from knowledge of this fact. It is important to understand that this need not be conscious or deliberate. Rather, it is simply a side effect of their commercial goals. People will be nudged toward knowledge when, and only when, there is profit to be made by nudging them in that direction.

In an age in which so many people get their knowledge from these sources, the extent of our knowledge is increasingly held hostage to commercial interests. We acquire all and only the knowledge that it is profitable for someone to share with us. This is not entirely new, of course. Even newspapers had to sell advertisements in order to make a profit. However, one thing has changed. A small number of firms now control the flow of an enormous quantity of information to a very large number of people. Consequently, the commercial interests of these particular firms threaten to restrict the dissemination of knowledge to many people to what is profitable for them to share. The problem is not just that these firms could disseminate misinformation. Rather, the problem is that they will tend to *exclude* knowledge that does not generate a profit, even if it is important knowledge, for other human purposes. One possible solution to this problem is for nations to invest in sources of information that are not held hostage to commercial interests. These nonprofit sources of knowledge will at least ensure that *some* sources of information are not driven by profit margins.

This concludes our discussion of propaganda, nudges, and Big Data. In summary, propaganda threatens human knowledge for two reasons. First, forming a belief by believing propaganda could easily lead to a false belief. Thus, even when an item of propaganda happens to be true, believing it does not constitute knowledge. Second, if propaganda is widespread in a society, then it is more difficult for people to get knowledge from reliable sources. That is because the existence of widespread propaganda in a society gives a person a defeater for any belief that, for all they know, might have come from propaganda. By contrast with propaganda, nudging can transmit knowledge. If the source of a nudge has true beliefs and reliably transmits those true beliefs, then nudges can transmit knowledge. That is because default options communicate recommendations to people. These recommendations are a kind of testimony, and so they can transmit knowledge in much the same way as testimony transmits knowledge. Finally, Big Data poses a significant threat to human knowledge. This is not just due to the possibility of misinformation but because Big Data restricts the dissemination of knowledge to what is profitable to share.

Study Questions

1. Suppose that a political action committee (PAC) vehemently opposes a certain political candidate. They hire investigators to research the candidate, and they discover that the candidate was once convicted of taking bribes. The PAC then creates an advertisement that states this fact and describes the candidate as "corrupt." Is this propaganda? Explain your answer.
2. If a person acquires a true belief by believing propaganda, then it seems they still do not *know* that their belief is true. Why not? What is it about propaganda that prevents the acquisition of knowledge?
3. Suppose that Sarah lives in a society full of propaganda, and she is aware of this fact. It just so happens that Sarah's local news outlet is generally reliable. Does the existence of propaganda in Sarah's society threaten her ability to get knowledge from this reliable news outlet? Explain your answer.
4. What is "nudging"? Give an example—either hypothetical or real—to illustrate nudging. Use this example to explain how nudging is different from propaganda.
5. What is Big Data, and how does it shape our beliefs and actions? Give an example, either hypothetical or real, to illustrate Big Data and how it influences us.

For Further Reading

For a deep dive into the nature of propaganda, see Randal Marlin's *Propaganda and the Ethics of Persuasion*, 2nd ed. (Peterborough, ON: Broadview Press, 2013). For an alternative view of propaganda, which sees it as essentially connected to harmful political ideology, see Jason Stanley's *How Propaganda Works* (Princeton, NJ: Princeton University Press, 2015). For an introduction to the concept of nudging and a defense of using it to improve behavior, see Richard Thaler and Cass Sunstein's book, *Nudge* (London: Penguin Books, 2008). For an excellent discussion of the epistemology of Internet technologies, see

Boaz Miller and Isaac Record, "Justified Belief in a Digital Age: On the Epistemic Implications of Secret Internet Technologies," *Episteme* 10 (2013): 117–134. For an approach to Big Data that sees it as less threatening, see Thomas Christiano's essay "Algorithms, Manipulation, and Democracy," *Canadian Journal of Philosophy* 52 (2022): 109–124. For a discussion of the problem of fake news, see Sanford Goldberg, "Fake News and Epistemic Rot; or, Why We Are All in This Together," in *The Epistemology of Fake News*, ed. Sven Bernecker, Amy K. Flowerree, and Thomas Grundmann (New York: Oxford University Press, 2021). For reasons to doubt that fake news plays a large role in shaping people's beliefs, see Daniel Williams, "The Fake News about Fake News, *Boston Review*, June 7, 2023.

CHAPTER SEVEN

Artificial Intelligence and Human Understanding

In March 2016, the computer program AlphaGo defeated the world champion Go player, Lee Sedol, a South Korean professional who had won eighteen world titles. Until that time, no computer had ever beaten a professional Go player, and many people would have deemed it impossible. Go is a strategy game in which two players take turns placing stones on a 19 × 19 grid. The goal of the game is to capture territory by surrounding it with your stones and prevent your opponent from capturing territory in the same way. While the rules of Go are quite simple, the game is enormously complex. There are 10^{170} possible positions in Go, and the strategies that professional players use cannot be reduced to a set of rules that can be programmed into a computer. Or so it seemed.

The most striking fact about AlphaGo's victory over the champion was how it achieved that victory. According to both its programmers and the AlphaGo community, AlphaGo played *creatively*. It introduced novel strategies that defied conventional wisdom. Thus, as Lee Sedol put it, "What surprised me the most was that AlphaGo showed us that moves humans may have thought are creative, were actually conventional."[1] According to Lucas Baker and Fan Hui, "AlphaGo's strategy embodies a spirit of flexibility and open-mindedness: a lack of preconceptions that allows it to find the most effective line of play."[2] This sort of thinking—*flexible*,

---

1. *AlphaGo*, directed by G. Kohs (United States: Reel as Dirt, 2017).
2. L. Baker and F. Hui, "Innovations of AlphaGo," Google DeepMind (blog), April 10, 2017, https://deepmind.com/blog/innovations-alphago/.

open-minded, creative—is precisely what many people would have deemed impossible for a computer. Nevertheless, that is precisely what AlphaGo appeared to do. Reflecting on the accomplishments of AlphaGo, the co-founder of DeepMind, Demis Hassabis, imagined something even greater. According to Hassabis, "These moments of algorithmic inspiration give us a glimpse of why AI could be so beneficial for science: the possibility of machine-aided scientific discovery."[3] Just five years later, Hassabis's lofty aspirations would come to fruition.

In July 2021, researchers used another DeepMind computer program, AlphaFold, to predict the structures of 350,000 proteins.[4] A protein molecule comprises a long chain of amino acids in which peptide bonds connect each amino acid to those beside it. Each specific type of protein is composed of a unique sequence of amino acids, and the amino acids in this sequence, together with the bonds between them, determine exactly how the amino acids fold into a specific, three-dimensional structure. That resulting structure determines many of the important properties of the whole protein molecule.[5] For decades, biologists have struggled to determine the structure of protein molecules based on the sequence of amino acids that compose them, but with little success. AlphaFold appears to have solved that problem. Moreover, the protein structures predicted by AlphaFold included most of the proteins produced by the human body. That discovery will be immensely useful to scientists searching for the cures to many human diseases. Commenting on the success of AlphaFold, Demi Hassabis said:

---

3. D. Hassabis, "The Mind in the Machine: Demis Hassabis on Artificial Intelligence," *The Financial Times*, April 22, 2017.
4. Paul Rincon, "AI Breakthrough Could Spark Medical Revolution," BBC News, July 22, 2021, https://www.bbc.com/news/science-environment-57929095.
5. B. Alberts, A. Johnson, J. Lewis, M. Raff, K. Roberts, and P. Walters, "The Shape and Structure of Proteins," in *Molecular Biology of the Cell*, 4th ed. (New York: Garland Science, 2002).

We believe this work represents the most significant contribution AI has made to advancing the state of scientific knowledge to date. And I think it's a great illustration and example of the kind of benefits that AI can bring to society.[6]

It appears that AI is already achieving Hassabis's aspiration.

There are also promising applications of AI in the practice of medicine. For example, there is evidence that AI might be good at interpreting medical images. In one study, a resident without expertise in radiology used an AI program to interpret chest radiology images. The resulting performance values were comparable to that of a board-certified radiologist.[7] If this succeeds, then it would enable general practitioners, and perhaps even physician assistants and nurse practitioners, to interpret medical images without the help of a specialist in the area. That could reduce medical testing costs that are otherwise very expensive.

The success of AI in each of these areas, as well as others, raises important questions about the relationship between artificial intelligence and human knowledge. How will AI affect human knowledge? Obviously, it has the potential to increase human knowledge. How much can it increase our knowledge? Will it eventually *replace* human knowledge? Or are there significant limitations on what AI can do for us? These are some of the questions that we will explore in this chapter. To focus our discussion, we will begin with this question: *Can AI help us make scientific progress?* As the CEO of DeepMind, Demis Hassabis, has often said, one of the principal aims of developing AI is to help us make progress in science. Can AI help us to achieve that? To answer that question, we need to understand what constitutes scientific progress.

What is scientific progress? When does a development in science constitute progress? According to one account, scientific progress

---

6. Rincon, "AI Breakthrough Could Spark Medical Revolution."
7. Pranav Rajpurkar and Matthew Lundgren, "The Current and Future States of AI Interpretation of Medical Images," *New England Journal of Medicine* 388 (2023): 1981–1990.

occurs whenever we gain more knowledge.[8] The goal of science is knowledge. Therefore, any increase in knowledge through science is an achievement of the goal of science. Progress is just achieving your goals. Therefore, scientific progress occurs whenever we gain more knowledge through science. Call this theory the *Epistemic Theory of Scientific Progress*. To illustrate the Epistemic Theory, consider a clear case of scientific progress—the development of the *Germ Theory of Disease*. In the 1820s, the Italian scientist Agostino Bassi set out to find the cause of the disease that was killing silkworms in Italy.[9] For the first eight years, he tried to prove the popular assumption that the disease developed spontaneously from something in the environment, such as the food or the atmosphere. However, through continued observation and experimentation, Bassi formulated a novel hypothesis—he concluded that the cause of the disease was a living agent, visible to the naked eye as a powdery substance on the silkworms. In 1834, a commission at the University of Pavia concurred with Bassi. That powdery substance turned out to be a microscopic fungus, which was subsequently named, in his honor, *Beauvaria bassiana*. In 1844, Bassi suggested that not only animal diseases but also human diseases are caused by living microorganisms. Thus, the Germ Theory of Disease was born. This was a clear case of scientific progress. Later scientists, like Louis Pasteur, built on Bassi's work to complete the theory as we have it today.

Bassi's discovery—that living microorganisms cause diseases—was a significant gain in knowledge. We know something that we did not know before. This comports well with the Epistemic Theory of Scientific Progress. If scientific progress consists in gaining more knowledge, then Bassi's discovery is a case of scientific progress. So far, so good. However, on further reflection, we can see that Bassi's discovery produced *more* than just an increase in knowledge. Before Bassi, one of the features of disease that puzzled people was the fact

---

8. This answer is developed and defended by Alexander Bird in "What is Scientific Progress?," *Nous* 41 (2007): 64–89.
9. J. R. Porter, "Agostino Bassi Bicentennial (1773–1973)," *Bacteriological Reviews* 37 (1973): 284–288.

that many diseases are *contagious*. People wondered: Why do diseases move from animal to animal and from person to person? One of the great achievements of the Germ Theory of Disease was that it *explained why* these diseases are contagious. If a disease is caused by a microscopic living organism, then if these organisms move from person to person, the disease will also move from person to person. In this way, the Germ Theory of Disease not only increased our *knowledge*, it also increased our *understanding*.

This brings us a to another distinct account of the nature of scientific progress. According to this account, not just any increase in knowledge constitutes scientific progress. Rather, scientific progress consists of an increase in *understanding*. On this account, the goal of science is not just to gain knowledge of new facts but to *understand why* those facts obtain. Following Finnur Dellsen, we will call this the *Noetic Theory of Scientific Progress*.[10] To understand the difference between the Epistemic and Noetic Theories, we need to understand the difference between knowledge and understanding. It is possible to know a fact without understanding why that fact obtains. Imagine a young student in a science lab who measures the volume, temperature, and pressure of a gas. Imagine that the volume of the container of gas is reduced while the temperature remains the same. The student then measures the volume, temperature, and pressure again. The student observes that the pressure of the gas is now greater. Even if the student knows these values, they might not understand *why* the value of the pressure changed from the first measurement to the second. Thus, knowing this fact—that the pressure changed from the first measurement to the second—is not the same as understanding why that fact obtains.

What is the difference between knowing a fact and understanding it? If a person understands a fact, then they are able to *explain* that fact, which means that they grasp at least one correct explanation of

---

10. See Finnur Dellsen, "Scientific Progress: Knowledge versus Understanding," *Studies in History and Philosophy of Science* 56 (April 2016): 72–83.

that fact.[11] Thus, understanding a fact requires more than just knowing it because understanding involves explanation. Suppose that the young student in the example above learns *Boyle's Law*, which says that the product of the volume and pressure of a fixed quantity of a gas is constant, given temperature. Suppose that the student then applies this law to their measurements and realizes that when the volume of a container of gas is reduced, and the temperature of the gas remains the same, Boyle's Law requires that the pressure of the gas increase. Using Boyle's Law, the student can now explain *why* the pressure of the gas increased. She has progressed from merely knowing this fact to understanding it. According to the noetic theory of scientific progress, scientific progress consists in gaining more understanding, not just more knowledge. Since understanding consists in grasping an explanation, this implies that scientific progress consists in being able to explain more facts. To understand what this entails, we need to understand the nature of scientific explanation.

There is a long-standing debate in the philosophy of science over the nature of scientific explanation, and several different theories have been proposed. For present purposes, I will focus on one specific feature of scientific explanations: their *generality*. Science explains particular facts and events by showing that they are instances of a general pattern. For example, science often explains a particular event by showing that it is an instance of a general law of nature. In the example of the young student in the lab, the increase in the pressure of the gas is explained by showing that it is an instance of Boyle's Law, which governs all gasses. Moreover, many other events involving the volume, temperature, and pressure of particular gasses can be explained in the very same way—by showing that all of these events are instances of the very same general law of nature. By showing that all of these events are instances of the same law, we *simplify* and *unify* our understanding of the world. That is the hallmark of a good scientific explanation. That is why many of our best theories in the sciences can be stated in terms of laws of nature—laws of physics, chemistry,

---

11. See Michael Strevens, "No Understanding without Explanation," *Studies in History and Philosophy of Science* 44 (2013): 510–515.

and biology, for example. Knowing these laws of nature enables us to see many distinct events as instances of the same general patterns.[12]

However, one might wonder if all good scientific explanations fit this model. Some scientific explanations simply identify the *cause* of an event. In some of these cases, it is unclear whether the explanation involves any general laws of nature. For example, when Agostino Bassi discovered that microscopic living organisms caused contagious diseases, the content of his discovery was not exactly a general law of nature. Rather, he discovered the cause of many particular events. Many scientific explanations seem to work in this way. Events stand in multiple relations of cause and effect with other events. Together, all the events in the universe form a *causal nexus*, in which each event is related to other events as either cause or effect. Some scientific explanations, like the Germ Theory of Disease, *locate* some events in that causal nexus of events. These explanations describe the causes and/or effects of some events.[13]

However, on closer inspection, even this kind of explanation involves generality. When a scientific explanation identifies the cause of some event, it always identifies that cause as an instance of a certain *kind* of thing. For instance, when Bassi first proposed the Germ Theory of Disease, he said that the cause of the silkworms' disease was an *organism*. An organism is a general kind of thing. Moreover, this kind or category—*organism*—is an essential part of the Germ Theory of Disease. It explained how and why diseases spread from organism to organism. Furthermore, it automatically suggested a possible way to fight disease—by killing the organisms that cause it. Thus, identifying

---

12. This way of understanding scientific explanation is captured in two prominent theories of scientific explanation—Carl Hempel's *Covering Law Model of Explanation* and Philip Kitcher's *Unification Theory of Explanation*. See Hempel, *Aspects of Scientific Explanation and Other Essays in the Philosophy of Science* (New York: Free Press, 1965); and Kitcher, "Explanatory Unification and the Causal Structure of the World," in *Scientific Explanation*, ed. Philip Kitcher and Wesley Salmon (Minneapolis: University of Minnesota Press, 1989), 410–505.

13. This is Wesley Salmon's theory of scientific explanation. See Salmon, *Scientific Explanation and the Causal Structure of the World* (Princeton, NJ: Princeton University Press, 1984).

the cause of disease as something that belonged to this general category—*organism*—was an important part of this explanation.

The relevance of some general kind or category to a causal explanation is not an accident. Whenever one event causes another event, the cause produces the effect *in virtue of being an event of a certain kind*. To see this, consider again the case of the young student in the lab. Suppose that the student reduces the volume of the gas by moving the gas from a large, round metal container to a small, square plastic container. Then the student measures the pressure of the gas again and sees that the pressure has increased. The event that caused this change in pressure—moving the gas—is an instance of many different kinds. It is an instance of *moving a gas from a metal container to a plastic container*. It is also an instance of *moving a gas from a round container to a plastic container*. However, if the student thinks that either of these general kinds is relevant to the pressure of the gas, then they will not have identified the real cause of the change in pressure. The relocation of the gas from one container to another caused the increase in pressure in virtue of the fact that the relocation of the gas was an instance of *reducing the volume* of the gas. It was only in virtue of belonging to *that* general kind of event—reducing volume—that the movement of the gas caused the increase in pressure. This illustrates a general principle—whenever one event causes another event, the cause produces the effect in virtue of the fact that the cause belongs to a certain general kind of event. The fact that the cause belongs to that particular kind is the reason why the cause produces the effect.[14]

Since causes produce their effects in virtue of belonging to a general kind or category, explaining an event by identifying its cause involves identifying the cause as something that belongs to a certain kind or category. Moreover, grasping the relevant kind or category of the cause is an essential part of understanding why the cause produces the effect. That understanding also makes it possible for us to design interventions that prevent the effect, as in the cause of diseases that

---

14. Some philosophers believe that there are exceptions to this rule. For present purposes, it will suffice to say that this is true in the majority of cases.

are caused by bacteria. In summary, then, scientific explanations all involve generality. A scientific explanation identifies an event as a particular instance of a general pattern. Even when we explain an event by identifying its cause, we identify the cause as something that belongs to some general kind or category, and in that way, we identify the cause as a particular instance of a general pattern. Not long after Bassi identified the cause of the silkworms' disease as an organism, he proposed that microscopic organisms also caused human diseases. He was able to make that inference precisely because he could see the silkworms' disease as an instance of a general pattern—microscopic organisms cause disease. His ability to see particular events as instances of general patterns in nature made his scientific explanation possible.

Now return to the question at hand. Can AI help us to make scientific progress? Suppose that scientific progress consists in greater understanding, and that greater understanding consists in explaining more facts. Finally, suppose that scientific explanations involve generality—seeing particular facts and events as instances of general patterns. Then, if AI can see particular facts and events as instances of general patterns in the relevant way, then AI can help us to make scientific progress. Thus, the relevant question is this: Can AI classify particular facts and events as instances of general patterns, in the same way that is involved in good scientific explanations? For those who are familiar with recent advances in AI, it might seem that the answer is clearly yes. However, on closer inspection, that is not obvious. In 1966, Joseph Weizenbaum observed that machines are "often sufficient to dazzle even the most experienced observer," but then, when their "inner workings are explained in language sufficiently plain to induce understanding, the magic crumbles away."[15] As we will see, Weizenbaum's observation might be as apt today as it was in 1966.

One might think that AI is clearly able to see particular events as instances of general patterns. How else could a program like AlphaGo beat the world champion at a game like Go? In order to determine

---

15. Quoted by Casey Fiesler in "AI's Biggest Challenges Are Still Unsolved," *Scientific American*, January 4, 2024.

if a program like AlphaGo could help us make progress in science, we need to understand how AlphaGo works.[16] AlphaGo trained on 28.4 million board positions and moves from 160,000 games played by professional players. Then it played 30 million games against other AI, each of which had trained on 100 million games or more. The network used those games to record the probability of any particular board state leading to a win.[17] Then, when AlphaGo plays a game, it uses a Monte Carlo tree search to simulate possible sequences of play. Figuratively speaking, a search tree is a map of a sequence of possible positions and moves in a game. As Marta Halina explains,

> the Monte Carlo tree search used in AlphaGo simulates games in order to determine the value of a move, given a particular board position. The simulation proceeds by first selecting a particular path and adding one or more valid moves to that path. One of these moves is then selected. . . .[18]

In this way, AlphaGo *simulates* possible sequences of play and then chooses the move with the highest probability of leading to a board state that is likely to lead to a win. As Halina argues, this simulation is analogous to the mental planning that often underlies human creativity. Prior to acting, we imagine how things might go. We simulate possible sequences of events in our minds, enabling us to identify novel solutions to problems. AlphaGo does something very similar when it uses the Monte Carlo tree search to simulate possible sequences of moves before choosing a move. In this way, AlphaGo's process is actually quite similar to one of the psychological processes involved in human creativity.

However, another type of process often underlies human creativity, which is absent from AlphaGo, and that is *domain-general understanding*. Domain-general understanding is the ability to reason about

---

16. The following summary is based on Marta Halina's explanation in "Insightful Artificial Intelligence," *Mind and Language* 36 (2021): 187–329.
17. Halina, "Insightful Artificial Intelligence," 322.
18. Halina, "Insightful Artificial Intelligence," 323.

objects in terms of their domain-general properties. Domain-general properties are properties that are causally and explanatorily relevant in many different domains. For example, the domain-relevant properties of physical things would include properties like weight, solidity, rigidity, and malleability. These properties of physical objects are causally and explanatorily relevant across multiple domains. Domain-general understanding is the ability to grasp this fact and reason about physical objects in terms of these domain-general properties. Moreover, this ability enables us to find novel solutions to problems. A simple example will illustrate. Suppose I want to hold my garage door open halfway in order to move some things out of the garage quickly. I see my large recycling bin standing beside the garage, so I place the bin underneath the garage door to hold it up temporarily. Of course, a recycling bin was not designed to be used in this way. However, by grasping the *solidity* of the recycling bin, I can infer that it will serve this purpose, even though it was not designed for it. In doing so, I have used my domain-general understanding of the solidity of a physical object to solve a problem. My understanding of solidity, as a property that remains constant across various uses of an object, enabled me to use the recycling bin in a novel way. That is the advantage of domain-general understanding.

AlphaGo does not do that. As Marta Halina explains,

> computer programs like AlphaGo are not creative in the sense of having the capacity to solve novel problems through a domain-general understanding of the world. They cannot learn about the properties and affordances of objects in one domain and proceed to abstract away from the contingencies and idiosyncrasies of that domain in order to solve problems in a new context.[19]

In its present state, AI is incapable of domain-general understanding. It cannot grasp the most general properties of objects in the way that is required to apply that understanding across multiple domains. Thus, when you ask Siri to add a liter of books to your shopping list,

---

19. Halina, "Insightful Artificial Intelligence," 326.

it does not hesitate to do so and confirm, "One liter of books added to your shopping list."[20] Siri does not understand the concepts *liter* and *book* in a domain-general way, and thus, Siri does not grasp the fact that these two concepts do not fit together in this way. In its present state, that is a general limitation on all AI programs. They lack domain-general understanding.

But then, how did AlphaFold predict 350,000 protein structures? Biologists working for decades were unable to do this. AlphaFold succeeded where they failed. How was that possible when AlphaFold lacks domain-general understanding? As with AlphaGo, AlphaFold begins with an enormous amount of data. More precisely, it begins with "three vast databases of experimentally determined DNA-to-protein mapping data."[21] It then uses that data to make predictions about the structures of other proteins. However, what AlphaFold does *not* provide is any explanation of *why* these proteins have the structure they do. Philip Ball explains:

> Since the pioneering work of Christian Anfinsen in the 1950s, it has been known that unraveled (denatured) protein molecules may regain their "native" conformation spontaneously, implying that the peptide sequence alone encodes the rules for correct folding. The challenge was to find those rules and predict the folding path. . . . AlphaFold has not done that. It says nothing about the mechanism of folding, but just predicts the structure using standard machine learning. It finds correlations between sequence and structure by being trained on the 170,000 or so known structures in the Protein Data Base: the algorithm doesn't so much solve the protein-folding problem as evade it. How it "reasons" from sequence to structure remains a black box.[22]

---

20. The example is due to J. Michael Bishop, "Artificial Intelligence Is Stupid and Causal Reasoning Will Not Fix It," *Frontiers in Psychology* 11 (2021).
21. Terry B. Bollinger, "Why AlphaFold Is Not Like AlphaGo," *Academia Letters* (2021): 1.
22. Phillip Ball, "Behind the Screens of AlphaFold," *Chemistry World*, December 9, 2020.

AlphaFold predicts how proteins will fold, but it does not *explain why* the proteins fold as they do. Since it does not give us an explanation of why proteins fold in the way they do, it does not increase our understanding. It increases our knowledge, to be sure, but not our understanding. If scientific progress consists in gaining new understanding, then the results of AlphaFold do not constitute scientific progress. Of course, the results of AlphaFold might help *us* to achieve more scientific progress, but that will be the result of what we do with these results, not the results alone.

Why doesn't AlphaFold provide an explanation of the folding of proteins? Arguably, it is because AlphaFold is not capable of the sort of domain-general understanding that is required for scientific explanation. That would also explain some of the apparent limitations of using AI programs to interpret medical images. Despite the success of such programs, there is evidence that they have some significant limitations. Studies have found that the performance of these AI programs worsens when they are applied to patients who differ from those in the AI's database. This is known as *dataset shift*.[23] This suggests that these AI programs struggle when they have to apply the information contained in their dataset to novel situations. This is exactly what we should expect if these programs are incapable of domain-general understanding. As Marta Halina points out, "Domain-general insightful problem-solving is powerful because it allows one to reason and intervene in the world effectively without having encountered that particular part of the world before."[24] In its present state of development, that is what AI cannot do for us. Even if AI cannot give us understanding, it can certainly give us knowledge. Thanks to AlphaFold, we now know the structures of many proteins we did not know before. Insofar as it is reliable, AI can give us knowledge in the same way a good thermometer can tell us the temperature. Moreover, there might be another way—a more fundamental way—in which AI can extend our knowledge. Consider the following

---

23. Rajpurkar and Lungren, "The Current and Future States of AI Interpretation," 1984.
24. Halina, "Insightful Artificial Intelligence," 327.

example, due to David Chalmers and Andy Clark.[25] The example involves three people—Inga, Mitzi, and Otto. Inga hears about an exhibition at the Museum of Modern Art and wants to go see it. Inga thinks for a moment, and she recalls that the museum is on 53rd Street, so she heads for 53rd Street. Now imagine Mitzi. Mitzi also hears about the exhibition, and she would also like to go and see it. However, Mitzi suffers from Alzheimer's. In order to cope with her Alzheimer's, Mitzi had a computer chip planted in her brain, which receives information from her laptop computer. On her laptop, Mitzi has stored lots of information that she might need at some point. Whenever she needs some information, Mitzi activates the chip in her brain, and it transmits the information from her laptop to her brain. On this occasion, Mitzi activates the chip in her brain, and it tells her that the Museum of Modern Art is on 53rd Street, so she heads to 53rd Street. It seems that both Inga and Mitzi *know where the museum is*. The only difference is that they store this information in different ways. Inga stores the information in a part of her brain, whereas Mitzi stores the information on her laptop, but they can both access the information readily. They both know where the museum is.

Finally, consider the case of Otto. In order to cope with his Alzheimer's, Otto carries a little notebook around with him, in which he has written information that he might need at some point. Whenever he needs some information, Otto looks in his notebook, where he finds the information. On this occasion, Otto looks in his notebook, and it tells him that the Museum of Modern Art is on 53rd Street, so he heads to 53rd Street. If Mitzi knows where the museum is because she can use the chip in her brain to access that information, then it seems that Otto also knows where the museum is since he can also access that information by looking in his notebook. Again, the only difference is that they store this information in different ways. Mitzi stores the information on her laptop, whereas Otto stores the information in his notebook, but they can both access the information.

---

25. A. Clark and D. Chalmers, "The Extended Mind," *Analysis* 58 (1998): 7–19. Clark and Chalmers discuss two people in their example. In what follows I have added a third character.

Thus, they both know where the museum is. The conclusion of the argument is that a person's knowledge need not be stored in their brain. If a person has information stored on a laptop or in a notebook, and they can access that information readily, then that information is part of what they know, just as if it were stored in their brain.

This view is called *The Extended Mind Thesis*. According to the Extended Mind Thesis, our minds sometimes extend outside our bodies and brains to include objects outside us. In the case of Otto, his mind extends to his notebook. If the Extended Mind Thesis is correct, then this opens up the possibility that AI will increase our knowledge in a very fundamental way—by extending our minds in such a way as to include the workings of the AI itself.

Is the Extended Mind Thesis correct? Clark and Chalmers argue that it is. Their argument is based on *The Parity Thesis*, which says that if something functions exactly like knowledge, then it *is* knowledge. The information in Otto's notebook functions exactly like the information in Inga's brain. Both Otto and Inga can access this information readily. Since Otto always carries his notebook with him, he can access the notebook just as easily as Inga can access her memories. Of course, it is possible that Otto loses his notebook, but it is also possible that Inga's memory will fail her. We can easily imagine that Otto's notebook is just as reliable as Inga's memory. Then, according to the Parity Thesis, if Inga knows where the museum is, then Otto also knows where the museum is since Inga's memory and Otto's notebook function in exactly the same way. The only difference between them is that Otto's knowledge is contained in his notebook, whereas Inga's knowledge is contained in her brain. Nonetheless, they both possess knowledge.

If that is correct, then it seems AI could extend our knowledge to include information that is located outside our brains, in much the same way that Otto's notebook extends his knowledge to include information that is outside his brain.[26] Let us suppose, for the sake of

---

26. Neil Levy defends this thesis in "Neuroethics and the Extended Mind," in *Oxford Handbook of Neuroethics*, ed. B. Sahakian and J. Illes (Oxford: Oxford University Press, 2011), 285–294.

argument, this is possible. Some would say that not just any information stored online or generated by an AI will extend our own knowledge. In the case of Otto's notebook, there is a relation of *mutual dependence* between Otto and his notebook. The information in Otto's notebook is information that he, himself, put there at some point in time. Thus, the information in Otto's notebook actually depends on Otto himself. Then, at a later time, Otto depends on the notebook. The information in the notebook is not produced in a way that is completely independent of Otto. That is an important part of the example.

Now imagine the following example. Suppose that a small child has access to the Internet and the ability to do a simple Google Search. Does that child, just by having the ability to do a Google Search, know everything that is stored somewhere on the Internet and searchable through Google? Some would say, "No, the child does not know something just because they can access it through a Google Search." According to this view, prior to doing a search, the mere availability of the information does not extend the child's knowledge to include everything that can be discovered through a Google Search. Why not? According to this view, the child has not *done anything* to contribute to the production of this knowledge. She has not played any active role in the production of the knowledge. Consequently, the mere availability of that information is not sufficient for her to count as knowing it. Is that correct? I will leave it to the reader to consider the matter further.

If that is correct, then it suggests the following standard: for AI to extend a person's knowledge, there must be a substantial degree of *interdependence* between the activity of the person and the activity of the AI in the production of that knowledge.[27] Here is a hypothetical example to illustrate the idea. Suppose we develop an AI program that can identify logical inconsistencies in a book or an essay. Suppose

---

27. This thesis is developed and defended by Karina Vold and Jose Hernandez-Orallo in "AI Extenders and the Ethics of Mental Health," in *Artificial Intelligence in Brain and Mental Health*, ed. F. Jotterand and M. Ienca (Berlin: Springer, 2021), 177–202.

the program is almost perfectly reliable, and it correctly identifies logical inconsistencies 98 percent of the time. Suppose I write an essay, and I submit it to this program to detect apparent inconsistencies. Suppose the program identifies three apparent inconsistencies. At that point, suppose I examine the apparent inconsistencies identified by the AI to see if I can find any obvious mistake in the AI's judgment. Now suppose that the result is as follows. On reflection, it is not obvious to me that these are genuine inconsistencies, but I can see no reason to doubt the AI. In other words, I can find no obvious mistake in the AI's reasoning. Given the nearly perfect reliability of the AI and my failure to find any mistake in its reasoning, I infer that these are, in fact, logical inconsistencies. Finally, suppose the AI is right—these are genuine logical inconsistencies. Then, once I believe that, do I myself *know* that these are logical inconsistencies? Arguably, the answer is yes. Obviously, the AI has played a large role in producing my knowledge, but I have *also* played a significant role. If I had found what seemed to be an obvious mistake in the AI's reasoning, then I would *not* believe that these were genuine inconsistencies. Thus, my knowledge that there are inconsistencies was produced by a process in which the AI and I both played a significant role. That is some reason to think that the results produced by the AI program are an extension of my knowledge.

In a similar vein, consider again the use of AI programs to interpret medical images. If those programs are sufficiently reliable, then a medical professional who lacks specialized knowledge of mental imagery might be able to extend her knowledge through the use of such programs. If the medical professional who uses such an AI program has enough medical knowledge to spot any obvious errors in the judgment of the AI, then the results of the AI program might be an extension of her own knowledge. She, herself, will know that what the AI says is correct. If so, then that would enable many medical professionals who lack specialization in specific imaging technologies to function just as effectively as those who do.

This concludes our discussion of the prospects of artificial intelligence for extending human knowledge. In summary, it seems that artificial intelligence can extend our knowledge, including much scientific knowledge. If the Extended Mind Thesis is correct, then under the right conditions, the products of artificial intelligence will be an extension of our own knowledge. However, in order for us to extend our knowledge in this way, there must be a relation of interdependence between the human being and the AI in the production of knowledge. However, even if AI can extend our knowledge in this way, it cannot, at the present time, give us scientific understanding. That is because understanding consists in grasping a correct explanation, and scientific explanations involve a degree of generality AI cannot yet achieve. For all its impressive accomplishments, AI is not yet capable of domain-general understanding, which is the kind of reasoning involved in grasping good scientific explanations. Thus, insofar as scientific progress involves an increase in scientific understanding, AI cannot make scientific progress for us. Perhaps that will change, but at the present time, artificial intelligence cannot fully replace human understanding.

Study Questions

1. What process does AlphaGo use to develop new strategies? Explain this in your own words.
2. The game of Go is played with small, round stones. Think of something that you could do with these stones—anything at all—other than playing Go. What kind of thinking is required in order to see that you can do this with the game pieces? If you asked AlphaGo to do this, would it be able to? What does this tell us about AlphaGo?
3. AlphaFold can predict the structures of many proteins. Could AlphaFold teach *us* how to predict the structures of even more proteins? Explain your answer.
4. What is the Extended Mind Thesis? Explain this in your own words. Think of an example, whether real or hypothetical, to illustrate this idea.
5. If a person can access some information on the Internet, then is that information part of what they know? Explain your answer.

For Further Reading

For an excellent discussion of whether AI could ever out-think us, see Uziel Awret, ed., *The Singularity: Could Artificial Intelligence Really Out-Think Us (And Would We Want It To?)* (Exeter, UK: Imprint Academic, 2016). For a deep dive into all the possible consequences of AI in the future, see Nick Bostrom's *Superintelligence: Paths, Dangers, Strategies* (New York: Oxford University Press, 2014). For an explanation of how AI can be integrated into other scientific practices in such a way as to generate genuine understanding, see Fridolin Gross, "The Explanatory Role of Machine Learning in Molecular Biology," *Erkenntnis* (forthcoming). For a discussion of some of the problems associated with dependence on AI for knowledge, see Inkeri Koskinen, "We Have No Satisfactory Social Epistemology of AI-Based Science," *Social Epistemology* (forthcoming). For a thoughtful attempt to allay these concerns, see Uwe Peters, "Science Based on Artificial Intelligence Need Not Pose a Social Epistemological Problem," *Social Epistemology Review and Reply Collective* (13) 2024.

CHAPTER EIGHT

Thinking about Conspiracy Theories

On August 29, 2005, Hurricane Katrina hit New Orleans, Louisiana, to devastating effect. The hurricane killed 1,392 people and caused about $190 billion in damages. Most of the deaths were caused by flooding that happened in the wake of the hurricane. Further investigation revealed that this flooding was the result of a faulty levee around the city of New Orleans.[1] However, among those who survived the hurricane, a different theory emerged. According to this theory, the destruction of the ninth ward of New Orleans, which was a predominately poor, black neighborhood, was done deliberately. Testifying before the House Select Committee on Hurricane Katrina, Dyan French testified that "I was on my front porch. I have witnesses that they bombed the walls of the levee, boom, boom! Mister, I'll never forget it."[2] Another resident, Leah Hodges, told the committee, "Certainly appears to me to be an act of genocide and of ethnic cleansing."[3] Gina Blandin, who lost her apartment in the flood, spelled out the theory in detail: "I think they blew up those levees and let the water come in. They were happy that this storm hit, to get all of us black people out of the city."[4]

---

1. Campbell Robertson, "Decade after Katrina, Pointing Finger More Firmly at Army Corps," *New York Times*, May 23, 2015.
2. Lisa Myers, "Were the Levees Bombed in New Orleans?" NBC News, December 7, 2005.
3. Myers, "Were the Levees Bombed in New Orleans?"
4. "Suspicions Fire Racial Tensions," *Chicago Tribune*, May 8, 2013.

According to this theory, people in power decided to use the hurricane to transform New Orleans from a poor, black city into a rich, white one. Before Katrina, New Orleans was 67 percent black and 28 percent in poverty. The poor, black citizens of New Orleans could easily imagine rich, white people looking for a way to remove them and finding this one. Harvard psychiatrist Alvin Poussaint explained that "such conspiracy theories are fueled by years of government neglect and discrimination against blacks: slavery, segregation and the Tuskegee experiments, during which poor blacks were used to test the effects of syphilis." According to Poussaint, "If you're angry and you've been discriminated against, then your mind is open to many ideas about persecution, abandonment, feelings of rejection."[5]

Theories like this one—that the levees of New Orleans were deliberately bombed—are often called *conspiracy theories*. In recent years, conspiracy theories have become the subject of both empirical investigation and philosophical debate. In this chapter, we will explore the epistemology of conspiracy theories. Is it ever rational to believe a conspiracy theory? If some conspiracy theory turned out to be true, would we say that its proponents *knew* that it was true, or were they just lucky? These are the questions that we will try to answer in this chapter. However, to answer those questions, we first need to define the concept of a conspiracy theory. What makes a theory qualify as a conspiracy theory? Unfortunately, even that question is hotly contested. The very definition of "conspiracy theory" is one of the subjects of heated debate.

With that in mind, here is how I will proceed. The recent debate over conspiracy theories has focused on whether it is ever rational to believe a conspiracy theory. One group of philosophers argues in the affirmative, while the other argues in the negative. In what follows, I will examine the arguments of one philosopher from each of these two groups. For that purpose, I have chosen Charles Pigden and Quassim Cassam. Charles Pigden argues that, contrary to conventional wisdom, it is sometimes rational to believe a conspiracy theory. By contrast, Quassim Cassam argues that, once they are defined

---

5. "Suspicions Fire Racial Tensions."

correctly, it is never rational to believe a conspiracy theory. As we will see, one of the issues between them is the correct definition of a conspiracy theory. However, as we will also see, the disagreements between them are not merely semantic. We will begin with Pigden's defense of the rationality of belief in conspiracy theories and then proceed to Cassam's critique of them. Finally, I will propose an alternative way of thinking about conspiracy theories, which differs from both Pigden and Cassam.

As Pigden understands it, the conventional wisdom is that no one should ever believe a conspiracy theory. Pigden opposes the conventional wisdom. According to Pigden,

> some conspiracy theories are sensible and some are silly, but if they are silly this is not because they are conspiracy theories but because they suffer from some specific defect—for instance, that the conspiracies they postulate are impossible or far-fetched. But conspiracy theories *as such* are not epistemologically unclean, and it is often permissible—even obligatory—to believe them. For sometimes the case can be rationally overwhelming.[6]

To understand Pigden's view, we must begin with his definition of a conspiracy theory. According to Pigden, a conspiracy theory is simply "a theory which posits a conspiracy—that is a secret plan on the part of some group to influence events by partly secret means."[7] If we accept Pigden's definition of a conspiracy theory, then the conventional wisdom—that no one should ever believe a conspiracy theory—is surely false. That is because

> history, as we know it, both from documentary evidence and the best historians, is choc-a-bloc with conspiracies. Thus, *if conspiracy theories are theories which posit conspiracies*, then to

---

6. Charles Pigden, "Conspiracy Theories and the Conventional Wisdom Revisited," in *Secrets and Conspiracies*, ed. Olli Loukola (Leiden: Rodopi, 2022), 2.
7. Pigden, "Conspiracy Theories and the Conventional Wisdom Revisited," 5.

accept the conventional wisdom and adopt the principle that we ought not believe or investigate conspiracy theories would lead to the conclusion that *history is bunk*, that much of what we thought we knew is not only unbelievable, but not worth investigating. . . . [I]t is not rational to adopt an epistemic principle with such catastrophic consequences.[8]

If a conspiracy theory is just a theory that posits a conspiracy, and we know that there have been many conspiracies throughout human history, then we should all believe some conspiracy theories. That is Pigden's argument.

There is no doubt that Pigden is right about the ubiquity of conspiracies in human history. Pigden's own writings are replete with examples stretching from ancient times to the present. Moreover, the fact that conspiracies have often occurred seems relevant to the rationality of believing in conspiracy theories. Consider again the theory that someone deliberately destroyed the levee around New Orleans. Many African Americans are aware of actual conspiracies that have harmed African American people in the past. Between 1932 and 1972, the United States Public Health Service and the Centers for Disease Control and Prevention conducted a study of untreated syphilis on almost 400 African American men. To motivate poor black men to participate in the study, these agencies promised free medical care. However, the men in the study were never informed that they had syphilis, and they were never treated for it. The men were told that the study would last only six months, but it was continued for forty years years.[9] For anyone aware of conspiracies like this, it is not hard to imagine white people bombing the levee around New Orleans to eliminate black neighborhoods. Moreover, there is actually a historical precedent for the theory that the levee was bombed. In 1927, the Great Mississippi Flood approached New Orleans from the north. The wealthiest and most powerful citizens of

---

8. Pigden, "Conspiracy Theories and the Conventional Wisdom Revisited," 15.
9. See Vann R. Newkirk, "A Generation of Bad Blood," *The Atlantic*, December 18, 2020.

New Orleans convinced the governor to dynamite one of the levees downriver to relieve pressure on the city's flood walls. The decision effectively destroyed low-lying black neighborhoods, like St. Bernard Parish, in order to save the wealthy white neighborhoods of New Orleans.[10] These examples illustrate Pigden's point. We now know that these conspiracies happened. Thus, every rational person should believe some conspiracy theories.

However, some would argue that there is a relevant difference between conspiracies that have now been confirmed with very strong evidence, and conspiracies that are alleged to have happened but without any supporting evidence. We can all agree that many conspiracies have happened in history. The question is whether that makes it rational to believe conspiracy theories that are, at present, unconfirmed. There appears to be a gap in Pigden's argument between the rationality of believing in conspiracies that are now well-confirmed and the rationality of believing in conspiracies that are presently unconfirmed.

Pigden has an argument to fill this gap. Here is the argument, in full:

> There are many theories which are not conspiracy theories now, though they were conspiracy theories in the past: the theory that the Kennedy administration conspired to overthrow Diem, the theory that CREEP [the Committee for the Re-election of President Richard Nixon] conspired to burglarize the Democratic headquarters in the Watergate building and that Nixon conspired with the mob to have peaceniks beaten up; the theory that Nixon and Kissinger conspired to overthrow Allende and connived at the subsequent murders and brutalities; the theory that the Reagan administration conspired to sell arms to Iran in order to fund the Contras, and the theory that suspected terrorists were kidnapped and tortured at the behest of the Bush administration—all these theories were once inconsistent with official opinion, though nowadays official opinion has managed to catch up with the facts. . . . Thus, it would have been

---

10. "Suspicions Fire Racial Tensions."

an epistemic mistake to have adopted this strategy [of never believing a conspiracy theory] in the past.[11]

If everyone in history had accepted the conventional wisdom and refused to believe any conspiracy theories, then they would have refused to believe many propositions that we now know to be true. They would have refused to believe that African American men were being used for experiments without their consent. They would have refused to believe that the wealthy white leaders of New Orleans facilitated the destruction of black neighborhoods in order to save white neighborhoods. Thus, the conventional wisdom would have led to a great deal of ignorance in history, as it often did.

However, it does not follow that there is any *better* policy than the conventional wisdom. Throughout history, there have been many conspiracy theories. Some of them turned out to be true, and some of them turned out to be false. With hindsight, we can often tell which were true and which were false, but at the time, it was very difficult, or even impossible, to tell that. If we accept Pigden's conclusion—that a person in the past should have rejected the conventional wisdom, then what alternative strategy should they have adopted? Suppose that they had chosen to believe most, or even all, of the conspiracy theories that were on offer at the time. Then they would have been led to many false beliefs since many of those past conspiracy theories were false. Although they would form some true beliefs by accepting the conspiracy theories that turned out to be true, they would also have formed many false beliefs by accepting the ones that were false. Is that really an improvement on the conventional wisdom? As Pigden himself notes, "An epistemic strategy should maximize the chances of truth, and minimize the chances of error." The problem is that it is not clear that there is any principled alternative to the conventional wisdom that maximizes the chances of truth and minimizes the chances of error *better* than the conventional wisdom. In reply, Pigden can argue that a rational person can distinguish between

---

11. Pigden, "Conspiracy Theories and the Conventional Wisdom Revisited," 24–25.

more and less plausible conspiracy theories and thereby devise a strategy that is better than the conventional wisdom. I will leave it to the reader to think about the prospects for this approach.

In sharp contrast to Charles Pigden, Quassim Cassam argues that "given what makes them special, Conspiracy Theories are unlikely to be true."[12] According to Cassam, the function of a conspiracy theory is "to promote a political agenda by spreading what is in fact . . . a bunch of seductive falsehoods."[13] To understand Cassam's position, we must begin with his definition of a conspiracy theory, which differs sharply from Pigden's. Cassam's definition of a conspiracy theory is much narrower than Pigden's definition. To mark this difference, Cassam always capitalizes the phrase *Conspiracy Theory* to distinguish the sort of theory that he is discussing. According to Cassam, a Conspiracy Theory has the following five traits: *speculative, contrarian, esoteric, amateurish,* and *premodern.* Each of these traits requires some explanation.

To say that Conspiracy Theories are speculative, is to say that "they are based on conjecture rather than knowledge, educated (or not so educated) guesswork, rather than solid evidence."[14] To say that they are contrarian is to say that they are "contrary to *appearances* or *the obvious* explanation of events."[15] To say that they are esoteric is to say that "once the obvious is ruled out, the far from obvious is ruled in. There is almost no explanation that is too bizarre for the Conspiracy Theorist's taste. . . ."[16] When he says that Conspiracy Theories are amateurish, Cassam notes that this is "not a comment on their intellectual merits, but on the qualifications of the amateur sleuths and Internet detectives who push them." According to Cassam, some Conspiracy Theorists do have qualifications in relevant fields, but they are a small minority. Finally, when Cassam says that Conspiracy Theories are premodern, he means that they are based on a worldview

---

12. Quassim Cassam, *Conspiracy Theories* (Cambridge: Polity Press, 2019), 7.
13. Cassam, *Conspiracy Theories*, 11.
14. Cassam, *Conspiracy Theories*, 16.
15. Cassam, *Conspiracy Theories*, 20.
16. Cassam, *Conspiracy Theories*, 22.

in which "complex events are capable of being controlled by a small number of people acting in secret, and this is what gives these events a deeper meaning."[17]

As Cassam defines the term, a Conspiracy Theory is a theory that has all five of these traits—speculative, contrarian, esoteric, amateurish, and premodern. If we accept Cassam's definition, then there is a very strong argument for the conventional wisdom—that no one should ever believe a Conspiracy Theory. As Cassam puts it, "Theories that have all five of the special features of Conspiracy Theories that I've listed are *unlikely* to be true, even if it is *possible* for them to be true."[18] That certainly seems correct. If a theory is not based on solid evidence, contrary to appearances, bizarre, propounded by people who are unqualified, and based on an archaic worldview, then it is very unlikely that it is true. Of course, it is always *possible* that it is true, but it is very unlikely. We should not believe things that are unlikely to be true. Thus, it follows that we should not believe Conspiracy Theories, as Cassam defines them.

One concern about Cassam's argument is that his definition of a conspiracy theory is doing all of the work in the argument. As Charles Pigden notes, arguments like this seem to say "it is irrational to believe conspiracy theories that [are] irrational to believe." But then, "As Horatio said, when confronted with a similar tautology, 'There needs no ghost, my lord, come from the grave, to tell us this.'"[19] However, Cassam illustrates each of the five traits in his definition with real examples of Conspiracy Theories that exemplify each. Cassam's argument is not based on his definition alone. Rather, it is based on the extent to which many conspiracy theories do exemplify these traits. Understood in that way, Cassam's argument is a simple inductive inference. All of the conspiracy theories that Cassam considers have the five traits that are included in his definition. Therefore, all conspiracy theories probably have these five traits. Since it is irrational

---

17. Cassam, *Conspiracy Theories*, 26.
18. Cassam, *Conspiracy Theories*, 29.
19. Pidgen, "Conspiracy Theories and the Conventional Wisdom Revisited," 30. The reference is to Shakespeare's *Hamlet*.

to believe a theory that has these five traits, all conspiracy theories are irrational.

However, in order to generalize from a particular sample of conspiracy theories to a generalization about all conspiracy theories, the sample must be representative of the entire population of conspiracy theories. In other words, the theories in the sample must be *relevantly similar* to the entire set of conspiracy theories. Perhaps Cassam's sample of conspiracy theories *is* representative of the entire population of conspiracy theories. However, it would require a much more thorough, exhaustive study of a much larger set of theories to justify that claim. Moreover, even if Cassam's sample of theories is representative, Cassam would also need to show that every theory in that sample actually has every one of the five traits and to the degree that he seems to assert. For each theory in the sample, Cassam would need to show that it was not supported by any real evidence, that it is contrary to appearances and the "obvious explanation of the events," that it tells bizarre stories, that its proponents all lack the relevant qualifications, and that it is based on an archaic worldview. Perhaps that could be done, but it would require an enormous amount of evidence—much more than Cassam provides. I will leave it to the reader to consider this further.

In the remainder of this chapter, I am going to suggest an alternative way to think about conspiracy theories. To really understand conspiracy theories, we need to be aware of the real-world contexts in which people believe them. Recent studies have found that believing conspiracy theories is typically associated with a range of adverse circumstances. People who believe conspiracy theories tend to have lower levels of education and be outside the labor force.[20] In a series of studies conducted in Australia, Bruno Casara and his colleagues found "a positive relationship between perceived economic inequality and conspiracy beliefs. . . . [P]articipants who perceived greater

---

20. Daniel Freeman and Richard P. Bentall, "The Concomitants of Conspiracy Concerns," *Social Psychiatry and Psychiatric Epidemiology* 52 (2017): 597.

economic inequality in Australia were more likely to doubt 'the official version of the events.'"[21]

In a more recent study published in October 2023, Zhao-Xie Zeng and his colleagues manipulated people's perceptions of economic inequality in a virtual society. They found that the subjects' perceptions of economic inequality shaped their moral evaluation of economically advantaged groups, leading to an increase in conspiracy beliefs. Zeng and his colleagues concluded that "perceived economic inequality predicts conspiracy theories about economically advantaged groups, and moral evaluations account for this effect."[22] More precisely,

> the moral evaluation of economically advantaged groups plays a mediating role in the relationship between economic inequality and belief in conspiracy theories about those groups. Specifically, the higher the perception of economic inequality, the lower people's evaluation of the morality of economically advantaged groups and the more strongly they believed conspiracy theories about those groups.[23]

With these studies, we can begin to see what a typical conspiracy theorist is like. A conspiracy theorist is usually a member of one of the lower classes in a society in which there is a great deal of economic inequality. The evidence shows that people in this situation tend to form a fairly low opinion of the people in the upper classes of their society. As it happens, there is some evidence that they are not entirely wrong. Some empirical studies have found that people in

---

21. Bruno Gabriel Salvador Casara, Caterina Suitner, and Jolanda Jetten, "The Impact of Economic Inequality on Conspiracy Beliefs," *Journal of Experimental Social Psychology* 98 (2022). In one of their studies, Casara and his colleagues found that conspiracy beliefs not only correlate with *perceived* economic inequality but with *objective* economic inequality as well.

22. Zhao-Xie Zeng, et. al., "How Does Economic Inequality Shape Conspiracy Theories? Empirical Evidence from China," *British Journal of Social Psychology* 63 (2023).

23. Zeng, "How Does Economic Inequality Shape Conspiracy Theories?," 482.

a higher social class (the rich) are more likely to lie and cheat than people in the lower social classes.[24] Be that as it may, members of the lower social classes in an unequal society are skeptical of the honesty and fairness of those above them on the socioeconomic ladder. Moreover, this evaluation of the people in the upper classes of their society increases their tendency to believe conspiracy theories.

Given their distrust of the upper classes, it is no wonder that people in the lower classes often challenge the authority of those in the upper classes. And that is the true function of a conspiracy theory. As Keith Harris points out, "Conspiracy theories are theories that allege conspiracies that are inconsistent with the claims of relevant epistemic authorities, where epistemic authority is possessed in virtue of credentials, professional positions, and the like."[25] An epistemic authority is a person who is alleged to be in a better position to know something than other people. Thus, an epistemic authority is, allegedly, someone who *should* be trusted because they are in a better position to know the truth of the matter.[26] Conspiracy theories contradict epistemic authorities. By contradicting the account of things that is propounded by people who are supposed to know best, conspiracy theorists are challenging the epistemic authorities.

As Harris notes, this does not entail that conspiracy theories are necessarily irrational. That is because

> an epistemic authority on a subject matter is not *necessarily* a reliable judge of claims concerning that subject matter. Rather, the reliability of relevant epistemic authorities depends on the

---

24. See P. K Piff, D. M. Stancato, S. Cote, R. Mendoza-Denton, and D. Keltner, "Higher Social Class Predicts Increased Unethical Behavior," *Proceedings of the National Academy of Sciences of the United States of America* 109 (2012): 4086–4091. See also M. W. Kraus, P. K. Piff, and D. Keltner, "Social Class, Sense of Control, and Social Explanation," *Journal of Personality and Social Psychology* 97 (2009): 992–1004.
25. Keith Harris, "Conspiracy Theories, Populism, and Epistemic Autonomy," *Journal of the American Philosophical Association* 9 (2023): 2.
26. We discussed the subject of epistemic authority in depth in Chapter 2, "Deferring to Experts."

extent to which credentials and positions are reserved for those who are reliable judges with respect to the subject matter.[27]

If the members of society who have the relevant credentials and hold the relevant positions are actually reliable, then they are *genuine* epistemic authorities, and they should be trusted. However, it is always possible that the people who have these credentials and hold these positions are not reliable, in which case they should not be trusted. Thus, the conspiracy theorist who contradicts the alleged epistemic authorities is not automatically irrational.

However, insofar as the people who have the relevant credentials and hold the relevant positions appear to be reliable, it certainly looks like the conspiracy theorist is being irrational. If someone is in a better position to know the truth about something than the rest of us, then we should trust that person, at least if we care about believing what is true. Thus, it seems that the conspiracy theorist is being irrational. However, this brings me to some surprising new research that promises to shed light on the nature of conspiracy theories. In a recent study, Kevin Reuter and Lucien Baumgartner examined the *language* that people use when they discuss conspiracy theories. They found that when people discuss conspiracy theories, they use language that is noticeably different from the language we use to discuss scientific theories. When people discuss scientific theories, they use words like "confirm," "prove," "disprove," "falsify," and "test." However, when people discuss conspiracy theories, they seldom use any of these words.[28] They seldom speak of testing or falsifying a conspiracy theory, or of confirming or disconfirming it. Thus, how people think about conspiracy theories seems to be different from how they think about scientific theories. Although some proponents of conspiracy theories try to prove them, those who consume conspiracy theories

---

27. Harris, "Conspiracy Theories, Populism, and Epistemic Autonomy," 2.
28. Kevin Reuter and Lucien Baumgartner, "Conspiracy Theories Are Not Theories: Time to Rename Conspiracy Theories," in *New Perspectives on Conceptual Engineering*, ed. Manuel Gustavo Isaac, Stefan Koch, and Kevin Sharp (Vol. 1–3, Synthese Library, forthcoming).

appear unconcerned about whether they can be proven or disproven. On that basis, Reuter and Baumgertner suggest that conspiracy theories are not really *theories* at all. They propose that we replace the term "conspiracy theory" with terms like "conspiracy story" or "conspiracy narrative."[29]

The language that people use when they discuss conspiracy theories tells us something about their state of mind when they entertain or accept them. The mental state of a conspiracy theorist seems to be different from the mental state of someone who entertains or accepts a scientific theory. This difference manifests in another fact that philosophers have noticed. The philosopher M. Giulia Napolitano points out that conspiracy theories are typically held in a very specific way; namely, they are held in a way that is *immune to revision by counter-evidence*.[30] Once a conspiracy theorist accepts a conspiracy, they refuse to accept any evidence as evidence against the theory. No matter what new facts they discover, they will refuse to see those facts as refuting the conspiracy theory. Napolitano infers that this is what makes conspiracy theorists irrational—they treat their conspiracy theories as immune to any counter-evidence. Very shortly, I will suggest an alternative interpretation of conspiracy theories and those who accept them.

Before I state my own proposal, here is one more fact to consider. At least one prominent conspiracy theorist explicitly denies that his theories are meant to be taken as literally true. In his online series, *Hush Hush*, Robert Barnes gives an alternative account of the purpose of a conspiracy theory. According to Barnes, the purpose of a conspiracy theory is

> to explore or examine either a past event, a current event, or predict a future event through a unique, alternative filter, prism, or frame. What if we took the conspiratorial interpretation?

---

29. Reuter and Baumgartner, "Conspiracy Theories Are Not Theories," 4.
30. M. Giulia Napolitano, "Conspiracy Theories and Evidential Self-Insulation," in *The Epistemology of Fake News*, ed. Sven Bernecker, Amy K. Floweree, and Thomas Grundmann (New York: Oxford University Press, 2021), 82–105.

> Where might that lead us? ... In this context, *I want to examine the possibility, just theoretically, hypothetically ... these are not episodes intended to be what reality is. ...*[31]

Barnes explicitly denies that his conspiracy theories are intended to be taken as literally true. Instead, he says that he is entertaining the *possibility* of these scenarios, in order to "see where it leads." In what follows, I will argue that Barnes is correct about the real function of a conspiracy theory and that the goal of this exercise—where it is supposed to lead to—is *skepticism*.

I am almost ready to state my own proposal. First, let us take stock of what we now know about conspiracy theories. Conspiracy theories are typically accepted by people in the lower classes of society, in a society in which there is a great deal of economic inequality. In an unequal society, the members of the lower classes distrust the members of the upper classes. To express their distrust, they tell conspiracy stories, and they embrace those stories. By embracing these conspiracy stories, the lower classes challenge the epistemic authority of the alleged experts in the upper classes, who claim to be in a better position to know the relevant facts. Second, the language used by conspiracy theorists indicates that they do not regard conspiracy theories the same way we regard scientific theories. Conspiracy theorists are much less concerned about whether these theories can be confirmed or disconfirmed, proven or disproven. Third, conspiracy theories are held in a way that is immune to counter-evidence. The conspiracy theorist refuses to see any new evidence as refuting the theory. Fourth, some conspiracy theorists explicitly deny that their theories are intended to be literally true. Now, what would explain these facts about conspiracy theories and those who accept them?

One way to understand a person's mental state is to notice how it functions in their overall thinking. How is this thought related to all their other thoughts? This is how we should approach conspiracy theories. How does the acceptance of a conspiracy theory function in

---

31. Robert Barnes, "Hush Hush, Episode 1," *Hush Hush* video series, January 15, 2021, https://vivabarneslaw.locals.com/content/videos/playlists/5/recent.

the overall thinking of a conspiracy theorist? This brings me to my suggestion. I suggest that a conspiracy theory functions as a *skeptical scenario*. In the remainder of this chapter, I will explain this hypothesis, argue in support of it, and then begin the task of evaluating conspiracy theories.

The best way to understand the idea of a skeptical scenario is to consider some famous examples from the seventeenth-century French philosopher René Descartes. Descartes wrote at a time when human knowledge was in crisis. The Protestant Reformation challenged the epistemic authority of the Catholic Church, and the Scientific Revolution was casting doubt on the way things appear to our senses. To the naked eye, it certainly looks like the earth is stationary and that the sun moves, but Copernicus and Galileo argued the contrary. At that point, some philosophers, like Michel de Montaigne, began to argue for skepticism—the thesis that we really do not have any knowledge at all. In this context, René Descartes wrote his famous *Meditations on First Philosophy* (1641). In the opening lines, Descartes says that when he looks back on his life, he sees that he has had many beliefs that turned out to be false. His intention for his book, he tells us, is to lay a new foundation for all human knowledge—one that will last because it is completely trustworthy. To achieve that, Descartes adopts his famous *Method of Doubt*—he will doubt everything that he can possibly doubt. Descartes's goal is not skepticism. His goal is to discover what *cannot be doubted* and use that as a foundation for all knowledge. However, to discover what cannot be doubted, Descartes first aims to doubt *as much as he can*. For that purpose, Descartes introduces two famous skeptical scenarios.

When you have a dream, you don't know that you are dreaming.[32] You think what is happening in your dream is real, even though it isn't. Some dreams can be very vivid. In a vivid dream, everything seems exactly as it does in real life. Now, suppose that you have a dream in which everything seems *exactly as it does right now*. In other

---

32. I assume you are not having a "lucid dream," in which you know that you are dreaming. For the purposes of this discussion, just imagine that the dream you are having is not a lucid dream.

words, imagine having a dream in which everything looks exactly as it does to you now, and everything sounds exactly as it does now, and so on, for smell, taste, and feel. If you had a dream like that, in which everything seemed exactly as it does to you now, then you would not be able to tell that you were dreaming. But then, *how do you know that you are not dreaming right now?* After all, if you *were* dreaming right now, then everything would seem exactly as it does to you now. So, the fact that it *seems* that you are awake does not prove that you are really awake since it would seem to you that you were awake even if you were dreaming.

The possibility that you are dreaming is what philosophers call a skeptical scenario. It is a situation in which everything seems to be a certain way, but nothing is really that way. It is a situation in which all of your evidence is *misleading*—it tells you that things are a certain way, but nothing is really that way. The defining feature of a skeptical scenario is that *if you were in a skeptical scenario, you would have no way of knowing that you were in it*. If a skeptical scenario is constructed well, then it would be impossible for anyone to know if they were in it. The point of a skeptical scenario is to challenge our ordinary claims to knowledge. Here is how they pose this challenge.[33] The most important part of the skeptical challenge is this: *in order to know that a proposition, P, is true, I must be able to rule out ways in which I could be mistaken*. To see this, consider an example, which is due to Barry Stroud. Suppose that you and I are out bird watching, and I see a small, yellow bird very briefly. Suppose that I say to you, "That was a Goldfinch." In reply, you tell me that there are also many Canaries in this area. Of course, Canaries are also small, yellow birds. Suppose you then ask me, "How do you know that the bird you saw was a

---

33. The following explanation of the case for skepticism is based on Barry Stroud's landmark study *The Significance of Philosophical Skepticism* (New York: Oxford University Press, 1984.). In what follows, I will use the letter "P" to stand for any *proposition*. A proposition is something that can be true or false and believed or disbelieved. Thus, the following are all examples of propositions: *that the earth is round, that smoking causes lung cancer, that the moon is made of cheese,* and *that Danny DeVito is taller than Lebron James*. Some of these propositions are true, while others are false.

Goldfinch rather than a Canary?" If I cannot rule out the possibility that what I saw was a Canary, then I do not *know* that the bird I saw was a Goldfinch. In order to know that I saw a Goldfinch, I need to be able to rule out the way in which I could be mistaken—that it was a Canary. This example illustrates a general principle—for any proposition P, in order to know that P is true, you must be able to rule out the ways in which you could be mistaken. These ways in which you could be mistaken are sometimes referred to as *possibilities of error*. To have knowledge, you must be able to rule out all possibilities of error.

Now here is how skeptical scenarios challenge our ordinary claims to knowledge. *Skeptical scenarios are possibilities of error that we cannot rule out.* One way in which my ordinary beliefs could be mistaken is if I were dreaming right now. So, in order to know that my ordinary beliefs are true, I must be able to rule out the possibility that I am dreaming right now. But, as we have seen, I *cannot* rule out the possibility that I am dreaming right now. If I were dreaming very vividly right now, then everything would seem exactly as it does to me right now. Thus, nothing in my experience proves that I am not dreaming right now. Consequently, I cannot rule out the possibility that I am not dreaming right now. If knowledge requires that I rule out every possibility of error, then I do not know that my ordinary beliefs are true. That is how skeptical scenarios seem to challenge our ordinary claims to knowledge.

It is important to notice something about this argument. In order to pose this challenge to ordinary claims to knowledge, skeptical scenarios only need to be *possible*. Given how the skeptic argues, she does not need any evidence that the skeptical scenario is actually true. It is very important to understand this. To see this, consider the birdwatching example. You asked me how I knew the bird I saw was *not* a Canary. Suppose I respond to your question with another question: "Well, what evidence do you have that it *was* a Canary?" Suppose I then add: "If you don't have any evidence that it was a Canary, then I *know* that it was a Goldfinch." Clearly, I have made a mistake. For me to know that the bird I saw was a Goldfinch, I need to be able to rule out the *possibility* that it was a Canary. If I cannot rule out that possibility, then I do not know that I saw a Goldfinch. The mere possibility that the bird I saw was a Canary is enough to call my knowledge into question. There does not need to be any positive evidence that it was a Canary for this possibility to threaten my claim to know. So it seems. Many philosophers reject this argument for skepticism. However, it has proven very difficult—some would say impossible—to show exactly where it is mistaken. We will return to that debate shortly.

My suggestion is that conspiracy theories function as skeptical scenarios that challenge our claims to acquire knowledge from epistemic authorities. The evidence for this claim is that it will explain many of the otherwise puzzling features of conspiracy theories and those who accept them. If conspiracy theories function as skeptical scenarios, then they do not need to be true in order to pose a skeptical challenge. That would explain why conspiracy theorists are often unconcerned about whether their theories can be confirmed or disconfirmed. To perform the function of a skeptical scenario, a conspiracy theory only needs to be possible. Thus, it need not be proven or disproven.

Likewise, if a conspiracy theory functions as a skeptical scenario, then the appropriate response to evidence that the theory is false is to construct a new, revised version of the theory that incorporates this new evidence. To understand this, consider how some people respond to one of Descartes's skeptical scenarios. Descartes says that it is possible that you are dreaming right now. You could be having a very vivid dream in which everything seems exactly as it does right now. In reply, some people say, "But I remember waking up this morning, getting out of bed, and being awake ever since then." In reply, Descartes will say, "Well, could you have a dream in which you wake up, get out of bed, and stay awake all day? Could you dream that?" The answer seems to be, "Yes, you could." Notice what Descartes has done here. The fact that you seem to remember getting up this morning is some evidence *against* the claim that you are dreaming right now. In reply, Descartes simply constructs another skeptical scenario, incorporating this evidence right into the scenario itself while retaining the possibility that you are dreaming right now. In this context, where the goal is simply to show that there is a possible situation in which you are dreaming, this response is perfectly appropriate. All that is required for that purpose is that the situation be possible.

If a conspiracy theory functions as a skeptical scenario, then we would expect the conspiracy theorist to respond to counter-evidence in the very same way, and that is exactly what they do. When experts testify against a conspiracy theory, then the conspiracy theorist replies that these experts are part of the conspiracy. When other facts do not fit the conspiracy theory, then the conspiracy theorist revises the theory in a way that incorporates these facts while retaining the basic claims of the conspiracy theory. If a conspiracy theory functions as a skeptical scenario, that is exactly what we would expect. More importantly, if a conspiracy theory functions as a skeptical scenario, then it is *appropriate* for the conspiracy theorist to respond in this way. Remember that the purpose of a skeptical scenario is to show that there is a possibility of error that we cannot rule out. For that purpose, it is acceptable to incorporate any known fact into the skeptical scenario. If the result is a possibility of error that we cannot rule out, then we have a good skeptical scenario, and that is what the conspiracy theorist aims to provide. The conspiracy theorist says, in effect, "It is possible that the epistemic authorities conspire to deceive you in the following way, and if they conspired in that way, then you would not be able to tell. This is a possibility of error that you cannot rule out." Thus, reasoning in the same way as the skeptic, the conspiracy theorist concludes that we do not really know that the statements of the epistemic authorities are true.

The hypothesis that conspiracy theories function as skeptical scenarios explains how conspiracy theorists think and speak about their theories. In addition, this hypothesis also explains the close relationship between conspiracy theories and the general distrust of the upper classes by the lower classes in an unequal society. Recall that conspiracy thinking increases with an increase in the degree of economic inequality in a society, *and* this is mediated by an increase in a general distrust of the upper classes in the society. If a conspiracy theory functions as a skeptical scenario, then it would provide a rational expression or even a rational justification for the general distrust of the upper classes by the lower classes in society. That is because a skeptical scenario forms the basis of an argument for skepticism, which denies that we have some kind of knowledge. If a conspiracy theory functions as a skeptical scenario in which the recognized authorities in society are deceiving us, then a conspiracy theory is well suited to the task of rationalizing the general distrust of the upper classes that seems to cause it. In summary, the hypothesis that conspiracy theories function as skeptical scenarios enables us to explain many facts about conspiracy theories and those who accept them, and that is some reason to accept it.

This brings us, at last, to the evaluation of conspiracy theories. If conspiracy theories function as skeptical scenarios in an argument for skepticism about epistemic authorities, then our response to conspiracy theories should be similar to our response to other forms of skepticism. One response to skepticism is that, on reflection, it has very implausible implications. In the case of conspiracy theories, this reply has been developed and defended by Neil Levy.[34] The conspiracy theorist denies that we acquire knowledge by trusting epistemic authorities. The reason is that we can easily imagine those authorities deceiving us as described by the conspiracy theory. Since the epistemic authorities could easily deceive us in the way imagined, we cannot know that they are telling the truth. The conspiracy theorist uses this reasoning to cast doubt on specific epistemic authorities. However, the very same kind of reasoning could be given for doubting any epistemic authority whatsoever. Thus, we have the same kind of reason for doubting any epistemic authority whatsoever. Consequently, the conspiracy theorist should really deny that we *ever* acquire knowledge by trusting epistemic authorities. However, as we have seen in Chapters 1 and 2 of this book, most of our knowledge comes from the testimony of other people, including experts. If we do not get knowledge by doing so, then we do not know much about anything at all. But that is very implausible. According to this objection, conspiracy theories imply a very radical degree of skepticism, which is simply implausible.

If the reasoning involved in conspiracy theories can be applied just as well to *all* epistemic authorities or even to most of them, then

---

34. Neil Levy, "Radically Socialized Knowledge and Conspiracy Theories," *Episteme* 4 (2007): 181–192.

this objection is correct. However, it is doubtful that the reasoning involved in conspiracy theories can be generalized in this way. The reason is that conspiracy theories are usually restricted to matters on which someone with power has a *motive* for conspiring and hiding the truth. That is why most conspiracy theories target people in positions of power, whether in the government or the private sector. There are very few, if any, conspiracy theories about your family doctor or your local mechanic. Thus, a conspiracy theorist is free to trust many, or even most, of the epistemic authorities in her own life. One way to put this point is to say that conspiracy theories are used to support a *local skepticism* about *some* epistemic authorities, not a *global skepticism* about *all* epistemic authorities. Thus, it seems that the conspiracy theorist can consistently trust epistemic authorities who are not in positions of great power or who have no motive for conspiring. So it seems.

Another reply to skepticism, in all its forms, rejects one of the premises of the argument for skepticism. Recall that one of the premises of the argument for skepticism is that in order to know that P, you must be able to rule out all of the ways in which you could be mistaken. You must be able to rule out all possibilities of error. Many philosophers argue that this premise is false. To have knowledge, you do not need to rule out every possibility of error. Rather, you only need to rule out the *relevant* possibilities of error. Consider the birdwatching example. In order to know that I saw a Goldfinch, I need to rule out the possibility that it was a Canary. That is because the possibility that it was a Canary is a *relevant* possibility. By contrast, suppose you said, "How do you know that it wasn't a tiny Pterosaur, which was disguised as a Goldfinch?" That would be a bizarre suggestion, and I would be right to say, "That is so unlikely that I need not rule out that possibility. It is not really a *relevant* possibility." This example illustrates a general principle—to know that P, you only need to rule out *relevant* possibilities of error.

When is a possibility of error a *relevant* possibility? It is difficult to define this concept in a general way. However, to a first approximation, here is one way to understand this concept. Every possible situation is either *similar to* or *dissimilar to* the real world—the world as it really is. Moreover, this relation of similarity or dissimilarity comes in degrees. Some possible situations are very similar to the actual situation, while others are less similar. We can illustrate this with the birdwatching example. Suppose that what I saw was actually a Goldfinch. Nevertheless, there is a possible situation in which the bird I saw was a Canary, and that situation could be *very similar to the actual situation in every other way*. The possible situation in which I saw a Canary is very similar to the actual situation. By contrast, the possible situation in which what I saw was a Pterosaur disguised as a Goldfinch would have to be *very dissimilar* to the actual world in many, many ways. This would have to be a situation in which Pterosaurs have not become extinct, in which some of them are very small, and in which they are sometimes disguised as Goldfinches. In all these ways, this possible situation is *very dissimilar* to the actual world. Whereas the possible situation in which I see a Canary is very similar to the actual world, the possible situation in which I see a Pterosaur disguised as a Goldfinch is very dissimilar to the actual world. Finally, that is why the former situation is a *relevant* situation, while the latter situation is an *irrelevant* situation. A relevant situation is one that is very similar to the actual world, and an *irrelevant* situation is one that is very dissimilar to the actual world.

If that is correct, then in order to know that P, I must be able to rule out possibilities of error *that are very similar to the actual world*. I do *not* need to rule out situations that are *very dissimilar* to the actual world. We are now in a position to apply these concepts to conspiracy theories. A critic of conspiracy theories can say that the possible situations described in conspiracy theories are *very, very dissimilar* to the real world, in many respects. This is one way to express the point that Cassam is making when he says that Conspiracy Theories are *esoteric*. They often postulate very bizarre events—events that do not happen very often, or at all, in the world as we know it. To the extent that a conspiracy theory postulates very unusual events, it describes a possible situation that is *very dissimilar to the actual world as we know it*. Thus, these possible situations are not *relevant* situations—we do not need to rule them out in order to have knowledge. If that is correct, then conspiracy theories fail to support the skepticism that they were intended to support.

The question, then, is this: *Are the situations described in conspiracy theories relevantly similar to the real world?* To that question, the ubiquity of conspiracies throughout human history is certainly relevant. As Charles Pigden pointed out, the sheer volume of known conspiracies in human history is quite large. To the extent that conspiracies happen frequently in human history, right up to the present, the situations described in some conspiracy theories seem to be relevantly similar to the real world. If that is correct, then conspiracy theories are possibilities that must be ruled out if we are to know that the official accounts of events are correct. In some cases, we can actually rule out these possibilities. For example, in the case of Hurricane Katrina, inspectors discovered that the flooding in New Orleans was caused by faulty engineering of the levee. However, if we embellish the conspiracy theory that the levee was bombed by including these inspectors among the conspirators and imagining that their testimony was part of the cover-up, then this conspiracy theory cannot be ruled out by their testimony. This brings us back to the relevant question—is this possibility relevantly similar to things that happen frequently in the real world? That is the underlying issue, and I will leave it to the reader to think about it.

Conspiracy theories cast doubt on epistemic authorities. Is that a good thing or a bad thing? That depends on the extent to which the epistemic authorities in a given society are reliable or unreliable. To the extent that the epistemic authorities in a society are reliable sources of information, casting doubt on them prevents many people from acquiring knowledge they could otherwise obtain. That is often very harmful. For that reason, some people now decry the public's loss of trust in epistemic authorities. In his best-selling book *The Death of Expertise*, Tom Nichols issues a scathing critique of Americans who doubt the experts. According to Nichols,

> Americans have reached a point where ignorance, especially of anything related to public policy, is an actual virtue. To reject the advice of experts is to assert autonomy, a way for Americans to insulate their increasingly fragile egos from ever being told they're wrong about anything. . . . People don't just believe

dumb things; they actively resist further learning, rather than let go of beliefs. . . . There is a self-righteousness and fury to this new rejection of expertise that suggest, at least to me, that this isn't just mistrust or questioning . . . *it is narcissism*.[35]

For Nichols, people who doubt the experts are fragile, self-righteous narcissists.

It is rather surprising that someone like Tom Nichols would make a statement like this. To understand why, you need to know a bit more about Tom Nichols. From 1997 to 2022, Tom Nichols was a professor of strategy, and a professor of national security affairs at the U.S. Naval War College. During that time, and speaking as an expert, Nichols was a staunch public advocate for the wars in both Afghanistan and Iraq. In a series of interviews, articles, and editorials, Nichols argued that the U.S. military strategy in Afghanistan was sound and that the invasion of Iraq was justified.[36] Both of those statements have turned out to be false.[37] By 2007, Nichols admitted that bad intelligence led to the Iraq war. In an editorial, Nichols even admitted that bias played a significant role in the reasoning that led people astray. According to Nichols,

> we accepted this disinformation because it told us what some of our officials wanted to believe. . . . Researcher bias is the simple tendency of all analysts to see what they want to discover, and to ignore what contradicts their theory.[38]

---

35. Tom Nichols, *The Death of Expertise: The Campaign against Established Knowledge and Why It Matters* (New York: Oxford University Press 2018), x.

36. See, for example, his contribution to the roundtable in *Ethics and International Affairs*, vol. 17, no. 1 (Spring 2003).

37. The *Afghanistan Papers*, released through a Freedom of Information Act request and published in the *Washington Post* in December 2019, revealed that the United States never had any realistic chance of winning the war in Afghanistan.

38. See Nichols's editorial "Bad Intelligence Led to Iraq War Mistake," *Gainesville Times*, updated February 2, 2008, https://www.gainesvilletimes.com/columnists/opinion-community-columnists/nichols-bad-intelligence-led-to-iraq-war-mistake/.

Thus, by his own admission, Nichols, *speaking as an expert*, made some very harmful mistakes, and he now recognizes both the fallibility of experts and the role of bias in many expert judgments. Nevertheless, he now chastises anyone who would doubt the experts as dumb narcissists.

Nichols's failure as an expert is just one of the many failures of expertise in recent years. In an article published in 2016, Paul Krugman, the erstwhile champion of unlimited globalization, admitted that he and his fellow economists made some very big mistakes about globalization.[39] In the months leading up to the 2008 financial crisis, many economists publicly declared that there was no serious problem in the housing market. These are just a few examples of the many harmful failures of experts in recent decades. If we want laypeople to trust the experts, then the experts need to be trustworthy. The first step toward restoring the public's trust in epistemic authority is for the epistemic authorities to get their houses in order.

However, that will not necessarily solve the problem of conspiracy theories. How should we respond to conspiracy theories? As we have seen, conspiracy theories are strongly correlated with economic inequality. As economic inequality increases, conspiracy theories proliferate. Moreover, the evidence indicates that this is mediated by a loss of trust between the lower classes and the upper classes in society. The more unequal society becomes, the more distrust there is between people in the lower classes and people in the upper classes. This, in turn, leads to more conspiracy theories. In one way, this is not surprising. There is empirical evidence that economic inequality causes many health and social problems. In their book *The Spirit Level: Why Greater Equality Makes Societies Stronger*, Richard Wilkinson and Kate Pickett found that economic inequality is correlated with anxiety, depression, drug and alcohol addiction, violent crime, teenage pregnancy, obesity, and even heart disease. These correlations obtain across twenty-four

---

39. See Michael Hirsh, "Economists on the Run," *Foreign Policy*, October 22, 2019.

countries and forty-eight U.S. states.[40] The best explanation of these correlations is that there is some causal connection between economic inequality and all these health and social problems. The empirical evidence concerning conspiracy theories suggests that we must add another harm to this list. Economic inequality breaks down the trust between members of the lower classes and members of the upper classes, and that leads to conspiracy theories. These conspiracy theories then cast doubt on the epistemic authorities in society, thereby preventing the transmission of knowledge that would otherwise occur. Thus, economic inequality causes *epistemic harms*.

Throughout this book, we have seen that human knowledge is a *social phenomenon*. We get most of our knowledge from other people, and we need to interact with other people in order to counteract the effect of our own biases. Thus, it is no surprise that human knowledge depends on having a healthy, functional society. If economic inequality makes a society *unhealthy* and *dysfunctional*, then that will have adverse effects on human knowledge as well. At this point, we have moved beyond epistemology and into social and political philosophy. However, for the reasons stated above, it seems that anyone who cares about human knowledge should also take time to think about the problem of economic inequality.

---

40. Richard G. Wilkinson and Kate E. Pickett, *The Spirit Level: Why Greater Equality Makes Societies Stronger* (New York: Bloomsbury, 2011).

Study Questions

1. Consider the theory that COVID-19 was manufactured in a laboratory. According to Charles Pigden, is this a conspiracy theory? According to Quassim Cassam, is it a conspiracy theory? In each case, explain your answer.
2. Consider again the theory that COVID-19 was manufactured in a laboratory. Would Charles Pigden say that it is rational to believe this theory? Explain your answer. What about Quassim Cassam—would he say that it is rational to believe this theory? Again, explain your answer.
3. Given what we know about most conspiracy theorists, would Bill Gates or Warren Buffett be likely to believe any conspiracy theories? Explain your answer.
4. What is a skeptical scenario? Explain this concept in your own words, and construct your own example to illustrate it.
5. Suppose that the theory that COVID-19 was made in a lab is a skeptical scenario. Then, what is the point of this story? What is it meant to prove? To determine whether it succeeds or fails, what would you need to consider?

For Further Reading

For Charles Pigden's most recent defense of his position, see "Conspiracy Theories and the Conventional Wisdom Revisited," in *Secrets and Conspiracies*, ed. Olli Loukola (Leiden: Rodopi, 2022). Quassim Cassam's position is developed and defended in his book *Conspiracy Theories* (London: Polity Press, 2019). For a recent discussion that makes some insightful connections to current politics, see Keith Harris, "Conspiracy Theories, Populism, and Epistemic Autonomy," *Journal of the American Philosophical Association* 9 (2023): 21–36. For an attempt to resolve the debate between Pigden and Cassam, see Matthew Shields, "Rethinking Conspiracy Theories," *Synthese* 4 (2022): 1–29.

CONCLUSION

Human knowledge is fundamentally social. Most of what we know comes from the testimony of other people. In many areas, we have to rely on experts to acquire knowledge for us and then pass it on to us. These processes—giving and receiving testimony, identifying experts, and relying on them—are social processes. They involve whole communities of people. Thus, human knowledge is seldom the achievement of a single individual. Rather, it is a collective achievement. Likewise, human ignorance is seldom the fault of a single individual. Bernie Madoff succeeded in deceiving many people because the whole regulation system failed. The SEC and the financial news outlets failed to scrutinize Madoff's claims. That is why his lies were believed. Thus, whether we achieve knowledge or languish in ignorance depends on the structure and activities of a whole community of people. In many cases, the way to achieve more knowledge and suffer less ignorance is to build and sustain the right kind of community.

For example, the case of Bernie Madoff shows that a reliable network of people needs at least a few doubters—people who thoughtfully and intelligently challenge conventional wisdom. The presence of such people makes it much more difficult for liars to succeed for any great length of time. Likewise, it is actually a good thing when an academic discipline includes a few members who dissent from the consensus opinion. This actually gives us *more* reason to trust the consensus opinion in that discipline because we know that alternative views are being considered seriously, and that they have been rejected by the majority of the experts in the discipline. In both of these cases, the presence of dissenters acts as a check against groupthink, which would otherwise threaten the reliability of experts.

There is another justification for why we need to reason together in groups. Recent work in empirical psychology has taught us that human reason is plagued by a multitude of cognitive biases. These biases threaten to undermine our ability to acquire knowledge. Even when we get true beliefs, it seems that we were just lucky to do so. The most promising antidote to cognitive bias is collective reasoning. People who reason together in groups perform better than even the smartest individuals reasoning alone. That is probably because human reason evolved to be used in a social context. For each individual, the function of reason is simply to persuade other people. Thus, when we reason alone, we tend to succumb to our self-serving cognitive biases. However, when we reason together in groups, other people challenge us, and that interaction helps us to overcome our cognitive biases. Consequently, we are more likely to form true beliefs when we reason together with other people.

Propaganda and political polarization both threaten knowledge precisely because they preempt the social, interactive processes through which we gain knowledge. Propaganda aims to circumvent our ability to think and reason about a subject in the way we otherwise would. Polarization involves an in-group bias that has very similar effects. Thus, propaganda and polarization are pathologies of the intellect because they disrupt the processes of interactive reasoning that we need to achieve knowledge. In the process, they place our pursuit of knowledge in the hands of fewer people. In the case of propaganda, our beliefs are shaped by the opinions and interests of the propagandist, whose opinions do not have to survive social scrutiny before they influence us. In the case of polarization, our in-group bias leads us to believe whatever the opinion-makers in our group want us to believe. Once again, the problem is that such beliefs do not go through the social, interactive, critical process required for us to be reliable.

In all these cases, we can see that we are at our best when we reason together, collectively, with diverse groups of people, including some dissenters. This process of collective, collaborative reasoning is the best way for us, as human beings, to achieve knowledge. Thus, we should foster this sort of process in society whenever we can, and we should form our own beliefs through this sort of process as often as possible. In every sector of society, we should encourage collective reasoning in groups that include at least some dissenters. Of course, this process of collective reasoning requires a certain amount of social trust in society. Some forces, such as economic inequality, seem to undermine social trust. If we are to achieve as much knowledge as possible, then we should seek to minimize those social forces that undermine social trust in our society.

INDEX

adversarial collaboration, 108
affective polarization, 111–112
agreement with consensus, as
    evidence of expertise, 39
Agrippa's Trilemma, 8n7
AI
    and domain-general
        understanding, 171–172
    and medicine, 164
    and scientific progress,
        164–174
    and scientific understanding,
        166–170
AlphaFold, 163, 173–174
AlphaGo, 162–163, 170–173
anchoring bias, 87–88
argumentative capacity, as
    evidence of expertise, 39

bias blind spot, 89–90
Big Data, 151–158
Bounded Rationality, theory of,
    96–97

Carter, President, 29–30, 34–35,
    40–43, 46–47, 52–55
Cassam, Quassim, 187–189
circular reasoning, 9–10
cognitive bias
    in criminal investigation,
        92–94

    as reason to doubt experts,
        51–53
    as threat to human
        knowledge, 86–95
coherentism, 9–10
Collins, Francis, 58–75, 78–81
Condorcet's Jury Theorem,
    47–51
confirmation bias, 88
consensus among experts, 47–51
conspiracy theory
    as challenge to epistemic
        authorities, 191–192
    definition of, 183–184,
        187–188
    and economic inequality,
        189–191, 194, 205–206
    as skeptical scenario,
        195–200
credentials, as evidence of
    expertise, 31, 35–36

Descartes, René, 195–196
disagreement, epistemology of,
    58–81
distributed cognitive network, 21
domain-general understanding,
    171–172

echo chamber, 118
epistemic peer, 62

Equal Weight View, of
disagreement, 67–77
evidence, and disagreement, 63–64
Evidentialism, 100–102
expertise
and cognitive bias, 51–53
definition of, 31
evidence of, 35–39
recognition of, 31–34
Extended Mind Thesis, 175–177
externalism, 41–45

Facebook, 137–142, 152–158
factual belief polarization,
112–120
feedback loop, 152
foundationalism, 10
framing effect, 88, 151

generality, problem of, 125n34
Google, 152–158, 177

heuristics, 87, 96–99, 117
Hitchens, Christopher, 58–81
human reason, function of,
103–105
Hurricane Katrina, conspiracy
theory about, 181–182
hypernudges, 152

ideological polarization, 112
infinitism, 8–9
in-group bias, 116–117, 120,
129–131, 210
internalism, about knowledge,
41–45

justification, of belief, 42n17,
96n24, 101n28

knowledge
fallibility of, xiv
and relevant possibilities of
error, 201–202
and reliable cognitive
processes, 122–129
requirements for, xii–xiv
skepticism about, 195–198

Mercier, Hugo, 103–106
Moderate Conciliationism,
about disagreement, 78–79
monitoring, of testimony,
17–19

Nichols, Tom, 203–205
normative deference, to experts,
47
Nudging, 148–151

overconfidence bias, 90

permissivism, 73–79
polarization, 111–135
and skepticism, 122–129
and social identity,
116–117
polarized political beliefs,
etiology of, 116–121
propaganda, 137–150
definition of, 142–145
effects of, 145–147
U.S. campaign of, 137–143

rational belief, goals of, 73–76
Regress Problem, 7–10
relevant possibilities of error,
    201–202
reliable cognitive network,
    19–20
reliable cognitive processes,
    122–129
Responsibilism, 95–100
Russell, Bertrand, 91

Safety Principle, 92
scientific explanation, 167–170
scientific progress, 164–170
scientific understanding,
    166–170
self-defeat, of Equal Weight
    View, 76–77
self-serving biases, 90
Shieber, Joseph, ix, 17, 19, 27

skeptical scenarios, 195–198
skepticism, 195–198
    and conspiracy theories,
        189–191, 194, 205–206
    local vs. global, 201
    about recognizing experts,
        45–46
    social interaction, as an antidote
        to bias, 103–108
Sperber, Dan, 103–106
Steadfast View, about
    disagreement, 77–81

testimony, epistemology of,
    1–26
trust, necessity of, 10–12

vision and testimony, analogy
    between, 14–16
Volcker, Paul, 29–30, 54